Californio Lancers

The 1st Battalion of Native Cavalry in the Far West 1863–1866

Californio Lancers

The 1st Battalion of Native Cavalry in the Far West 1863–1866

Tom Prezelski

University of Oklahoma ⁂ Norman

Publication of this book is made possible through the generosity of Edith Kinney Gaylord.

LIBRARY OF CONGRESS CATALOGING-IN-PUBLICATION DATA
Prezelski, Tom, 1970–
Californio Lancers : the 1st Battalion of Native Cavalry in the Far West, 1863–1866 / Tom Prezelski.
pages cm —
Includes bibliographical references and index.
ISBN 978-0-87062-436-0 (cloth)
ISBN 978-0-8062-5752-8 (paper)
1. United States. Army. California Cavalry Battalion (1862–1865)—History. 2. California—History—Civil War, 1861–1865. 3. United States—History—Civil War, 1861–1865—Participation, Mexican American. 4. United States—History—Civil War, 1861–1865—Regimental histories. I. Title.
E497.4.P74 2015
979.4'04—dc23
2015001398

The paper in this book meets the guidelines for permanence and durability of the Committee on Production Guidelines for Book Longevity of the Council on Library Resources, Inc. ∞

Some 300 of this class have seen two years' service in the Native Battalion, and make hardy and docile soldiers, exactly fitted, when commanded by officers who speak their language and understand their habits, for this very Mexican frontier or Apache service. The English have Afghans and other Asiatic sepoys; the French, Algerians and Turcos; the Austrians, Slavs and Croats; and Maximilian his Austrians and Belgians; and out of the 10,000 or 12,000 Mexican Americans below San Jose it is singular if we could not get as many as we wanted for this kind of frontier and Indian service, and mix them with Americans to increase their intelligence and fighting capabilities.

SAN FRANCISCO BULLETIN
JULY 18, 1865

Contents

Illustrations

Figures

Maps

Table

Preface

During the years of the Civil War, more than 16,000 California men volunteered for service as soldiers in the Union army. More than 5,000 of these volunteers were posted to Arizona at one time or another during their enlistment. Though far removed from the bulk of the fighting, these soldiers saw active service in bringing some semblance of order and peace to the largely unsettled territory while the regular army was otherwise occupied.

Of all the California Volunteers, perhaps the most unusual unit was a four-company squadron called the 1st Battalion of Native Cavalry. During their service across the state, these men were charged with pursuing bandits, supporting a campaign against Indians in the northern counties, and securing the roads that crossed the southern deserts. While based at a squalid post on the Mexican border in Arizona, they patrolled against Apache Indians and guarded the frontier against potential incursions by Emperor Maximilian's partisans. Most importantly, they, like the other California volunteers, were the face of U.S. authority in the region, and their presence helped maintain the West for the Union during the rebellion.

While most of the volunteers were recruited in the northern part of the state among Anglo-Americans who had emigrated from the East, the Native Cavalry were to be recruited largely in the so-called cow counties of Southern California and the Central Coast. As implied by the unit's name, the intention was to recruit volunteers from among the "Californios," the state's Spanish-speaking natives, also known as "Native Californians" in the vernacular of the day. The hope was that the legendary horsemanship of these men could be put to good use in the federal service.[1]

Also unusual was the battalion's armament. When telling people about my research on the Native California Cavalry, the few who had actually heard of the battalion most often asked, "Did they really carry lances?" These cavalrymen did indeed. Though the concept seems fanciful and somewhat out of character given the American military tradition that largely rejected the flash of European-style cavalry, the presence of the weapon is confirmed by official correspondence and newspaper accounts. Other lancer units joined both the Union and Confederate armies during the Civil War, but only the Native Cavalry retained the lance for the duration of its service. This was obviously a nod to romantic notions about the Californios as well as to the weapon's historical place in the military traditions of California and the entire Spanish-speaking world.

I have been working on this book in one way or another for more than a decade. There have been numerous interruptions, including a six-year stint in the Arizona state legislature. I first became interested in the battalion while taking a class by Professor Harwood P. Hinton at the University of Arizona many years ago. During one lecture, he made a passing remark about a unit of "Mexican lancers from California" that was briefly posted near Tubac during the Civil War. This got me curious, and a few days later, I searched through a copy of Richard H. Orton's *Records of California Men in the War of the Rebellion,* found the entry for a "Battalion of Native Cavalry," and assumed correctly that this must be the unit Dr. Hinton mentioned. But Orton had little to say about the battalion's service since the official records were, in his words, "very incomplete." This negligence on the part of the battalion's officers would prove to be an important part of the story.

From time to time over the next few years, I would look here and there for anything more about the battalion, but the information was sparse. Other than mentions in Constance Altschuler's *Chains of Command,* Aurora Hunt's *Army of the Pacific,* and an unpublished paper by Sidney Brinkerhoff, there was almost nothing in print, a circumstance that was tantalizing rather than frustrating. Mark Santiago of the Arizona Historical Society in Tucson encouraged me to pursue the topic further, which eventually led to a paper in the *Journal of Arizona History.*

My interest did not end there, however. The article attracted correspondence from California, mostly from a fellow named David Jackson, an amateur researcher in Los Angeles. It quickly became clear that I had made numerous errors and omissions, primarily due to my near-total ignorance about California. I continued to work on the research, with varying levels of commitment, in hopes of expanding on what I had already written and correcting my mistakes.

Other issues made the idea of actually completing this project seem even more urgent. My time in the Arizona legislature confirmed my longstanding suspicion that ignorance of history, particularly with regard to my own state's Mexican heritage, had led to a lot of bad public policy. Subsequent events compounded this. Too much of the debate is driven by the impression that the Mexican community is new and foreign, without a claim to a share in the nation's heritage. The fact that Spanish-surnamed Americans have long served in the military with distinction, sometimes in disproportionately high numbers, certainly argues against this but is almost unknown in the popular imagination. Arguably, this contribution can be traced back as far as the Civil War, when as many as 10,000 Hispanics served on both sides, although primarily with the Union. Their service has too often been ignored or, as in the case of the New Mexico volunteers, unfairly maligned.

Historian Leonard Pitt wrote that the mere fact that Californios volunteered for the U.S. Army during the Civil War was far more important than anything that the Native Cavalry did during its service, something that could arguably be applied to the other Mexican Americans who did the same in Arizona, New Mexico, and Texas. Pitt argues that their participation, not quite a generation removed from the violent conquest of a good portion of what had been their native country, in the fight to preserve the Union represented a transition from active resistance to U.S. rule to a different kind of struggle within the new order.[2] While not assimilated in the conventional sense, Mexican Americans were no longer merely a conquered people but a constituency who demanded a seat at the table as fellow Americans.

Of course, these broader political implications were only barely recognized at the time by a few community leaders and some of the battalion's officers. For the most part, the rank-and-file recruits, who eventually included immigrants from Mexico, Latin America, and Europe, enlisted for their own reasons, which often had something to do with poverty or boredom. Because so few of these men could speak English and even fewer were literate, much of their story can only be read between the lines of newspaper accounts and official correspondence. Though they largely did not fight (except with each other), they suffered from the same privations that have afflicted most soldiers throughout history: bad food, boredom, disease, loneliness, and too often the frustrations of service under officers who were sometimes unworthy of their rank.

In writing this book I set out to tell the strange story of an interesting and unique unit of soldiers in the Civil War. I hope that in doing so, I will have done justice to the service and contributions of not only the Native California Cavalry but also Mexican Americans in general.

Acknowledgments

This book would not have been possible without the help of many people over the years. First, I need to thank David R. Jackson of Los Angeles, who shared his substantial research and insights about the Native Cavalry. Likewise, the late Constance Wynn Altschuler of Tucson gave me access to her notes before her passing. I would have been lost without the generosity of either one of these dedicated researchers.

This could not have succeeded without the work of archive and museum professionals. Those deserving recognition include the collections and library staff at the Arizona Historical Society in Tucson, Anita Badertscher of Tumacacori National Historical Park, Cynthia Chamberlin and David Hayes-Bautista at the Center for Latino Health and Culture at the University of California, Los Angeles, David Cheever of the Maine State Archives, Wanda Guibert at the San Juan Bautista Historical Society, Shaw Kinsley at Tubac State Park, Marianne Leach and the staff at the California State Library, Crystal Miles and the staff of the Bancroft Library at the University of California, Berkeley, Susan Ogle at the Drum Barracks Civil War Museum, Monica Orozco and the staff at the Santa Barbara Mission Archives, and Charles Wommack of Special Collections at the University of Arizona Library.

There are others whose assistance, insights and encouragement kept this project going. Dawn Santiago read over an early version of the manuscript and provided useful suggestions. My mother, Carmen Villa Prezelski, helped to translate some of the Spanish primary sources. Tom Jonas provided beautiful and concise maps and was a pleasure to work with. Also helpful were Gustavo Arellano, Jack August, Jr.,

Mark Barnes, Sidney Brinckerhoff, Frank Barrios, Nick Blesser, Elisa Brooks, Dan Buckley, Celesste Bracamonte, Cristina Cardenas, Allison Cobb, Jeff Coleman, Rick Collins, David Devine, David Ellis Dickerson, Bruce Dinges, Rob Ferrier, L. Boyd Finch, Alice J. Flick, Arnie Franks, Al Gonzales, Jim and Loma Griffith, Diana Hadley, Skip Heller, Mari Herreras, Patricia Ann Howe, Father Kieran McCarty, Ernesto "Neto" Portillo Jr., Jennifer Powers, Ian Record, Jennifer and Jon Rauhouse, Mark Santiago, Karen Seger, Wayne Sherman, Melanie Sturgeon and Jay Van Orden.

Finally, I need to thank Charles Rankin, Stephanie Evans, Emmy Ezzell, and the rest of the staff at the University of Oklahoma Press for showing this novice author so much patience. In particular, long-suffering copyeditor Kevin Brock deserves praise for his grace and professionalism.

A Note on Language

Having been born under the Mexican flag but finding themselves coming of age in a territory recently conquered by the United States, the generation represented by the Native Cavalry was the first that could be truly called Mexican American. This is reflected in the colloquial language, which as in other parts of the western United States at the time blended to varying degrees English and Spanish. This presents some interesting problems for the writer.

Some correspondence and contemporary writing, in particular the letters of Captain Porfirio Jimeno, are written in both languages. Retaining this code-switching, however, seems to put a reader unfamiliar with Spanish at a disadvantage. For this reason, translations of quoted Spanish-language portions are presented in the endnotes.

Most of the Native Cavalry soldiers worked in cattle ranching in one capacity or another in their civilian lives. In modern American language they would be called "cowboys," but this term was not yet commonly used in California. English-language sources sometimes use the terms "drover," "herder," or "herdsman" to describe such workers, but the Spanish term "vaquero" for one who works with cattle ("vacas") was far more common, even appearing in official military records, and thus is used in this work.

The rolls also use the word "ranchero" to describe the civilian occupation of many Native Cavalry soldiers. Though it has different, sometimes derogatory, connotations in modern Mexican usage, the term literally translates to "rancher." It seems that in the context of the time it simply meant an individual who worked in ranching, not necessarily someone who owned a ranch.

Contemporary sources identify Mexicans born in California with the Spanish term "Californios" or the English term "Native Californians," and I use these interchangeably. The phrase "Native Cavalry" may have been as much an allusion to the "native" units in some European colonial armies as it was to the Native Californians who filled its ranks. The term "native" should not be considered in the context of the modern phrase "Native Americans," even though a fair number of tribal people, primarily Yaquis from Sonora and California Mission Indians, were among the Native Cavalry's enlistees. To avoid confusion, the term is avoided in favor of the names of individual tribes or, where this is impossible, the word "Indian," which is still considered acceptable.

Correspondents of the time used the Spanish word "rancheria" to describe an Indian community, and the term still remains in limited use in modern California. I retain its usage in this book where appropriate.

CHAPTER 1

The Californios and the Rebellion

On the following day, a large meeting of Mexicans and their sympathizers was addressed by F. P. Ramirez, Esq. His speech was delivered in Spanish. In the course of it, he strove to impress upon his audience that a deep feeling of sympathy was felt by the American Govt towards Mexico in its current struggle, and that it was the duty of resident Mexicans to aid in the support and defence of the Federal Govt against the rebellion now seeking its overthrow.

ALTA CALIFORNIA

In 1861 some observers worried about California remaining firmly in Union hands. In the most recent national election, the state had gone for Abraham Lincoln by only a narrow plurality. Its popular governor, Irish-born John Downey, was a Democrat who in the past had been associated with his party's Southern-leaning "chivalry" faction, as had his lieutenant governor, Pablo de la Guerra. While citizens of the well-populated corridor from Sacramento to the San Francisco Bay area largely remained loyal to the Union in the face of secession, those who favored the Confederacy were vocal and ever present, particularly in the southern counties.

The loyalty of California's Spanish-speaking population was a source of some doubt too. The "Californios," as they called themselves—known as "Native Californians" to their English-speaking contemporaries—had numbered some ten thousand to fifteen thousand when what had been a frontier province of Mexico was forcibly annexed by the United States in 1848. Thereafter they were quickly outnumbered by the rush of new settlers from the eastern states as well as Europe and Latin America.[1]

Left to right: Pablo de la Guerra, Salvador Vallejo, and Andrés Pico in 1856.
Photo courtesy of Bancroft Library, University of California, Berkeley.

In terms of language, culture, and religion, the Californios were essentially Mexican, but in the years before the conquest, they were more likely to identify themselves with their home province rather than the mother country. New arrivals from *la otra banda* were, at least initially, disparaged as *cholos* and regarded as ill mannered and racially suspect despite the mixed-race origins of many Californios, even the most prominent. Nominally they were Roman Catholic, but religious ritual had largely become the province of women, and with some notable exceptions, there was generally little patience for the institutional church. Those who concerned themselves with politics were republican in sentiment, outwardly embracing nineteenth-century liberalism in theory, but not necessarily in practice. In reality, life and political power were largely about family, and the patriarchs at the center often ruled their kin and households with an apparent dictatorial authority that astonished many outsiders.

Ranching dominated the state's preconquest economy. Men thus were nearly "always on horseback" and could "hardly go from one house to another without mounting a horse." Outsiders writing of the Californios frequently described them as being among the best horsemen in the world. A merchant seaman who visited California in the 1830s wrote that they were "put upon a horse when only four or five years old, their little legs not long enough to come half-way over his sides," and would simply be left there until their legs grew to reach the stirrups.[2] The same writer described the Californios' aggressive and often brutal horsemanship:

> When they go on long journeys, they ride one horse down, and catch another, throw the saddle and bridle upon him, and, after riding him down, take a third, and so on, until the end of the journey. . . . [T]hey make no use of their stirrups when mounting, but striking the horse, spring into the saddle as he starts, and, sticking their long spurs into him, go off on the full run. Their spurs are cruel things. . . . The flanks of the horses are often sore from them, and I have seen men come in from chasing bullocks, with their horse's hind legs and quarters covered with blood.[3]

Anglo-American outsiders regarded the Californios with a mix of romanticized admiration and derision. Patriarchs like Pío Pico and Mariano Vallejo were praised for their hospitality, generosity, and genteel manner, but were also described as some sort of landed nobility who did little but dabble in politics and engage in petty feuds. Though they bore the important responsibility of maintaining their family and property, English-speaking correspondents did not regard this as real work. Likewise, while the hard-working *rancheros* were admired for their skill in the saddle, their indulgent pastimes, the *fandangos,* cockfights, bear-baitings, and other "kinds of amusement and knavery" were offensive to the protestant sensibilities of observers from the United States. Generally, even to their admirers, the Californios were regarded as decadent and their traditions were seen as quaint at best.

After the conquest Californios did not accept the new order quietly but were in little position to resist or even assert themselves. Not only were they quickly overwhelmed in terms of population, but the fact that their wealth was almost entirely in cattle and land made them ill prepared for the new cash economy. Even the most prominent Californios found their influence greatly diminished as their ranchos were reduced piece by piece as they were legally outmaneuvered or forced to sell property to pay debts. In the "cow counties" south of San Jose, which generally attracted fewer Anglo-American settlers than other areas and where ranching was still economically important, the Native Californians were able to retain a portion of their land and their clout. A handful, through a combination of charisma, respect, and political skill, even remained prominent in public life. But the overall decline was nonetheless precipitous. The "nativist" political movement of the mid-1850s, which culminated in the brief rise of the Know-Nothing Party both nationally and in California, was also a great blow to the community. Discriminatory laws, like the so-called Greaser Act of 1855, were ostensibly designed to target immigrants but did not spare the native-born Californios. The worst passed within a few years, however, and the Native Californians were able to recover a bit of their political standing by finding solidarity with immigrants from Mexico and other parts of Latin America. By the time of the attack on Fort Sumter, not even a full generation after the conquest, the once-proud Californios had largely become, in the eloquent words of former governor Pío Pico, foreigners in their own land.

Anglo California, meanwhile, was increasingly preoccupied by the issues dividing the country, though the question of slavery seemed secondary to sectional sympathies. Word came to San Francisco by Pony Express on April 24, 1861, that Fort Sumter had fallen, but the coming of the war was long obvious even on the West Coast, where public

Californio vaqueros lassoing a grizzly bear.
From Browne, "A Dangerous Journey," pt. 2.

demonstrations by secessionist sympathizers had been occurring in communities around California for weeks. Brigadier General Albert Sidney Johnston, commander of the U.S. Army's Department of the Pacific, had already resigned his commission as the first step in his eventual defection to the Confederacy, and more Southern officers would soon follow. Even though many soldiers in the army remained loyal, it was clear by the end of the month that most of them would be withdrawn to the fight in the East. There seemed a very real possibility that California, with its gold and strategically important ports, could be lost to the rebels.

Because of Governor Downey's political alliances and ambivalence about slavery, there were those who doubted his loyalties. Nonetheless, in July, when the Pony Express brought a request from Secretary of War Simon Cameron for the state to provide one regiment of infantry and four companies of cavalry to secure the overland route across

Mormon-dominated Utah, Downey enthusiastically and even personally took to the task of raising these volunteers. In August the governor and his entourage were on the road to New Almaden when he met the geological-survey party of Professor Josiah Whitney. There, he offered a volunteer commission to one of its members, a twenty-one-year-old Californio named José Juan Francisco de Jesús Guirado, who also happened to be Downey's brother-in-law.[4] In September Guirado was mustered in as first lieutenant of what became Company B of the 1st Regiment of Cavalry, California Volunteers.[5]

Downey's initial success led the War Department to request additional units, and by the end of August, the call was increased to include five regiments of infantry and two of cavalry, more than 7,000 officers and men. The mission of these volunteers likewise expanded. In response to civil unrest in Southern California and a Confederate invasion of New Mexico, Guirado's company was first sent south, then east across the desert as part of the California Column, a brigade of 2,350 men, including infantry, cavalry, and artillery, to secure the Southwest for the Union. During the course of the war, there would be some 16,000 California volunteers, serving as far north as the Columbia River and as far east as the Rio Grande. For the most part, these men would be Anglo-Americans and European immigrants recruited in the San Francisco Bay area and from the mining camps of the Sierra Nevadas, regions where Union sentiment was strong. For the time being, few if any Californios served in the ranks, and Guirado would remain the only Spanish-surnamed officer.

Distant from both the active theaters of fighting and the issues behind the conflict, Native Californians were ambivalent about the Union cause. Given the litany of wrongs they had suffered since the American conquest, their lack of enthusiasm was understandable. Additionally, many Californio community leaders, particularly in Southern California, had allied themselves with political elements sympathetic with the Confederacy, though this was largely the product of expedience rather than sentiment.[6]

Events south of the border played some role in breaking this complacency. In January 1862, with the United States distracted by the rebellion, France landed an expeditionary force in Mexico and intervened on behalf of a conservative faction in an ongoing civil war there. By the summer of 1863, Mexican president Benito Juárez had been forced to flee northward, moving his government to El Paso del Norte, within sight of a U.S. Army garrison across the Rio Grande, while the French controlled the national capital and most of the key cities. The insurgents declared a monarchy in July and eventually offered the imperial crown to Archduke Ferdinand Maximilian, an Austrian nobleman, who accepted and arrived to take power the following May.[7]

In California these events were followed closely by the press, particularly the Spanish-language newspapers. This popular excitement was not entirely an accident, for Juárez had agents in San Francisco actively working to raise money and recruits for his *Republicano* cause, and stirring up popular support suited their purposes. Nonetheless, the celebration that followed the victory of a Mexican force over the French at Puebla on May 5, 1862, was sincere. In their enthusiasm Spanish-speaking residents of all stripes organized "patriotic clubs" across the state and rallied around what they saw as the struggle for the sovereignty of the Americas against an arrogant European colonial aggressor.[8]

The first anniversary of this victory was celebrated in various places around California, marking the earliest observation of what would become known as Cinco de Mayo, a holiday of sorts among Mexican Americans. One such celebration, staged by a local chapter of La Junta Patriótica Mexicana, a club founded to promote Mexican solidarity, occurred one evening in 1863 on a prominent hill overlooking Los Angeles. It was a well-organized affair attended by a reported four hundred "resident Mexicans and native Californians" who gathered around a bonfire and large portraits of President Juárez and the late general Ignacio Zaragoza Seguín, hero of the fifth of May. Festivities included an honor guard of militia, speeches, music, musket volleys, and pyrotechnics. When it was over, the assembled walked down the hill and processed respectfully through the town. A group of some twenty-five Frenchmen assembled and marched through the streets as well, and for a time it appeared that the evening would end violently. Fortunately, however, the Mexicans remained orderly while the French expatriates restricted their display to singing "La Marseillaise"; there was no confrontation.

For the Spanish-speaking participants, the "patriotic commotion" did not end there. The next day the junta called a "large meeting of Mexicans and their sympathizers." There, firebrand attorney Francisco P. Ramirez addressed the assembled in flowery and eloquent Spanish. He called upon the crowd of Californios and immigrants from Mexico, Chile, Colombia, Peru, and Central America to stand united behind Juárez. He went a step further and made a thinly veiled call for the audience to take a stand in the struggle faced by their new country: "Fellow citizens! You have the sympathies of all the good citizens of the United States. Mexicans of California! Be always faithful and loyal citizens! Do not stain yourselves with treason against the country of Franklin, of Adams, and of Jefferson."

While Confederate ties with the Imperialists in Mexico were well known, this did not figure into Ramirez's speech. Instead, he focused on the importance of maintaining the Union, a sentiment expressed over and over again in similar public gatherings across the state. This meeting concluded with the assembled forming in procession behind a band and a color guard, then marching through the streets with the flags of Mexico and the United States side by side.[9]

By this time an effort was already underway to provide more substantive support to the Union effort. State senator Romualdo Pacheco of San Luis Obispo and Santa Barbara Counties was a passionate supporter whose loyalties led him to abandon his Democratic Party for the Unionist ticket.[10] A general in the state militia, he seems to have been the first to suggest that a battalion of volunteers could be raised from among the Mexican American population of Southern California and the Central Coast. Eager to showcase the patriotism of his fellow Californios, Pacheco believed that their legendary horsemanship skills could be put to good use in Texas.[11] In December 1862 Brigadier General George Wright, commander of the Department of the Pacific at San Francisco, forwarded a request by telegram to Washington, D.C., for authorization to raise a four-company battalion of "native cavalry" in and around Los Angeles. He received permission from the War Department a month later.[12]

At some point in planning, the notion arose that this unit should be armed with lances. This was not out of parsimony or a misguided effort to keep firearms out of Mexican American hands, for at least one company later would be armed with state-of-the-art carbines. The weapon had a storied past in California, extending back to the earliest days of Spanish settlement, when mounted *soldados de cuera* imposed a new religion and the rule of a distant king upon the local tribes at the point of the lance.

Later, ad-hoc companies of lancers raised from among the citizenry fought for one side or another during the numerous petty rebellions that occurred with regularity following Mexican independence. Likewise, in the absence of a competent regular army, such militias formed the core of the forces that were organized against Indians and, eventually, invaders from the United States.[13] After the American conquest, this tradition continued as prominent Californios would organize volunteer lancer companies to pursue bandits or Indians or to otherwise maintain the peace. *Lanceros* in fancy traditional dress remained a common sight in local parades.

In the U.S. Army the lance was a bit of a novelty, though there were veterans who championed its use after having witnessed its effectiveness in the hands of the enemy in Mexico. As a result of this interest, the manual of the lance was included in some cavalry drill books, and there were official specifications for lance design for Federal service based on an Austrian model George McClellan had brought back from Europe in the 1850s.[14] The weapon used by the Native Cavalry was manufactured at the Federal arsenal at Benicia. The bulk of its length was a nine-foot-long ash shaft. At one end was a steel ferrule, or buttcap, which would fit in a socket on the right stirrup to make it easier to carry on the march. At the other was a head consisting of a narrow eleven-inch steel triangular blade attached to the shaft by two steel flanges that also ostensibly served to protect the wood against saber blows in combat. The head was festooned with a red linen pennon, which tended to give the weapon a flamboyant appearance but originally served a more gruesome purpose, namely to wick up the blood that would otherwise run down the shaft and make it too slick to handle securely.[15] Cavalrymen were to supplement the lance with the more conventional saber and Colt pistol.

Early on officials suggested that Andrés Pico, described as a "patriotic gentleman," be commander of the new unit. This choice was both inspired and a little ironic, for Pico had led the force of Californio lancers that had humiliated Brigadier General Stephen Watts Kearny at San Pasqual in December 1846.[16] Despite his battlefield success, Pico recognized that the fight against the *yanqui* invaders could not long be sustained, and as commander of California's military forces, he agreed to articles of capitulation at Cahuenga Pass that ended the fighting a little over a month later. Under the new regime, Pico remained prominent as

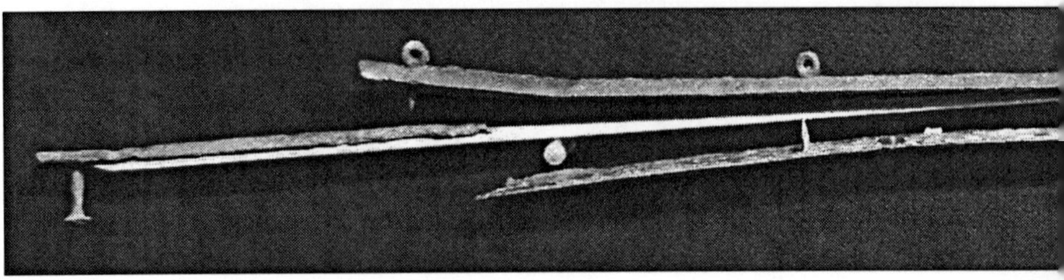

a member of the legislature and in leading ad-hoc companies of citizen-lancers organized from time to time as trouble threatened the peace of the territory. His loyal service was recognized by his appointment as a brigadier general in the state militia in 1858.[17]

Like other prominent Californios, Pico faced more than his share of bigotry and was frequently involved in legal battles over the rights to his land. Despite this, he was, like Pacheco, a staunch supporter of the Union whose sympathies eventually led him away from the Democratic Party. When, at the dawn of the Civil War, a stand of militia arms was spirited away to Texas by Confederate sympathizers with the help of Los Angeles County sheriff Tomas Sanchez, Pico was put in charge of securing what remained. This duty consisted mostly of sorting through what turned out to be years of incomplete and confused paperwork neglected by an increasingly unpopular adjutant general. Pico was assisted by his adjutant, Major William P. Reynolds. They were successful in recovering most of the state's arms in Southern California, but many others were damaged or had been long since lost.

Pico was offered a commission as major and command of the Native Cavalry in February 1863. But at fifty-three, he was in declining health and no longer able to ride a horse. Pico turned down the commission and, except for a failed attempt to return to the state senate, largely retired from public life. This left the new organization without a commander for what turned out to be most of the year.[18] Major Reynolds, however, took an active interest in the battalion, assisting in its recruitment and training. He was a longtime California resident whose military experience went back to his time in Colonel John C. Frémont's volunteer battalion during the U.S. conquest. Reynolds was well respected among both civilian and military authorities and had a reputation as "the best drill officer in the state."[19]

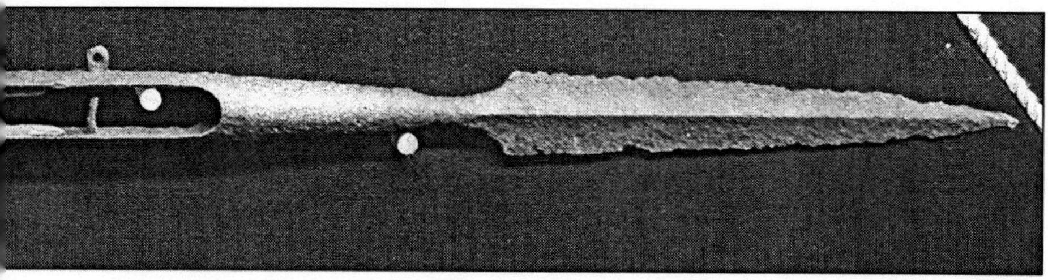

A Native Cavalry lance head found near Rio Rico (Calabazas), Arizona, on display at Tubac Presidio State Park. *Photo by author with permission of park staff.*

The recruitment of the battalion was well underway by December 1863 when Salvador Vallejo accepted a commission as major. This was an odd choice, for few Native Californians expressed more grievances against the United States. Vallejo had spent well over a decade in a fruitless struggle against squatters who had taken his land with the help of what he saw as a corrupt legal system. He had a clear patrician contempt for Anglo-Americans and remained high handed, confrontational, and often ill mannered. Like Pico, his military experience extended back to Mexican times, when he led brutal and extensive campaigns against the tribes of Northern California as commander of the presidio at Sonoma. His relentless and hard-riding life in the field took a stiff toll on his body. By the time he was in his late twenties, Vallejo "had broken two ribs and fractured both thighs, the one in two places, and the other in three, so that now he had very little left in reserve but his neck."[20]

During the Bear Flag Rebellion at the dawn of the war with the United States in 1846, Salvador and his brother General Manuel Guadalupe Vallejo were seized and held as prisoners by Frémont and his band of armed colonists. The indignities and outright abuses they suffered in captivity further soured Salvador's attitude toward the United States. After the conquest he remained largely uninvolved in public affairs, military or otherwise, concentrating instead on his fight to retain his property in and around Napa Valley. By the mid-1850s, however, his finances exhausted and lacking faith that he could find justice from "squatter juries," "squatter sheriffs," and "squatter judges," Vallejo more or less retired with his family to a relatively modest home in Napa to "spend a few years of a quiet life" occupied with educating his children and "fishing and hunting."[21]

Given Salvador's continuing bitterness and cynicism, it is surprising that he came out of retirement several years later to wear the uniform of the United States. His prominent brother Mariano, with whom he frequently clashed, was universally respected and had great faith in American institutions. He seems a more obvious choice for the command but does not seem to have been considered, likely because he was already well into his fifties and largely out of public life. But at least one member of the family had already joined the war effort. Mariano's nephew Platon, a medical student at Columbia University, served as a volunteer surgeon with the Union army and in that capacity witnessed the carnage of First Bull Run.[22] Perhaps the influence of his brother or the example of his nephew inspired Salvador. It seems more likely that, at age forty-nine, the former presidial captain was simply bored and decided that he had one more fight left in him.

For his own part, Salvador wrote many years later that his support for the Union was drawn not from any ill will toward the South or from sympathy with what the bigoted *patrón* called the "negro element." Like Ramirez and other prominent Californios, it seems that Vallejo set aside his grievances with the new order not only out of a sense of civic responsibility but also in solidarity with the then-ongoing struggle of the Mexican republic. Echoing these now familiar sentiments, he said his support came from a desire to "put an end to the fratricidal strife" and to consolidate "the great union of the United States of America, a Republic very properly considered the bulwark of safety against european [*sic*] despotism."[23]

For whatever his specific reasons, Vallejo accepted a commission as major by the outgoing Governor Leland Stanford in December 1863 and command of what would become the 1st Battalion of Native Cavalry, California Volunteers. By this time two companies were already being organized in San Jose and San Francisco. The motives for these new recruits would be many and varied.

CHAPTER 2

Company A: San Jose

My son, José R. Pico, is desirous of raising a company of Cavalry for the service of the government. I should be very happy to learn of his success in the matter, and to some extent should feel a sense of pride in knowing that a Company of Native Californians were enlisted in the military arm of our Country.

ANTONIO M. PICO

José Ramón Pico was an audacious nephew of Andrés Pico. As a young man he accompanied his uncle at the 1846 battle of San Pasqual and later reported having been wounded there.[1] Years later he told the tale of being captured by the American forces shortly afterward, then released when peace was made at Cahuenga Pass. The proud horseman spoke of the experience with some resentment, not for his captivity, but because he was left without a horse and forced to return to his comrades on foot.[2]

Described as being over six feet tall and "of large and imposing physique," Pico had an outsized personality to match. Known as one of the best horsemen in California, in the fall of 1860 he bet a fellow resident of San Jose $2,500 that he could ride 150 miles in six and a half hours. It was reported at the time that no one but Pico himself believed that he could do it. In the end he famously won the wager, using thirty horses at a race track in Santa Clara, clocking in at six hours, sixteen minutes, and fifty seconds, an accomplishment characterized as an "unparalleled feat" of "courage and skill" as well as "speed and endurance on the part of horse and rider."[3]

Captain José Ramón Pico wearing a borrowed colonel's uniform. *Courtesy of Wayne and Pamela Sherman, Los Angeles.*

The short-tempered Californio had a bit of a checkered past as well. In 1855 he was arrested at Santa Clara for shooting down his own cousin in a dispute about the ownership of a horse. He was later acquitted of the murder.[4]

Hearing news of the proposed Native Cavalry battalion, the bombastic and arrogant thirty-two-year-old did not wait for the unit's authorization from the War Department to write to Governor Stanford in January 1863 demanding a commission in the new organization:

> Permit me to intrude upon your precious time and ask a favor. I am very anxious to obtain a captain[']s commission to raise a cavalry company of Californians; I can get a great many to join a company with me. I most respectfully ask your Honor to recommend me for that position. I would not have dared to place myself before your Honor, but I consider that I have a sort of claim on your Honor, as a partisan. I am and have always been a republican, since I have had the right of Suffrage. I was one of your strong supporters in Santa Clara county when you was elected to the office of Gov. of this State. I consider myself a competent person to fill the position I ask for, if I have the good fortune to obtain a commission.[5]

His request was supported by a number of prominent citizens, including Senator Pacheco and both of his home county's state senators, who praised him as "active" and "energetic."[6] Pico received his commission as captain in late February. About a week later, on March 3, he began

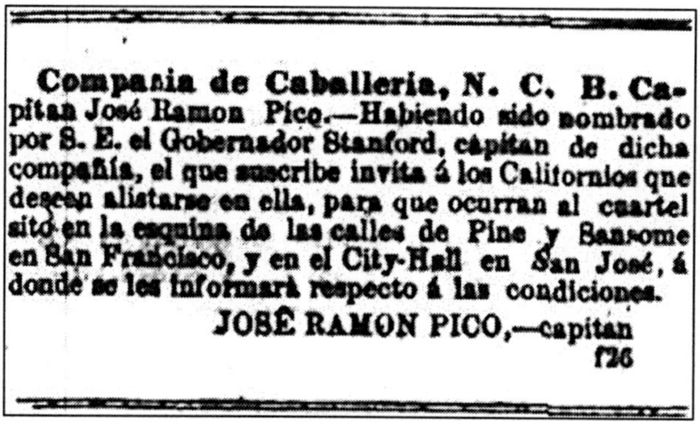

Compania de Caballeria, N. C. B. Capitan José Ramon Pico.—Habiendo sido nombrado por S. E. el Gobernador Stanford, cápitan de dicha compañía, el que suscribe invita á los Californios que deseen alistarse en ella, para que ocurran al cuartel sito en la esquina de las calles de Pine y Sansome en San Francisco, y en el City-Hall en San José, á donde se les informará respecto á las condiciones.

JOSÉ RAMON PICO,—capitan

f26

A recruitment advertisement appearing in *El Voz de Méjico,* a Spanish-language newspaper in San Francisco, March 3, 1863. *Courtesy Center for the Study of Latino Health and Culture, University of California, Los Angeles.*

his recruitment drive with a notice that appeared in a San Francisco Spanish-language newspaper alongside war news from Mexico and among advertisements for restaurants, clothing stores, musical instruments, and a vendor of yerba maté.[7]

Pico followed up later that evening by leading a torchlight rally on the plaza in San Jose, where he spoke in "soul stirring strains."

> My Fellow Countrymen: We convene here to-night on an important matter. The Captain's commission which I here display before you authorizes me to form a company of California cavalry, to be composed of a hundred able-bodied men, to serve the Government of the United States of America. Those among you who are willing to enlist under my command will not regret their choice. I have sworn to defend this beautiful flag, the Star Spangled Banner, the emblem of Truth, Liberty, and Justice, and would also take another oath to guard the personal rights of each and every volunteer under my command.
>
> Sons of California! Our country calls, and we must obey! This rebellion of the southern states must be crushed; they must come back into the union and pay obedience to the Stars and Stripes. United, we will, by the force of circumstances become the freest and mightiest republic on earth! Crowned monarchs must be driven away from the sacred continent of free America![8]

The local press marveled at the horsemanship of his new volunteers, noting their horsemanship and skill with their "lassoes [*sic*]," described as "novel weapons of offence [*sic*] . . . which they are exceedingly expert at using on horseback." Pico attracted about forty recruits in a little over a week, and they would camp on the plaza while awaiting formal induction into the army.[9]

But the initial enthusiasm quickly waned, and recruitment soon slowed considerably. It would be said later, without citing any specifics, that Pico was "unaided by Government funds" and was therefore forced to rely "upon his own means" while his efforts were disrupted by local Confederate sympathizers. Similar frustrations would be faced by those organizing the other Native Cavalry companies. It would be months before his company quota was complete.[10]

Over the next several months, recruits would be regularly ferried by steamer across the bay to the Presidio of San Francisco, which would be their new home until the end of the year. Established in 1776 by the same expedition that brought Captain Pico's Spanish ancestors to California from Sonora, the Presidio was emerging from decades of varying levels of neglect under Spanish, Mexican, and American rule. War had prompted a construction boom, and the Native Cavalry recruits arrived as the post was expanding from a handful of windswept adobes and newer wood-frame cottages set among gentle hills and swampy flats to a neat and orderly installation consisting of dozens of modern buildings. The Presidio had largely functioned as a depot for soldiers awaiting other assignments. But as the war progressed, it grew in importance as the center of San Francisco's harbor defenses while troop detachments from time to time dealt with occasional civil unrest in the city. As for Pico's recruits, their time at the Presidio was spent in becoming soldiers, with assistance from the officers and men of the 9th U.S. Infantry already stationed there.[11]

The first twenty-nine recruits were formally mustered into the service on April 23 "to serve for a period of three years, unless sooner discharged." This was well short of the regulation compliment of ninety-eight enlisted men, so for now the only officer officially mustered in would be 2nd Lieutenant Marcelino Erasmo Jimenez, a bilingual, highly literate, and ambitious twenty-nine-year-old Chilean immigrant who had settled in San Jose. By all accounts Jimenez carried out his duties with "commendable zeal," and he quickly endeared himself to the Anglo-American regular officers at the Presidio.[12]

It is unclear when the enmity between Pico and Jimenez first emerged, but it seems to have happened fairly early. There was little if any interaction between the captain and the lieutenant during this period. Ostensibly busy with the continuing work of organizing the company, Pico was

The entrance gate of the Presidio of San Francisco in 1869, shortly after the post's Civil War–era expansion. Image by Eadweard Muybridge. *Courtesy California History Room, California State Library, Sacramento.*

rarely if ever at the Presidio, so a number of the recruits, having never seen the captain, knew no officer other than Jimenez. Officially in command of the company for the time being, the lieutenant coveted the rank of captain, but there was no means of promotion as long as Pico retained the commission. Whether due to professional rivalry, issues with Pico's conduct, or simple personal dislike, Jimenez quickly grew to resent his captain and began to seek ways to have him removed.

In early May, on a steamer taking recruits from San Jose to the Presidio, the lieutenant sat in the dining room eating breakfast with Sergeant Prudencia Garcia while another soldier, Private Marianna Rodrigues, napped on a nearby bench. The conversation must have been in Spanish since neither the sergeant nor Rodrigues, who reported the incident later, spoke English. Garcia, apparently alluding to a promise that had been made earlier, said to Jimenez, "My lieutenant, you know what I enlisted for." Jimenez replied, "never mind Sergeant. If you help me to break Capt Pico and as soon as I be myself the Captain of the Company, I shall give you my epaulettes." In the coming months the lieutenant's scheming would become more open and brazen, and his divisive behavior would exacerbate the company's troubles.[13]

Of course, it did not help matters that Captain Pico's own conduct in running his company was irregular to say the least. A strange incident that illustrates this involves Benigno Pico, his twenty-six-year-old cousin from San Luis Obispo. Officially mustered in at the Presidio as the company's first sergeant in April 1863, in reality the younger Pico had asked another man to answer to his name so he could remain in his hometown on what the captain later claimed to be "Recruiting Service," an ostensible mission that yielded few if any additional men. His extended absence gave him time to marry Anna Mary Forrester, a Scottish American, at the Mission San Luis Obispo on January 6, 1864.

The ruse only came to light when 1st Sergeant Pico, having been officially designated a deserter in July 1863, was arrested and returned to the company in February 1864. The captain wrote to the adjutant general to plea for leniency for his cousin since he was never properly mustered in. He also admitted to his own role in the deception, claiming, in what would become a familiar excuse during his career, that he was "ignorant of the rules of the service" and "was not aware that any wrong was committed." Apparently, the issue was favorably resolved as Benigno Pico, having been reduced to the ranks, served out the rest of his enlistment without any further trouble.[14]

As recruitment continued, Captain Pico's efforts spread out beyond San Jose to surrounding Santa Clara County as well as to the Bay Area and the Central Coast region. During this time, he engaged in his share of carousing and otherwise enjoyed the trappings of an officer's commission, such as presiding over a Fourth of July parade and cotillion given in San Francisco.[15] These may or may not have distracted him from the already difficult duty of recruitment. For his own part, Pico largely blamed the slow pace of his efforts on finances. The California legislature had set aside money to assist organizers of volunteer units with the expenses incurred in recruiting. As will be seen, this fund would prove to be less than adequate or timely for some of the Native Cavalry's officers, including Captain Pico, who would have to dip into their own pockets to meet these costs. Because many of his recruits were destitute, Pico had become responsible for furnishing their lodging, board, clothing, and occasionally even spending money.

An example, though an extreme one, of the sort of expenses incurred in recruiting comes from Private Francisco Ibarra, one of Pico's initial volunteers who signed on in the spring of 1863. Ibarra later testified that the captain had made big promises to get him to join, including that he "would have no taxes to pay on [his] property in Los Angeles," and plied him with liquor. While still in San Jose, the new recruit was showered with gifts by Lieutenant Jimenez, including a sack of flour, half a pound of chocolate, twenty yards of calico, and a parasol, the latter two items being for the man's wife. Private Ibarra, who claimed that he enlisted under false pretenses and while drunk, was later dishonorably discharged after deserting twice.[16]

It was not until June 1863, three months after his speech on the plaza in San Jose, that Pico finally received $900 from the state to help him recoup his expenses, a sum well short of the estimated $1,200 he had spent. The officer's subsequent efforts to address this shortfall would lead to trouble for himself and his company over the next several months.

It was not until September 7 that the company, now designated Company A, 1st Battalion of Native Cavalry, California Volunteers, was considered sufficiently full for Pico to be mustered in officially as captain.[17] Along with him was a new first lieutenant, thirty-five-year-old Crisanto Soto, who was the son of a presidial soldier and spoke little English. During the war with the United States, the young Soto had joined Californio forces to fight the invaders and may have seen some active service, though he later accepted the new order once the cause was lost.

This came full circle in 1856, when the newly formed Republican Party nominated John Frémont for president of the United States. Soto was one of a number of prominent Native Californians who supported the candidacy of "Juan Carlos," attaching his name, along with more than two dozen other Californios from the northern counties, to a letter to a Los Angeles Spanish-language newspaper attesting to the colonel's credentials as a friend of the community. This stance was controversial. Frémont's conduct during the war, and his behavior toward the Native Californians in particular, got him branded a bandit and even worse. Nevertheless, Californio support in the 1850s was understandable in light of the new party's "liberal principles," Mexican Amercians' distaste for the institution of slavery, and domination of the state's Democratic Party by nativists and riffraff. It seems natural, then, that Soto embraced the Union cause and accepted an officer's commission a few years later.

But it seems that poverty may have driven his decision almost as much as patriotism. Official correspondence makes it clear that Soto's priority was seeing to the welfare of his young wife and two children, as though they had no means of support other than his salary, and they accompanied him to the Presidio. When the company was ordered to leave the post in December, Captain Pico, lamenting "the state of" the lieutenant's family, wrote to department headquarters asking that Soto be allowed to stay behind to take care of them. Instead, the lieutenant remained with the troops, and his family would continue to follow him throughout his service in California.[18]

Soto's arrival may have proved a frustration to Lieutenant Jimenez. Not only was Jimenez no longer in charge of the company, but with a first lieutenant in place, he would not enjoy temporary command in Pico's absence either.

The new company was not quite what Senator Pacheco had in mind when he had proposed the battalion the year earlier. Instead of a unit composed of Native Californian vaqueros recruited in Southern California, the press described its eighty-two rank-and-file troopers as a "mixture of colors and tongues" that included "native Californians . . . , Mexicans, Chilenos [*sic*], Sonorians [*sic*], California and Yaqui Indians, Germans, Americans, etc."[19] Significantly, the company had already lost eleven men to desertion.

Captain Pico had been lobbying for promotion to major of the battalion since shortly after his uncle Andrés declined the commission in March. At one point he even partly blamed the troubles he had recruiting on the vacancy.[20] Expecting Pico to be promoted, a number of officers at the Presidio recommended Jimenez to become captain of Company A.[21] By November, however, Pico had abandoned this notion and had joined others in endorsing Salvador Vallejo for the appointment. Despite an abortive attempt by Jimenez to get a commission in another company, neither the second lieutenant nor the captain gained promotion.

In September the men of the Native Cavalry received the pay that they were owed for the previous two months. One soldier, Private Lucas Galea, was confined in the Presidio's guardhouse at the time but was released long enough to stand in line at the paymaster's table with the rest of his company. Immediately afterward, Captain Pico ordered him to hand over his money to him. Galea understood that Pico was going to hold it until he served his punishment. Upon release, he asked for his money, but the captain told him that he had used it to pay off the private's debts from as far back as March, when the recruits were still in San Jose.[22]

When the company was paid again two months later, Galea, who apparently could not long stay out of trouble, was again in confinement, this time in the custody of the provost marshal's guard in San Francisco. He had made arrangements with Sergeant José Leyva to draw his money in his absence. But declaring that the sergeant was not authorized to receive another soldier's pay, Captain Pico took this as well.[23]

Once again, Pico would maintain that Galea's money was put toward old debts. A portion of the confiscated funds went to pay off both the captain and Lieutenant Jimenez for cash loans, while much of the rest went to merchants, a baker, and a barber in San Jose who had extended credit to Galea and other recruits—about thirty-seven dollars total. When Galea returned from confinement, Pico gave him fifteen dollars in greenbacks and dismissively declared that they "were square."[24]

The soldier did not understand the arrangement, and the captain's sometimes high-handed behavior was probably not helpful. Seeking assistance in this matter, Galea approached Sergeant Prudencia García, who said there was nothing he would do. In frustration the disgruntled private turned away and walked toward the post hospital, where he stopped Major Andrew Bowman of the 9th U.S. Infantry, the Presidio's commander, with a similarly predictable lack of results. In the coming two years, Galea would continue to maintain that the captain owed him the balance, with García and Lieutenant Jimenez taking his side in the argument.

Leyva seems to be the only soldier who complained at the time. On one occasion Leyva, accompanied by Sergeant Garcia, brought his grievances to Pico, telling his captain that "he did not dislike him, but that he had taken his [Leyva's] money."[25] In the coming months, though, two other soldiers would gripe about having their pay withheld, and it is likely that there were others. Pico's practice was certainly irregular and presented great opportunities for misunderstandings and potential abuse. The captain, in his arrogance and impatience, at the very least was playing fast and loose with the rules.

In December E. Marchande, the proprietor of San Francisco's Union Hotel, wrote to Major E. Sparrow Purdy in the Adjutant General's Office to complain about an unpaid bill "of $165, for meals, lodging, and monies loaned." Pico, said Marchande, had "frequented" the hotel since receiving his commission and was extended credit "solely on the fact of his being an officer." The businessman said he was reluctant to bring the matter to the department, but after two months of excuses from the captain "such as wait till tomorrow, etc.," he wrote to Purdy "in the hope that means may be adapted to induce Capt Pico to maintain the character a U.S. officer should have."[26]

Referring to Pico's "unfortunate actions," Major General Irvin McDowell forwarded the complaint to the captain, who responded within a few days. He called Marchande's letter "*Entirely false*" and went on in some detail about the money he had paid as "settlement" for his "account" at the hotel. Pico further went on to boast in his usual manner, "There is no man can say that I or any of my Family ever owed a dollar but what was paid." He admitted to having no receipts, as his transactions were "as one Gentleman with another," because he regarded Marchande as "a man of honor," though in this he stated he found himself to be "very much mistaken."[27]

Marchande responded within a day. His letter to Lieutenant Colonel Richard C. Drum reflects not only his understandable and justifiable frustration with the Californio captain but also his unfortunate bigotry:

San Francisco, December 9, 1863

R. C. Drum.
Adjutant Gen. USA.

Dear Sir:
I have just seen a letter addressed to you by Capt Pico, of the *native* Cal. Cavalry, in which he says that my statement of Dec. 2 1863, "is entirely false." Capt Pico's memory must be very defective—so much so as to disqualify him from occupying an honorable position—or he is a wilful [*sic*] and deliberate liar. As he is in the US. service and is, in time of war, not held amenable to civil process for debts incurred, I have not sought a legal remedy. And, besides, I have no wish to disgrace the uniform he wears. But I suppose that, in consequence of his absolute denial of being indebted to me, in order that

others may not be victimised [*sic*] by the Captain of the *native* Cal Cavalry, herewith I enclose a memorandum, from my books, in which you will observe the manner by which the indebtedness has been contracted. The Captain speaks of "settlements," when there has not been, at any time, a settlement in full. It is the first time I ever heard of part fragments being made synonymous with "settlement." However, as he is a *native,* some allowance should be made to one who does not know what honor means in English. Sir, I am not the only one who has been trifled with, and when the *native* Captain alluded to his pecuniary resources, in a manner that ever characterises [*sic*] a "Jeremy Diddler," he promised that his tongue had deceived all but me. In this he was mistaken, as he will be apt to find out to his disgrace.

Very Respectfully,
Your Obt Serv't
E. Marchande.
Union Hotel[28]

A few days later the proprietor of another San Francisco establishment, the Union Bar, wrote to the adjutant general to report that over the previous months, Pico had run up a tab of six dollars for "liquor for self & recruits" and had failed to pay despite repeated promises to do so.[29] It is unclear if this issue was ever resolved, but this would not be the last time the captain would be involved in such a dispute.

By the end of 1863, recruitment efforts for other Native Cavalry companies were underway in San Francisco and Los Angeles. Officials were eager for the new battalion to take shape so it could be sent out of state where it was needed, but its organization had already taken longer than anybody expected. Meanwhile, more than twenty men of Pico's Company A had grown weary of the wait and deserted.[30] When the new year arrived, it would be a greatly reduced unit that would finally be sent to its first assignment in the field.

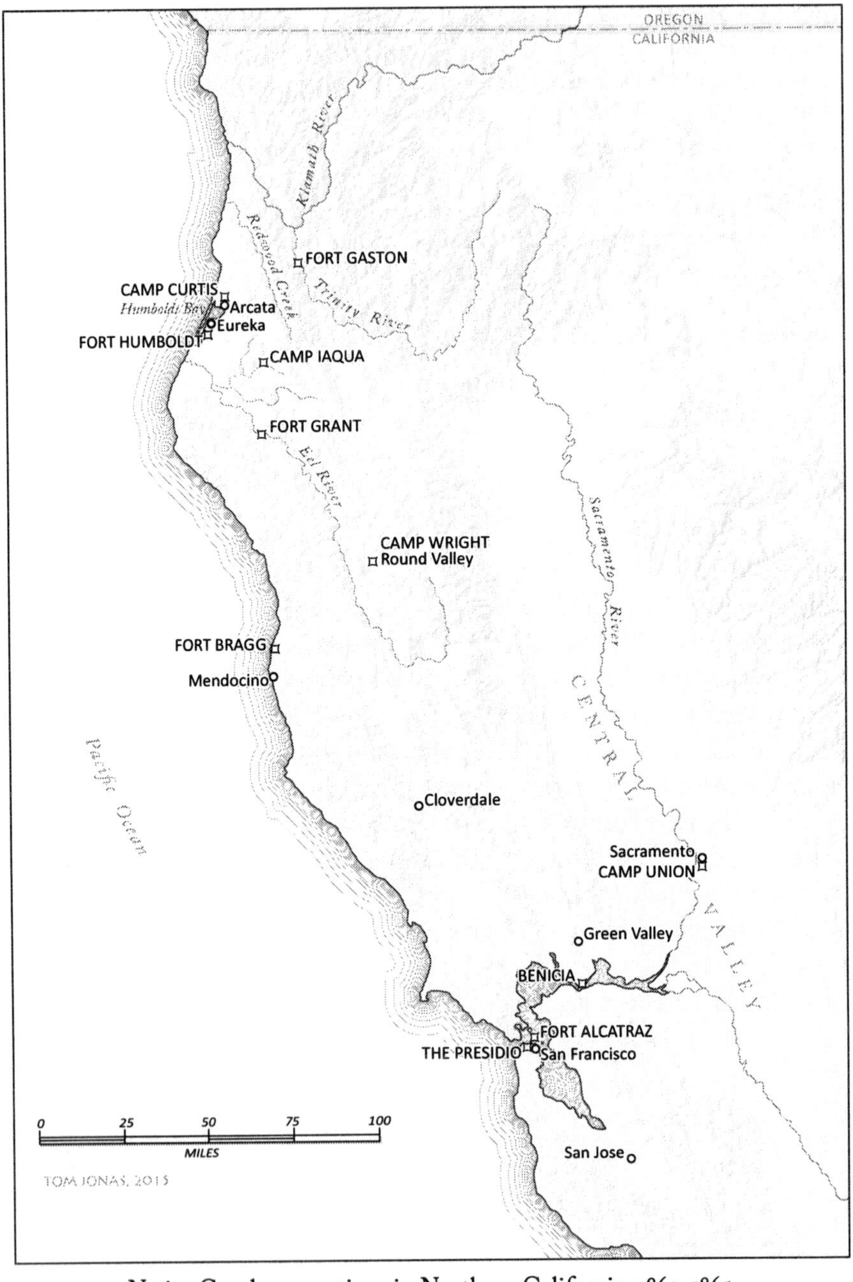

Native Cavalry operations in Northern California, 1863–1865.
Map by Tom Jonas. Copyright © 2015 by the University of Oklahoma Press.

CHAPTER 3

Service in the Northern Counties

Never mind Sergeant, the man that puts me out of the Service requires to have a larger pair of balls than I have, for he will have to fight me.

CAPTAIN JOSÉ RAMÓN PICO

After a few months of drilling and garrison duty at the Presidio, orders arrived in December 1863 for Company A to join an ongoing campaign in Northern California against a coalition of Hupa Indians and their allies.[1] For the duty ahead, the Californio troopers turned in their lances in exchange for Sharps carbines, the standard shoulder arm of the Federal cavalry.[2] On January 2, 1864, the officers and 53 men boarded the northbound steamer *Panama* for Humboldt Bay.[3] After three days the company disembarked at Eureka and reported to Fort Humboldt. Two weeks later they marched inland for Fort Gaston, where the Native Californians joined a force of 350 men, including elements of a special volunteer unit of light infantry called the 1st Battalion of Mountaineers, which was being assembled for a series of operations against the tribes of Northern California.[4]

This campaign was merely the latest phase in a longstanding conflict that began in the 1850s as the various tribes of far northern California put up intermittent armed resistance to Anglo-American settlers. In addition to the usual issues of encroachment, the newcomers further antagonized them with raids on their rancherias to support an illicit trade in Indian slaves as well as occasional massacres and other atrocities committed by local militias. War had erupted by 1860, with regulars and militia engaged in constant combat with warriors of no fewer than nine different tribes. By 1863 the Hupa had emerged as the most prominent of these, having organized their fighters into at least three well-armed bands known as "gun gangs," totaling an estimated 150 men. Though woefully outnumbered by the federal forces, they proved far more familiar with the rugged country than even the locally recruited mountaineers and were ably supported by an intelligence network that included spies among the army's Indian scouts.

One commander described the challenges of service in the Humboldt District in a letter to department headquarters:

> This country alone contains some 3,000 square miles, and is made up of steep mountain ridges and covered, three-fourths of it, with dense forests, packed full of undergrowth and chaparral, all but impenetrable to white men, and with no communications but rough and difficult mountain trails in many places next to impassable. The task of bringing in the Indians scattered over such a country as this, stealthily moving about in small parties, never traveling in the known trails, always unseen, though constantly watching our movements by their spies and scouts; hiding when they stop in the most inaccessible places, would be like the task of bringing in all the ground squirrels or the foxes, and will have to be performed somewhat in a similar way.[5]

An example of the frustrations faced by the army in prosecuting the campaign came in December 1863, weeks before the Native Cavalry's arrival in the district. A force of mountaineers, supported by a howitzer, laid siege to a band of Hupas holed up in a small compound of blockhouses in the middle of a swampy prairie. After exchanging fire with the Indians for two days, the soldiers stormed the fort on the morning of the third day only to find that the estimated three hundred Indians had stolen past the pickets and disappeared into the forest sometime during the night.

Lieutenant Colonel Stephen G. Whipple, commander of the district, immediately made use of the new force he had assembled at Fort Gaston, sending detachments on daily and nightly patrols of the surrounding Hoopa Valley. After nearly two weeks, Whipple received intelligence that the gun gang led by a Hupa known as "Big Jim" was at a rancheria called Tseweñaldiñ less than half a mile from the post. The colonel sent a force of mountaineers to attack the Indians at night, while Captain Pico's company was posted on the east bank of the Trinity River to prevent the Hupas from escaping. But Big Jim and his band were warned of the soldier's approach in time to make an orderly withdrawal, and the soldiers found no one in the rancheria but children and old women and supposed the fighting men had entirely abandoned the area. This was not the case, however, as Corporal José Picasso, an Italian immigrant who was one of Pico's initial recruits, was shot through the chest by a sniper who fired from concealment in the brush on the opposite bank of the Trinity. Though "several Indians" were spotted fleeing into the hills, efforts to pursue were to no avail as the elusive Hupas melted into the forest. Picasso at first was assumed to be mortally wounded, but he soon recovered and was back on duty. Meanwhile, the mountaineers put Tseweñaldiñ to the torch.[6]

Pico's unit was praised in the local press as "active and energetic," while the captain himself spoke of his men "in high terms as efficient and well drilled soldiers." Despite this rosy assessment, however, internal strife continued to shadow Company A.[7]

It took little time for serious discipline problems to emerge. In February 1864 Lieutenant Soto found himself dealing with a minor mutiny. In command of a detachment near Redwood Creek, Soto ordered Private Pedro Seguin to help drive the detachment's horses into camp. Seguin refused the order three times, turning away and saying "no quiero."[8] When Soto disarmed the soldier and ordered his arrest, another private, Marcos Leon, handed Seguin his pistol "for the purpose of resisting" the officer. Others joined Leon and Seguin, but a serious incident was avoided when cooler heads prevailed. Three soldiers—Leon, Seguin, and bugler Henry Dumont—were convicted by a subsequent court-martial at Camp Iaqua and each sentenced to hard labor with a twelve-pound ball chained to their legs. Seguin and Dumont later deserted.

Though it had diminished significantly since the company had left the Presidio, desertion remained a serious discipline problem. On February 4, four French-surnamed troopers absconded from Fort Gaston with their arms and a number of horses, including one of Captain Pico's personal mounts, a black with white legs named Jack. Fleeing south, they broke into a house belonging to a prominent citizen of the lower Eel River, and "capsizing the contents of bureaus, closets, and overturning beds on the floor," they made off with clothing, a carpet bag, "provisions," and a gold watch, all with an estimated value of $200–250. Four days into their flight, three of the men were captured near Camp Grant on the mail route to Mendocino and taken under arrest to Fort Humboldt. Meanwhile, the captain's horse was recovered near Arcata but was not returned to the company for nearly a month, having become lame from the rough treatment by the soldiers during their escape.

Months later, from confinement at Fort Alcatraz, the deserters wrote to Major General Irvin McDowell, now commander of the Department of the Pacific, to plea for leniency and to address some of the problems in Company A. Unable to speak Spanish, they confessed to having difficulty understanding their orders and spoke of physical abuse at the hands of Captain Pico. Significantly, the prisoners mentioned that prior to their flight, they had appealed to Lieutenant Jimenez, who had tried to intervene on their behalf.[9] The three eventually were allowed to return to the company but soon deserted again.

In mid-February Colonel Henry M. Black arrived at Fort Humboldt with three companies of his own 6th California Infantry, totaling some 250 men, and assumed command of the district from Whipple. By this time it had become clear that mounted troops were of limited usefulness in the thick forest and rugged terrain of the redwood country, thus the Native Cavalry's duties were greatly curtailed.[10] On March 6 Black ordered Pico's company to escort a government train returning from Fort Gaston to Arcata on Humboldt Bay, then to report to what would become their new duty station at nearby Camp Curtis. From there, detachments were to shuttle back and forth to Fort Gaston to escort prisoners to the coast. This would remain their mission for the time being.[11]

In the interior the campaign continued. Though for the most part the army was unable to force the enemy into open battle, the constant movement of soldiers began to wear on the hostile bands. By the end of April, the leaders of the most active gun gangs had grown "tired of the mountains" and were negotiating terms for peace. The war in the redwoods was now all but over. Nevertheless, the Native Cavalry continued escorting prisoners to and from the Humboldt Peninsula. By May at least three hundred people remained confined there while authorities elsewhere discussed their fate.[12]

It was while the company was stationed at Camp Curtis that what should have been a minor dispute arose regarding Captain Pico's horse. After Jack was returned in March after recovering from its ordeal with the deserters, Pico was able to use the horse for only a brief time before

Arcata, California.
This lithograph dates to 1857, when the town was still known as Union.
Courtesy California History Room, California State Library, Sacramento.

he was again lame. In the meantime, the captain purchased a yellowish roan that he called Baby from a "French doctor" in Arcata. Pico, however, soon decided that he preferred to ride one of the government horses and left Baby among the horses set aside for the rank and file. Adding to any potential confusion was the fact that Jack carried a "US" brand, the result of the captain carelessly having left him in the corral with the soldier's horses at the Presidio months earlier.[13]

A number of soldiers mistakenly, but perhaps understandably, believed that Pico had appropriated a government horse as his own. This was chief among of a number of complaints that Lieutenant Jimenez made concerning the captain's conduct in April, prompting Colonel Black to order the commander at Camp Curtis, Captain Eugene Gibbs, 2nd California Infantry, to investigate. Gibbs's report led to no further action, though these matters would lead to more trouble for Pico over the next year. Meanwhile, Corporal José Villa was riding Baby while serving with an escort detachment of ten cavalrymen under Sergeant José Leyva. As Jack had been at the Presidio, the yellow roan was branded under orders from the post quartermaster while Leyva was at Fort Gaston in June.[14]

Another dispute with Pico involved money yet again. Because of the district's relative isolation, troops stationed there were paid less than regularly, and merchandise was usually available only at inflated prices. As he had in San Jose and at the Presidio, the captain occasionally loaned money to his men and even saw to the needs of the troops by buying goods for them from a civilian sutler at Fort Gaston, including boots, bowie knives, pipes, sardines, sewing needles, shirts, and tobacco. Later at Camp Curtis, Pico withheld money from his indebted soldiers to cover their loans. At least two men, Sergeant Francisco Higuera and Corporal Picasso, back on duty after recovering from the wound suffered in January, misunderstood the rather haphazard arrangement, which Pico apparently never fully explained, and complained that he had stolen from them. Captain Gibbs looked into this while investigating the matter of the horse and apparently found nothing that warranted further action.

By the end of the summer, the Hupas were allowed to return to their valley pending the organization of a reservation. The mission in the Humboldt District thus shifted from one of active campaigning to one of peacekeeping. In far-off San Francisco, department officials were increasingly concerned with maintaining law and order in more populated parts of the state with the approaching elections, especially since the three-year enlistments of many in the 2nd California Infantry were due to expire. Thus they issued orders in September to withdraw most of the forces then in the district. Colonel Whipple, who was once again in command, disagreed with the order and argued that maintenance of the reservations would require at least one company of infantry in addition to the scattered Mountaineer Battalion and a company of the 2nd California Infantry that remained. He suggested instead that the Native Cavalry, whose duties were so limited that the unit was "no material increase to the force" under his command, be withdrawn from the district instead. In the end Whipple's request was not granted, but during the subsequent reorganization of his forces, Pico's company was moved to Fort Humboldt.

During this otherwise idle time, Pico requested one month's leave to return to San Jose for the election. On the eve of his departure, he delivered a windy statement to his men, urging them to support the Union ticket:

> In my absence it may be attempted to lead or influence you from the path you have voluntarily chosen. I therefore ask you to be steady in the opinion

> you have formed and expressed in regard to the coming election. Soon will come the day when you will be called upon to exercise your rights as civilians in the selection of a man for the Chief Magistracy of the Nation. On such a momentous occasion it is hoped and believed, from your intelligence and patriotism, and love of order, that you will sustain the defenders of the Union and the cause of liberty; it is believed that more will be unnecessary to show you how dishonorable it would be to serve as instruments of the demagogues who are trying to link us to the cause of the Rebellion. No! it is not possible that Calif should go back a single step, after giving so many proofs of her loyalty and patriotism; what would she gain by a change? Let me say to you then, sustain forever the noble Union party.[15]

After journeying south via the coastal steamer *Panama,* Pico was warmly received in his hometown. Speaking to the local press, he praised "his company in high terms." But the captain also hinted at some impatience with the dullness of service in the Humboldt District when he "expressed the hope that he may soon be ordered to a more active field of duty where his native Calif troops may have an opportunity of winning more distinction than can be acquired in camp life."[16]

Frustrated as he may have been with his stint in the north, Captain Pico had certainly returned to his element in San Jose. On the eve of the election, some three hundred Native Californians paraded through the streets of his hometown to assemble for a torchlight rally. There, Pico gave a speech calling on them "to vote for the Union ticket, and thus prove their devotion to their country and the cause of freedom." The speech ended with the crowd giving him "loud vivas" as he was "showered with bouquets by the loyal ladies of San Jose," followed by the presentation of a "silk sash as a token of appreciation" from the community "for his services in the Union cause."[17]

Meanwhile, concerns regarding the upcoming election required Company A to move to a remote post called Camp Wright at Round Valley, about 160 miles by road south of Fort Humboldt across "an unbroken succession of mountains and can[y]ons." Round Valley itself was described as "a charming sight . . . hidden among the spurs of the Coast Range" at an altitude of some eighteen hundred feet. During the summer, the place was regarded as picturesque, "dotted with groves of magnificent oaks intermixed with leafy dells and shaded glens." Yet during the winter, which was when the Native Cavalry was there, "the lower parts of the valley were little better than swamps and quagmires," with "almost constant rain" rendering even the smallest creeks "nearly unfordable."[18]

Camp Wright itself consisted of a parade ground surrounded by a handful of log structures and tents dwarfed by enormous oak trees. The post was commanded by Captain Charles D. Douglas, a competent and earnest, if somewhat humorless, officer. Douglas had come to Round Valley nearly two years before with his own Company F, 2nd California Infantry, to establish the post and impose martial law to maintain peace between less than one hundred Anglo-American settlers and some 300–500 Wailaki and Yuki Indians on the adjacent Round Valley Reservation. Though Douglas would continue to enforce a ban on selling liquor, martial law was lifted after only a few months. Nevertheless, tensions lingered, and the captain harbored doubts about the loyalties of some settlers.

Rumors of a secessionist conspiracy to disrupt the upcoming elections abounded in California in the latter half of 1864, even in the northern counties. For his part, Captain Douglas, citing a report from a militia captain, wrote to department headquarters in August to tell of a "well organized party" of "disloyal men" who planned to attack Camp Wright to seize the supplies there. He believed that they were "only waiting the approach of the November election and a signal from their leaders to inaugurate a guerilla warfare in these valleys and mountains." Specifically, Douglas singled out a hard-drinking Round Valley resident named Smith Gamble, with whom the captain had a longstanding feud, as a suspected conspirator but admitted being reluctant to arrest him until he received authorization. In the meantime Douglas expressed concern that his small, isolated garrison would be unable to defend the post and requested an additional company as reinforcement.[19]

Apparently, Colonel Whipple did not consider this an urgent problem, so it was perhaps fortunate for the fate of the Republic that the conspiracy apparently did not go off as Douglas had supposed. Not until November 10, two days after the election, did Whipple order Company A south to Camp Wright under the command of Lieutenant Soto.

Meanwhile, difficulties in scheduling a northbound steamer caused Captain Pico to request an extension of his leave. It was not until November 21 that he stepped off the steamer *Oregon* at Eureka and finally reported at Fort Humboldt, where he was handed a package of letters that included one to Lieutenant Jimenez from Major Vallejo at Drum Barracks.[20] Pico accompanied a small train of pack mules and its escort as far as the Eel River, where the condition of the roads due to "continuous rain" forced him to abandon much of his baggage, though he intended to send for it all later.[21] After many "trials and difficulties," he finally arrived at Camp Wright to resume command of his company on December 10.

Lieutenant Jimenez was now the post adjutant and was working closely with Captain Douglas, in whom he found a more receptive audience for his complaints about Pico than he had in Colonel Black or Captain Gibbs the previous spring. As a result, Pico's conduct was now under far more scrutiny so that even relatively minor incidents would have serious consequences. One such matter involved the letter from Major Vallejo. Upon arrival at Camp Wright, Pico let Jimenez know about the letter without realizing that it had been misplaced at some point on the road. By this time, both officers were doing what they could to avoid speaking to each other, so the matter was forgotten until the letter finally turned up in mid-January 1865. The captain quietly placed it in one of the pigeonholes in Jimenez's office while the lieutenant was elsewhere.[22]

Douglas had left for San Francisco at the beginning of the month, leaving Pico in command of Camp Wright. The feared guerilla campaign still had not materialized, so the garrison was left with little to do. For his part, Pico amused himself by riding around Round Valley demonstrating his Californio horsemanship by "lassoing hogs" and "throwing cattle by the tail." While the settlers were entertained, some of the officers at the post reportedly found this conduct scandalous.[23]

Always gregarious, Pico socialized with the local civilians, many of whom had less-than-savory reputations, including a reputed horse thief. Among them too were men who had been arrested for expressing, or had been suspected of having, Confederate sympathies, including Smith Gamble. Other officers in Douglas's command, however, had not shared their captain's opinion of Gamble and had been purchasing butter and eggs from him for years. As for Captain Pico, Gamble and some of the others were old acquaintances of his father, so they were welcomed into "his quarters in a spirit of gentlemanly kinship" and invited to share his hospitality and his whiskey.[24]

Around the time Pico assumed command, the garrison found itself low on ammunition, with his own company being out altogether.[25] The captain had sent for a resupply, but it would take about two weeks for the shipment to arrive from Fort Bragg, the nearest post, some eighty miles away by waterlogged mountain trails. Meanwhile, word of the garrison's predicament had gotten out, with some of the officers believing that Pico had told Gamble and his friends while intoxicated, though even Jimenez later admitted that there probably was not enough whiskey there for any of them to get drunk.[26]

Two other incidents occurred during Pico's tenure as acting post commander that, to his detractors, seemed to reflect badly on his judgment, though it could be argued that his actions were understandable in the circumstances. The first happened on the night of January 4, when Lieutenant William H. Noyes of the 2nd California Infantry as officer of the day was making his rounds among the guard posts. Private Emilio Gerard, a Frenchman from San Jose, had been posted for the night in front of the guardhouse, situated among the trees at the edge of Camp Wright. Gerard was "subject to fits" that would sometimes make him faint "like a dead man." As Noyes approached the guardhouse, the soldier collapsed in front of him. As officer of the day, he ordered that Gerard not be put back on guard duty. Sergeant Alejandro Laurier, another French-speaking volunteer from San Jose who was in charge of the guards, assumed the post. But he must have misunderstood or later ignored the order, for Gerard was soon back on duty.

Once again making the rounds a little before reveille, Noyes found the post abandoned. Laurier told the lieutenant that Gerard had had a second fit and that he was looking for another soldier to take his place. Continuing his rounds, Noyes found that Private José "Joseph" Wilhem had walked away from his post near the Native Cavalry's company campfire. Finding him near the cook's tent, the officer took the trooper's belts and ordered him arrested. Noyes made a brief report about the two errant troopers to Captain Pico, telling him that he believed that Gerard, while unfit for duty, did not deserve punishment since his problem was "something he could not avoid."

At this point some confusion occurred, but it is unclear where the disconnect was. Noyes understood that Pico had ordered him to release Wilhem from the guardhouse when he apparently meant that Gerard, who was not at this point under arrest, was to be freed. The lieutenant freed Wilhem, but the captain ordered him rearrested once the mistake was discovered. Again there was a misunderstanding, and both privates were placed in the guardhouse for three days before they were both ordered released. Noyes later attributed the matter to the fact that the sergeant and corporal of the guard who assumed duty that morning were Anglo-Americans "who did not understand French or Spanish" as well as his own failure to understand that Wilhem was following instructions when he left his post, having been ordered to wake up the cooks for breakfast.

The second incident happened a little over a week later and also involved Noyes. A Round Valley resident named J. B. Owens came to the lieutenant to report that some soldiers had killed one of his cows. Noyes passed this on to Pico, and the captain mounted a brief but futile search for the perpetrators. The next day Owens came back with an Indian who was able to identify two of the culprits, both troopers of Company A. Pico put the men in the guardhouse, though he did not consider an Indian to be a competent witness and initiated a cursory investigation and search for a "responsible person" to "come forward." Finding nothing after two days, the captain dismissed the whole matter as "frivolous and unsubstantiated," released the men from confinement, and did not pursue it further. Before the end of the month, the implicated soldiers had deserted.

Captain Douglas returned to Camp Wright on January 24 and received from Lieutenant Jimenez what was doubtless a debatably subjective account of Pico's conduct during his absence. He ordered Jimenez to place Captain Pico under arrest two days later for "neglect of Duty and conduct unbecoming an officer and a gentleman." The *chileño* lieutenant was pleased with this turn of events, calling Sergeant García behind a tent one evening to tell him, "now Sergeant we have it, he is under arrest now, and I shall not cease until I have discharged him from the service." Alluding to the promise he had made on the steamer from San Jose nearly a year and a half earlier, he added, "as soon as I do that, you get my epaulettes."

While Jimenez saw the arrest as an opportunity for an almost certain promotion, it would have the opposite effect on Pico. It was clear at this point that Major Vallejo would be resigning his command of the battalion, and prominent San Jose friends of the captain, citing both his service in the field and his efforts on behalf of the Union ticket during the recent election, were already lobbying for his appointment to the expected vacancy. Pico's arrest effectively removed him from consideration.

Relieved of command of Company A, the proud Californio was left to stew while confined to his quarters. Bitter, he reportedly declared, using a phrase that does not easily translate into English, that Captain Douglas and all the other Anglo-American officers were "damned goats" *(cabrones?)* who would not drive him from the service, "that he did not wish and would not serve with or under such damned goats." He reportedly stated this on at least two occasions in the presence of Sergeants Laurier and García. García later reported that Pico became even more defiant, declaring that Douglas would need to have "a bigger pair of balls" than him, for he would have to fight the Californio if he wanted to force him out of the army. Even though under arrest, said García, Pico promised "with an air of animosity" that "when he was free," he would make Douglas pay, "God damn."

Toward the end of the first week of his arrest, the captain had calmed down sufficiently to articulate his grievances in a more civil manner. Given Pico's usual impatience with the rules of the service and his uneasiness with written English, it is likely that he had some help, perhaps from another officer at the post, in asserting his legal rights in correspondence. Eight days having passed without his having been served a copy of the specific charges, the captain demanded his release under army regulations and wrote to General McDowell to further request a court of inquiry, a military equivalent of a grand jury, to investigate the charges to see if they actually warranted action.

Douglas responded by presenting Pico with a list of six charges supported by twenty-two specifications. These composed the complete litany of Jimenez's complaints about Pico since his enlistment and ranged from frivolous to quite serious. First, "Conduct prejudicial to good order and military discipline" referred to his having withheld Private Galea's pay at the Presidio nearly a year and a half earlier. Next, "Conduct unbecoming an officer and a gentleman" concerned his financial dealings with Sergeant Higuera and Corporal Picasso, his relationship with Smith Gamble, and his having lassoed hogs and thrown cattle by the tail "to the great scandal of his Brother officers and the enlisted men of his command." A third charge of "Neglect of duty" was about the men whom he freed from the guardhouse while in command of Camp Wright.

Charges four and five, "Using contemptuous and disrespectful language in speaking of his Commanding Officer" and "Using violent and threatening language against his Commanding Officer," both derived from his intemperate outbursts while under arrest. Finally, the captain was charged with "Fraud" in the matter of the branding of his horse.

Douglas urged department headquarters to reject Pico's request for a court of inquiry, arguing that the "expenses of sending the prisoner and witnesses to San Francisco would be much greater than the *value* of Captain Pico to the service." Instead, he requested permission to convene a court-martial at Camp Wright, though even suggesting that Pico be "summarily dismissed from the service, to which *he is a disgrace*."

A week later Pico again wrote to McDowell, this time in an effort to avoid a court-martial by resigning his commission. For his part, the Californio blamed some of his difficulties on "the inconvenience of a want of knowledge of the English language." To this Douglas pointedly added that Pico needed help in writing the letter, something that, in his opinion, made him "highly *incompetent* to *properly* discharge the duties *necessarily attached* to the profession of a Captain." No action was taken on the resignation, and Pico remained confined to quarters under arrest at the end of March, when his father wrote, in Spanish, to the general to plead for intervention.[27]

McDowell, of course, had many other priorities, among them plans for Pico and his company. By mid-February it was well known that the four companies of the Native Cavalry were to be assembled as a battalion and sent to Arizona for service against the Apaches.[28] By the end of the month, department headquarters issued orders for Company A to march to Benicia Barracks, more than 170 miles to the south, and from there continue to Drum Barracks near Los Angeles to join the battalion. Captain Pico's arrest, among other issues, would delay this movement for well over a month.

Meanwhile, the company's rank and file languished in relatively dull garrison duty under the command of Lieutenant Soto, though Jimenez would have temporary command during Soto's frequent absences. The soldiers spent some of their ample idle time entertaining themselves with athletic contests. One day in early April, a "noted racer" known as Plough Boy appeared at Round Valley to challenge the garrison to a footrace. The soldiers put forward their best runner, a sergeant of the

Native Cavalry. A one-hundred-yard track was improvised as a "great crowd" gathered. The betting was furious as some "three or four thousand dollars" and "several horses" changed hands, with odds running 100–20 against the sergeant.

After three false starts, the race began in earnest. Just after the judge's shout of "go!," the sergeant abruptly stopped, apparently thinking this was another false start, before starting again and almost overtaking Plough Boy with twenty-five yards remaining. Suddenly, as his opponent was about to pass him, Plough Boy "over-reached himself and fell." As the Californio crossed the finish line, his comrades "threw up their caps, and gave three cheers for Uncle Sam's Boy, and went to their quarters." The civilians who had bet on Plough Boy, however, were suspicious that the race was fixed.

The controversy remained unresolved when the Native Cavalry, still under Lieutenant Soto, finally left Camp Wright and the Humboldt District for Benicia Barracks two days later. Captain Pico accompanied them but remained under arrest, to Lieutenant Jimenez's delight. One day while on the march, Jimenez, "under the influence of liquor," reportedly drew his saber on the captain while insulting and threatening him.

The march to Benicia took ten days, during which much would happen in the world beyond California. On the evening of April 9, word came by telegraph to San Francisco of General Robert E. Lee's surrender at Appomattox Court House, Virginia, leading to spontaneous celebrations in the streets of loyal Union towns like Sacramento.[29] This news would not arrive in some outlying areas for a few days yet, so it is unclear when Company A was informed that the rebellion was all but over.

The wires carried very different news when the company arrived at Benicia on April 15. President Lincoln had been shot by an assassin the previous evening and had passed away that very morning. Riots broke out in San Francisco as word spread through the city. Police, militia, and soldiers were mobilized and quickly restored order. Uncertainty, however, continued to reign for weeks as rumors spread that McDowell was suppressing bad news, including "riots all over the East"; that Governor Frederick Low had been assassinated; and that "anonymous letters threatening all the State and milty [*sic*] authorities with death" had been found in the streets. At the same time, reports of varying credibility came in of "bloody riots" all over the state.[30]

The Native Cavalry was mobilized as part of the larger effort to deal with this unrest. Green Valley, a squatter settlement a little over fifteen miles north of Benicia, was long known to be "infested with some of the boldest Secessionists" on the West Coast who were "open and loud-mouthed in their abuse of the Government" and had for years threatened pro-Union citizens and army recruiters, sometimes at gunpoint. On April 22, after local officials received word that the Green Valley secessionists had "held a jubilee" to celebrate the assassination of the president, Lieutenant Jimenez and a detachment of twenty-five troopers moved out to arrest the ringleaders.[31]

As the Native Cavalry arrived at the settlement, the instigators retreated to a fortified brick farmhouse in the upper part of the valley. When the soldiers approached the house and demanded that the men surrender, the secessionists let loose with a volley that left two cavalrymen wounded. The troopers returned fire with their carbines, wounding two of the men inside. The "secesh party" quickly surrendered, and Jimenez's bluecoats arrested ten men, who were brought back to Benicia the next day to be held for a trial by court-martial.[32] Of the two wounded soldiers, Private Juan Leon was soon able to return to duty, while Private Antonio Guellman, seriously injured in the foot, would eventually be discharged.[33]

Meanwhile, the long-awaited court of inquiry for Captain Pico had finally convened. A substantial post of modern brick buildings, Benicia Barracks had, unlike Camp Wright, a garrison sufficiently large to provide enough officers for a proper panel. Pico himself would be represented by counsel, a San Francisco attorney and family friend named A. C. Campbell.

The proceedings started on April 25 and lasted nearly two weeks. True to Douglas's concerns, of the witnesses the court intended to call, four would not appear. Three of these, Camp Wright's post surgeon and two civilians, were apparently unable to travel from Round Valley, while the fourth, Sergeant Laurier, had deserted the day before the company took up the line of march.

Lieutenant Jimenez was the first witness, and his testimony was the longest, taking up most of the first two days. The written record makes his evidence appear quite matter of fact, but Campbell later characterized him as showing "excitement and anxiety." Counsel's attempt to impugn the lieutenant's motives at this point were blocked by procedural motions, as they would be later when Sergeant Garcia was called to the stand.

An interpreter was called in to take testimony from Lieutenant Soto and from some enlisted men of the Native Cavalry. Often these statements were confused and self-contradictory. In some cases the soldiers seemed to misunderstand the questions and occasionally had nothing to say at all. On the issue of the horse, for instance, different witnesses were clearly talking about different animals. A few of the charges and specifications were never even addressed during the lengthy proceedings. Campbell, though frequently frustrated when the court ruled against him, was able to score a few points on behalf of his client. For instance, he was able to get Sergeant Higuera, Corporal Picasso, and Sergeant Leyva to admit that they owed Captain Pico money by producing receipts and promissory notes.[34]

General McDowell, for his part, was anxious to see the inquisition end so he could start his planned operations in Arizona. On the eighth day his adjutant, Colonel Drum, sent a telegram from San Francisco ordering that the court "sit without regard to hours, the necessity of the service requiring Pico's Company to move." Meanwhile, the department had sent a quartermaster officer to Benicia to inspect the Native Cavalry's horses in preparation for field service.[35]

The proceedings continued for the next two days. Ironically, testimony by some of the same Anglo-American officers whom Pico had allegedly insulted, Captain Gibbs and Lieutenant Noyes of the 2nd California Infantry and Captain Trittle of the 6th California Infantry, generally supported the defense's case. Finally, on the last day Campbell was able to introduce evidence of Jimenez's motives when he called Private Rodrigues was to the stand. Rodrigues, as it happened, had been a witness to some of Jimenez's conversations with Sergeant García promising a commission in exchange for García's help in getting Pico discharged. Even more damning than this was the soldier's statement that, just three days before, Jimenez had cornered him at the post's stables to tell him that if he were "to give any testimony in favor of Capt Pico, he would work until he would get me to Alcatraz Island wearing a 30 lb ball on each leg."

Pico did not testify in his own behalf, Campbell instead summing up the captain's case with a twelve-page written statement. In it he refuted the charges one by one and once again reiterated his attacks on Jimenez.

His wrap up included some familiar sentiments regarding Pico's often irregular approach to command:

> In conclusion I would respectfully submit to the honorable the Court that I am fully satisfied in my own mind and hope that your honors are also satisfied from the whole testimony as taken in this case that the charges made against Capt. Pico are untrue in fact that they have been instituted on the part of the real prosecutor Lieut. Jimenez either from malicious motives or else to subserve private ends.
>
> Stating at the same time that if Capt. Pico has in the slightest manner violated the military law I hope your honors will come to the conclusion that it has been more an error of the head than of the heart and that by the decision of this Court Capt. Pico may be honorably acquitted and returned to the command of his Company to do such duty as may be required of him by our Country.

The panel of officers found that, even though some of the charges were "frivolous and malicious," the record as a whole merited that a full court-martial move forward. One officer on the panel dissented, however. Captain Edgar W. Hillyer of the 4th California Infantry, who acted in the case as a judge advocate, cited the issue about the horse as "the only matter meriting serious attention." Even this, he acknowledged, may have been mere irresponsibility. The record of the case, he said, bore "unmistakable marks of malice both on the part of the officers preparing the charges and Lieut Jimenez," which tended to "taint the whole proceeding with the spirit of persecution." General McDowell, impatient to get his plans for Arizona moving, repeated Hillyer's arguments in a May 12 letter ordering that Captain Pico be released from arrest and restored to command.[36]

Two weeks later Pico and Company A, desertion having reduced its strength to a little over half of what it was when mustered in two years earlier, were marching south to join the battalion.

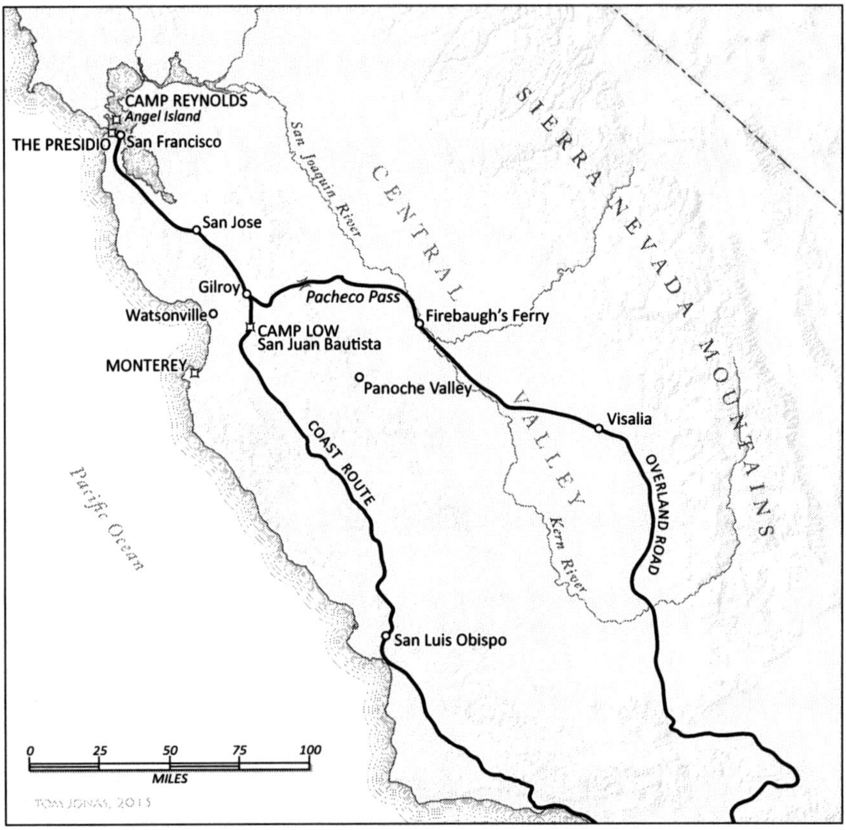

Native Cavalry operations in Central California, 1863–1865.
Map by Tom Jonas. Copyright © 2015 by the University of Oklahoma Press.

CHAPTER 4

Company B: San Francisco and the Central Coast

Uncle Sam's Paymaster has paid us a visit recently, and the troops have all been paid off. Greenbacks are plenty as drunken soldiers, for they would have had a spree anyway; but they sobered off in a few days, and now all are straight and sober.

A RESIDENT OF SAN JUAN BAUTISTA

While Pico's Company A was at the Presidio, another unit, which would be designated Company B, began organizing in the Bay Area. This command was similarly troubled, though it was very different in many ways. Most notably, a majority of its initial recruits were largely French, not Native Californians or Spanish-speaking immigrants.[1]

Tens of thousands of Frenchmen had immigrated to California since the American conquest, driven by the havoc that followed the Revolution of 1848 and drawn to the opportunities of the gold rush. By the time of the Civil War, they had a well-established and significant presence in California, particularly in San Francisco, where there were numerous French fraternal societies and francophone newspapers.

Though not nearly as substantial, there was a French expatriate community in San Jose as well. One such resident was Ernest Hypolite Legross, a twenty-five-year-old clerk at a French-owned mercantile firm.[2] His friend Captain Pico, citing Legross's "undoubted ability" and "considerable influence with the Native Californians," recommended him for a commission as captain, proclaiming that "he would be able to raise a company in a very short time."[3]

Legross received his commission at the end of September 1863 and opened a recruiting office in San Francisco shortly thereafter.[4] Very little happened for the next few months. In January 1864 Major Vallejo, also headquartered in the city, expressed his frustration with Legross in a letter to Brigadier General John Sanford Mason, provost marshal of California, and hinted at some of the ethnic tensions in California at the time: "it has now been between five and six months [since] he received his commission as Capt Company 'B' Nat Cav up to the present time he has succeeded in raising but 26 men and out of that number but three or four are native Californians the balance being Frenchmen this being one great objection to him the natives having no desire to serve under a French Captain."

Vallejo further stated that Legross had refused to give "any account" of "over $200" that he had gotten from the recruiting fund, though the major was "credibly informed" that the money was "spent in dissipation." Concluding that the officer was "far more of a detriment to the Battalion than a benefit," he suggested that Legross be removed as captain and that the men he had recruited be transferred to a new company being raised north of San Francisco by José Fitch.[5] General Mason, who officially oversaw all volunteer recruitment efforts on the Pacific Coast, recommended that Legross be mustered in as a first lieutenant until he had enough recruits for a full company.

For his part, Legross blamed his lack of progress on his subordinates. His first lieutenant was Edward Bale, the twenty-year-old son of Edward Turner Bale, an English physician who had arrived in California in 1837, and Maria Ignacia Soberanes, the niece of Major Vallejo. Legross said that Bale had not been heard from since he received $115 from the recruiting fund and left San Francisco. The captain had gone so far as to forward charges against the errant lieutenant. Vallejo apparently had been in regular contact with his grand-nephew and reported that the lieutenant was recruiting in Napa for Fitch's company. Nothing ultimately came of either the charges against Bale or of Fitch's company.

At the end of March, there were finally enough recruits for the Legross's command to be formally mustered as Company B, 1st Battalion of Native Cavarly at the Presidio. Of the unit's eighty-six initial volunteers, nearly half were French surnamed while only eight had recognizably Spanish names, the remainder being from other parts of the United States or Europe. One newspaper later commented on this substantial French presence, noting that one soldier was a nine-year veteran of the French army who had served in the Chasseurs d'Afrique in North Africa and the Crimea.[6] There were other ways in which the recruits for the new company were less than ideal: one of the new sergeants was McKelvie J. Unger, who had just two weeks before been a lieutenant in the 2nd California Cavalry until he was cashiered for fraud.[7]

At the Presidio the new soldiers received instruction. Presumably, this included the use of lances, though it is unclear when the troopers received them. Records indicate that at this point, the company's privates were issued only sabers, while Colt Navy pistols were issued only to sergeants. Other soldiers would be given pistols from the ordnance room for guard duty, patrols, and target practice, but these would be returned to the ordnance sergeant afterward.[8] There is no mention of lances during the company's service at the Presidio, though subsequent reports of the men having been well drilled in that weapon's use imply that they had received training at some point while there.[9]

They would remain at the Presidio for the rest of the year as the garrison expanded to an unprecedented strength of more than 1,600 men. The troopers of Company B were occupied mostly with drill and garrison duties, though this routine was broken from time to time as soldiers would be detached to serve in the provost marshal's guard patrolling the city or to meet the occasional crisis. One such excitement occurred during the November elections, when the Presidio was put on full alert, the troops ordered to be ready to move at a moment's warning, in response to rumors that Confederate sympathizers intended to disrupt the polls, a threat that never materialized.[10]

Other purported threats to the coast emerged, such as persistent reports of Confederate privateers operating in the Pacific. Early in 1864, as war raged in Mexico, officials in California reacted with alarm to intelligence of increasingly aggressive French naval activity and credible reports of French designs on the province of Sonora.[11] This prompted department officials to step up the expansion of harbor defenses around San Francisco. In July 1864 a detachment of twenty Native Cavalry troopers were sent from the Presidio to Camp Reynolds on Angel Island in San Francisco

Bay.[12] There is little record of their duties, but presumably they joined the other soldiers there in constructing the artillery works and protecting Federal property against civilian squatters, loose livestock, and feral dogs. The post, described by Samuel Clemens, a young journalist who visited while the cavalrymen were there, as "a pleasant little village" of "white houses," would remain the detachment's home until October.[13]

While Company B was posted at the Presidio, the troopers generally fared well in inspections, but there were signs of serious trouble. The unit suffered nearly fifty desertions, which amounted to a rate averaging more than one per week. Even the detachment at Camp Reynolds was not immune to this problem, though how soldiers absconded from an island tests the imagination. Well over half of the company's deserters were French surnamed, with the bulk of the remainder having English or German names.[14] Private Francois Malet, who deserted along with a dozen other French-surnamed soldiers in April 1864, later testified that he left because he was misled as to the nature of the command. He said that he had enlisted with the understanding that he was signing on with a French company but was dismayed to find that his compatriots included "some Mexicans, some Spaniards, some Germans and some English-people from all parts of the world." For his own part, Captain Legross blamed the high number of desertions on the roguish Sergeant Unger, who along with "several others" unable to speak Spanish, "worked against the Interest of the Company.

Recruitment would continue to address this attrition. Early on, Captain Legross had bemoaned his lack of a second lieutenant for recruiting duty, leaving him to do the task entirely by himself.[15] This changed in May when the vacant position was finally filled, though it seems that the new officer would be little more help to the company than the errant Lieutenant Bale. Lieutenant Zebina Nathaniel Streeter was one of the more colorful individuals to be associated with the Native Cavalry. Born in Genoa, New York, in 1838, Streeter ran away from home at age eleven and went to sea for seven years. Later as a civilian contractor, he followed Brigadier General Albert Sidney Johnston's column during the campaign against the Mormons in Utah in 1857 and from there drifted to Santa Barbara, where his estranged father was married into a locally prominent Californio family. After working as a clerk for a few years, Streeter was commissioned second lieutenant of Company B on May 8, 1864.

Given his family connections and the fact that he was bilingual, Streeter was probably at first regarded as an asset to his overwhelmed captain. Yet this would not last long. In June he was sent to Los Angeles on recruiting service, remaining there for several weeks.[16] On August 13 the lieutenant went on a drunken spree in Wilmington, a waterfront town twenty miles to the south, becoming "shamefully and grossly intoxicated." After behaving "disgracefully" in public, he collapsed in full uniform in the street, where he remained until the local provost guard dragged him back to the neighboring army post of Drum Barracks. A subsequent court-martial ordered him dismissed from the service, which was made final in October.[17] Though Streeter was no longer an officer, the Native Cavalry had not seen the last of him.

The other new officer would prove to be more effective. Lieutenant Bale, with whom Legross apparently did not get along, resigned in late June to accept command of another Native Cavalry company that had been raised in Los Angeles. Within days he was replaced by a twenty-nine-year-old former prizefighter named John Lafferty. Born in Oneida, New York, Lafferty had previously served as superintendent of the state insane asylum in Stockton before accepting his commission as first lieutenant.

As was Streeter before him, Lafferty was shortly sent on recruiting service, ordered to enlist only "Californians, or those of Spanish descent," a directive that brought him some small frustration. His efforts were aided by officers detailed from other regiments, and their efforts ranged as far north as Placerville and as far south as Monterey. By the end of the year, more than forty new recruits had joined Company B, which meant a majority of the troopers were no longer the French-surnamed volunteers mustered in just eight months before.

In keeping with the order, most but not all of the new soldiers were Spanish-surnamed, including Californios and immigrants from Mexico, Chile, and other parts of Latin America. Things came full circle in some way in the end, however, as among the last of the recruits were four French-surnamed veterans, three of whom were born in Algeria, of the ongoing conflict in Mexico.[18] In all likelihood these were deserters from the imperial army who had taken refuge north of the border. One newspaper later characterized Company B as being "composed of representatives of many races," including a handful "thought to be of pure Indian blood."[19]

In the meantime, as the company continued with mundane garrison duty at the Presidio, problems emerged with Legross's "irregular" management, issues similar in some ways to those with Company A. The captain was in the habit of taking, "borrowing" in the words of one soldier later, overcoats and boots from the company's storeroom. When a discrepancy in the clothing stores was discovered by Sergeant Charles Marstrand in July, Legross was reportedly overheard telling him "that the deficiency could easily be made up by charging it . . . to deserters." Similarly, when a few pistols turned up missing, the muster rolls were altered to show that the weapons had been issued to deserters.

In an even stranger move, Legross would, from time to time, order that bales of hay and sacks of grain be removed from the Presidio's stables and left out in the open at the company's corral, with the understanding that "certain men" be allowed to take these away. By August an estimated 4,000 pounds of hay and 7,000 pounds of barley had vanished from the unit's stores. At one point the forage situation was so acute that Company B's horses were briefly put on half-rations, though it was later noted that the captain's own horse was well fed and remained "in excellent condition."

Also in July, a soldier named Fermin Ayala, a nineteen-year-old waiter from Panama, had a disagreement with Legross about his bounty, accusing the captain of withholding about twenty-five dollars that he was due. The incident was an apparent misunderstanding, but matters were not helped by what was later characterized as "the difficult position [Legross] occupied as commander of a company composed of so many different nationalities" and "the personal enmity of his subordinates." Eventually, Ayala would desert, but not before he found someone who was willing to take his grievance seriously enough to make trouble for his captain.[20] As was the case with Captain Pico, it was a matter of some dispute as to the degree to which these incidents were the result of neglect, incompetence, or outright theft.[21]

In November 1864 Company B was ordered to join two other Native Cavalry companies at Drum Barracks in Southern California. Preparations for the move had not been completed on January 10, 1865, when they received orders to instead occupy San Juan Bautista, a town more than one hundred miles to the south.[22] Taking to the saddle two days later, the line of march would take the company through Legross's hometown of

San Jose, where the lancers made camp on the plaza on the night of the fourteenth. The local press praised their bearing, showing that, despite the unit's problems, the men had been well drilled during their time at the Presidio: "the company marched through the streets performing on horseback various military evolutions with precision, the horses seeming to understand the word of command, so admirable was their training and management."[23]

Company B resumed the march after two days, arriving at San Juan Bautista on January 18. The lancers' new posting lay in the rolling country below the eastern flank of the Gabilan Mountains. Remote as it was from the county seat at Monterey, the area was considered somewhat lawless, and its population was generally regarded as being sympathetic with the Confederacy. The modest adobe town clustered around three sides of the plaza of the large eighteenth-century mission church from which the community got its name, the fourth side being the escarpment of the San Andreas Fault. It owed its relative prosperity not only to the fact that it was central to a number of small mines in the surrounding hills but also to its position as a stop along the Coast Route and its proximity to two critical passes, Pacheco and Panoche, which connected the coast to the interior. For its longstanding regional importance, historians thus refer to the town as "the crossroads of California." The army recognized it as a "grand central geographical strategic point" whose "occupation would be beneficial" to control of the Central Valley. This would be the Native Cavalry's mission for the next few months.[24]

The immediate cause for Company B's deployment was a series of depredations by a group of cutthroat bandits called the Mason-Henry gang. John Mason and a man calling himself Jim Henry were two drifters with troubled pasts who, in the spring of 1864, briefly fell in with a rancher and former judge from Merced attempting to form a band of pro-Confederate guerillas. Leading a gang that at times numbered as many as twenty men, Mason and Henry quickly abandoned all but the pretense of fighting for the Confederacy and went on a spree of robbery and murder from Watsonville to Visalia. Law enforcement was hard pressed to deal with the gang, and some suspected that locals were in sympathy with their cause. Pursuit of the bandits thus became a matter for the army.[25]

Major Michael O'Brien, with two companies of his 6th California Infantry, had already been ordered to San Juan Bautista and had made

The plaza of San Juan Bautista Mission in the early 1860s.
Courtesy San Juan Bautista Historical Society.

arrangements to rent the National Hotel, an empty two-story hostelry at the northwest corner of the plaza, for use as a barracks nearly a week before the Native Cavalry's arrival.[26] The new post, which eventually included rented space for officers at the more well-kept Plaza Hotel and spread out to a bivouac on the plaza, was named Camp Low in honor of Governor Frederick Low.

Already well known for their spectacular horsemanship, the troopers of Company B made a special impression on the citizens of sleepy San Juan Bautista:

> [When] the soldiers came inside of the town, the children ran out bare-headed crying out "Mother! Mother! Here comes the soldiers." Not even a pair of drawers, shirt, or chemise was left hanging on the clothes lines as the *gay and gallant Spanish lanceroes* [*sic*] came dashing through the town with the lances in hand, a flag flying from each of them. I assure you they presented

National Hotel *(top)* and Plaza Hotel *(bottom)*, San Juan Bautista, in the 1860s.
Both images courtesy San Juan Bautista Historical Society.

> a war-like appearance, the people here thought their time had come, as a greater portion of them had never seen a soldier in their lives—Yes sir! They even stampeded the Spanish cattle that were so poor before that they could scarcely stand alone.[27]

At first the community, dominated by "copperheads," were hostile to the presence of Federal troops. In January, upon hearing the rumor that the town was to be the site of a post, one resident wrote to the Democratic-leaning *Pajaro Times* of Watsonville to express some of the cynicism that was doubtless common in San Juan:

> Mr. Editor, for what purpose? Are we in a state of rebellion? or is it to enrich a few contractors and renting a worn-out hotel, to pay high for water and fuel, and freighting forty miles, while our veterans are wanted and needed so much elsewhere. Besides, there are two infantry and two cavalry companies in Santa Cruz and Monterey Counties, well equipped and drilled, at a large expense to the State, who are always ready and willing to protect Government property and keep peace in our peaceable counties.[28]

Hostile at first, the local population warmed up to the soldiers after the occupation proved a boon to local business, particularly the town's numerous saloonkeepers. Kemp's Saloon, across the street from the National Hotel and owned by a prominent local Democrat, regularly held "a big, steep poker game" where the officers and men of Company B were "stripped of their salaries by the male members of San Juan's elite society."[29]

Many mornings found rowdy Native Cavalrymen in an abandoned adobe which was commandeered for a guard-house. For the most part, this was for simple drunkenness, but occasionally the problems were more serious. In February, Private Francisco Boronda was near-fatally shot during a dispute with a French surnamed comrade who claimed "that he was not aware the gun was loaded." In April, Corporal Juan Perras shot and killed a local Indian named Capistrano during another drunken argument, and was eventually sentenced to "death by musketry."[30] Overall, however, the Native Cavalry were eventually regarded as "royal good fellows" by residents.[31]

Within days of their arrival, O'Brien had sent the Native Cavalry into the field against the bandits. Having received word that the outlaws' "hiding place had been discovered," at 3:00 A.M. on January 22, the major dispatched Lieutenant Lafferty and twelve lancers in pursuit.[32]

Their efforts were unsuccessful, however, and ten days later a frustrated O'Brien reported being unable to track down the gang despite having "scoured the country thoroughly."[33]

On February 10 Captain Legross was relieved of command and placed under arrest on charges of fraud and misappropriation of government property from the previous summer. Major O'Brien convened a general court-martial three days later. During the four-day hearing, the company's ethnic tensions again showed themselves as German- and Spanish-surnamed soldiers were called to testify for the prosecution, while the accused's witnesses were all French surnamed. Legross represented himself in the trial and in the end tried to shift blame to Lieutenant Lafferty; the roguish Sergeant Unger, who testified for the prosecution; and several other enlisted men who, he maintained, "formed them selfs into a plot to accomplish my ruin." The court nonetheless convicted the captain of wrongdoing and recommended that he be cashiered and made to "return all money entrusted to him for the payment of men under his command."[34]

These findings were forwarded to department headquarters, but in the time it took to receive a reply, a strange situation arose because of some confusing orders. In late January O'Brien received instructions to reestablish a post at the old Presidio of Monterey.[35] While the order was apparently written with the intention of allowing the major to exercise some judgment in how to divide his command between the two locations, the muddled language left him puzzled. After nearly three weeks without clarification, O'Brien took all three companies to the new post, leaving only a token guard of Native Cavalry under a sergeant "to protect govt property" at Camp Low.

Legross, in the meantime, remained under arrest at San Juan Bautista. He had attempted to resign his commission via telegram to department headquarters during the court-martial. General McDowell, who had not yet received word of the proceedings, accepted the resignation on February 20. An official letter to this effect, addressed to "Commanding Officer, Camp Low," arrived at San Juan on the evening of the twenty-third. Since there was no official commander at Camp Low at this point, the only officer present, Lieutenant William McKay Owen of the 6th California Infantry, accepted the letter and forwarded it to Legross. Because the telegraph office in Monterey was closed, Owen

The trail through the Gabilan Mountains from San Juan Bautista to Monterey. From Browne, "A Dangerous Journey," pt. 1.

was unable to reach Major O'Brien until the next morning, by which time Legross had boarded a stage for San Jose.

O'Brien was furious. The major was the commander of the forces in Monterey County, and the lieutenant had no business opening the letter, much less acting upon its contents on his own. O'Brien telegraphed San Jose to inform Legross that his resignation was not accepted and ordered his immediate return to Camp Low.

In the end McDowell, upon reviewing the court-martial report, disapproved "the severe findings and sentence" as excessive. Ascribing Legross's difficulties to his "ignorance of the rules of service"; the unruly, polyglot nature of his company; and the "enmity of his subordinates," the general ordered that the captain's resignation be accepted and made effective on March 10 "for the interest of the service" without further action. Lieutenant Lafferty was left in acting command of Company B, which returned to San Juan the same day to resume active patrols of the countryside.[36]

On March 17 Company B's new captain, twenty-four-year-old Porfirio Jimeno, arrived to take command after a week's ride from Los Angeles. Promoted from Company C, which had been organized in Santa Barbara the previous summer, the new captain was one of eleven children born into an elite Californio family in Monterey. His father, Manuel Jimeno Casarin, was prominent in politics during the Mexican era, even serving occasionally as acting governor of Alta California. His mother, Angustias de la Guerra Ord, was a member of one of the leading families of Santa Barbara, though her relationship with her siblings was strained.[37] The elder Jimeno and Angustias separated in 1852, and he died of cholera in Mexico City a year later. In 1856 Angustias married Dr. James Ord, a surgeon who had come to California with the U.S. Army during the conquest.[38] These influential connections in Californio and Anglo-American circles would serve the younger Jimeno well.

In 1850 he and his brother Antonio were sent east in the company of a family friend, Lieutenant William T. Sherman, to see to their education. Sherman would continue to arrange for financial support for Porfirio during his time in boarding schools in Boston, New York, and Washington, D.C., including a brief stint at Georgetown.[39] Captain Jimeno was by far the best educated of the Native Cavalry's officers but was also clearly a man of two worlds. During his service, he wrote eloquent letters home in both English and Spanish, often switching between the two languages midparagraph.[40]

Commissioned a second lieutenant in June 1864, Jimeno characterized his life in the army as lonely and sad. Though he expressed love for his family, even sending much of his salary to his mother, he also frequently lamented the lack of a response from home, occasionally in bitter tones:

> Dear Aunts,
> If you were not so lazy, I would write to you more. But I have written two letters to you two, and neither one have answered, and for this I do not want to write any longer. You know how to send my letters so that if you want to write if not, go to hell, pigs. Some day you will pay me. Good bye, good bye. Greetings to all.
>
> Your nephew,
> Porfirio

This was, however, unusual. For the most part, his letters revealed great affection for his family and largely detailed the privations of the service. A more typical example of his oft-expressed sentiments comes from a letter he wrote to a relative in Simi:

> Dear Aunt,
> I received your little letter of the 13th today and since you said that I had forgotten to write, so as not to forget I am doing so now.
>
> I am fine, sad and without enough to buy a cigar and since they do not pay us until the end of this month, I have to smoke pipe tobacco, but we will tolerate it.
>
> The little pastries (thanks for them) are lovely. Captain Copely left by the steamer the day before yesterday. My uncle [Captain] Ant[onio] M[aria] left for Los Angeles with my uncle [Major] Salvador Vallejo yesterday, and I do not know when they will return.
>
> When I was in Simi I invited you to come visit us when you come to Los Angeles. I hope I did not forget to do that. On the 15th they will operate on Jose Antonio's [de la Guerra] leg. I hope to God that he heals soon.
>
> Dear aunt, do not forget that all the news about home is a joy for the absentee and I hope that you will write to me soon and tell me about everything that happens. Tell my aunt Concepcion that her little boy is fine.
>
> I wrote to Francisco and to J. and also to Clotilde and no one answered. That is the way they remember their cousins.
>
> Regards to them and do not fail to write to me. I remain your nephew who wishes to see you (as they say).
>
> Porfirio Jimeno[41]

Monterey, California.
From Bartlett, *Personal Narrative,* vol. 2.

Shortly after taking command, Captain Jimeno began sending the lancers of Company B into the countryside. The beginning of the Confederacy's surrender in April did nothing to curb either the Mason-Henry gang's depredations or the Native Cavalry's pursuit of the outlaws. Jimeno vowed to "keep up the hunt until Mason" was "either killed or captured." On April 11 the captain received a report that the gang had been "committing depredations" near Firebaugh's Ferry and ordered Lafferty and five lancers to ride out in pursuit, hoping to head them off at Pacheco Pass.

At 7:00 A.M. the next day, Lafferty's detachment surprised Mason "at the head of the Great Panoche Valley." In the ensuing running fight, Lafferty shot Mason in the hip, wounding both the bandit and his mount. The outlaw ultimately escaped, though the cavalrymen captured his horse. Lafferty and his men rode back into Camp Low that evening, and Jimeno soon sent another detachment in pursuit.[42]

Though they never caught the gang, Company B's constant activity did eventually force the bandits to focus their operations farther south.

Major John C. Cremony.
Courtesy Maine State Archives, Augusta.

By May the gang was being reported in the Kern Valley and around San Bernardino, where soldiers from Drum Barracks would take to the field against them, but Mason and Henry would no longer be a menace to northern areas nor a concern to the men of Camp Low. The Native Cavalry was credited with bringing a semblance of law and order to the vicinity for the first time since the American conquest.[43]

By March it was common knowledge that Company B was soon to move south to join the other Native Cavalry companies at Drum Barracks and from there proceed to what would be their new posting in Arizona Territory. In preparation, Major John C. Cremony, a veteran of service in the Apachería, was transferred from the 2nd California Cavalry to take command of the battalion. He arrived at San Juan Bautista from San Francisco, where he had been recruiting, by mid-April. Though an Anglo from New England, the major was fluent in Spanish and was by all accounts a capable officer. But Cremony had numerous detractors who considered him pompous, some even comparing him to the noted eighteenth-century yarn-spinner Baron Munchausen.[44]

The major arrived in time to participate in the town's memorial observance for President Lincoln. Cremony, Jimeno, and Lafferty led a catafalque, accompanied by an honor guard of soldiers from the Native Cavalry and the 6th California Infantry and a delegation of prominent local citizens, on a solemn procession through the streets. It seemed that the community had, if only briefly, moved past the bitterness that had divided the nation.[45]

But these sentiments were not universally held. Over the next few weeks, the soldiers of Camp Low enforced a departmental order by arresting a handful of men "for rejoicing over the death of" the president. The sweep went as far afield as Gilroy, where Lieutenant Lafferty arrested a "notorious secessionist" on May 13. Those apprehended were held in Camp Low's makeshift guardhouse. One correspondent hoped that these men would eventually be given "an opportunity to pace the Island," a euphemism for imprisonment at Fort Alcatraz.[46]

With peace restored in San Juan Bautista, the men of Company B resumed their preparations for the anticipated arrival of their comrades and the orders that would ultimately send them to Arizona.

CHAPTER 5

Company C: Santa Barbara

We were cavalrymen . . . , and we were terribly excited. We thought we had the finest cavalry outfit in the whole country. Probably we did. Such horses we had!

JUAN JOSÉ DE LA GUERRA

Even as Native Cavalry companies were being raised in the central and northern parts of the state, a series of disasters devastated Senator Pacheco's former constituency, leaving the "cow counties" of Southern California in little shape to raise such troops.[1] In January 1863 an epidemic of smallpox started in Los Angeles and eventually spread across the adjoining counties. The outbreak hit Mexican American and Indian communities hardest, with hundreds or possibly thousands dying by the following spring, when it had run its course. The region was already in the throes of a drought, which by the spring of 1864 would leave the corpses of thousands of cattle littering the countryside. According to some estimates, as much as two-thirds of the livestock in Southern California was lost, and even the most prominent families faced ruin. By the time community leaders were able to summon the wherewithal to organize a company of volunteers, the proud vaqueros idled by the collapse of the big ranches were eager to enlist simply for the prospect of regular meals and a soldier's pay of thirteen dollars a month.

Scholars tend to point to this as the historical moment when the old order ended in Southern California, but it is unlikely that many realized this at the time. While not entirely untouched by the wave of immigration that transformed other parts of California in the years after the American conquest, the southern counties maintained much

Captain Antonio María de la Guerra. The handwritten caption reads: "Don Antonio Maria de la Guerra—Capitan de la Compania de Santa Barbara durante la Guerra civil entre el N. y el S." ("Don Antonio Maria de la Guerra—Captain of the Santa Barbara Company during the Civil War between the N[orth] and the S[outh].") *Courtesy Santa Barbara Mission Archive, Santa Barbara, Calif. Used with permission.*

of their Californio character. Despite their financial reverses, some of the old families who had dominated the region since Mexican times still retained much of their influence.

Nowhere was this more true than in Santa Barbara. The town and surrounding county had a population of some four thousand, of whom only about three hundred were Anglo-American, and the de la Guerra family remained dominant. Even in the face of declining financial fortunes, the family retained control of the local Democratic Party machinery, and de la Guerras served in elected office at all levels. The family patriarch, Don José de la Guerra y Noriega, still commanded such respect that *Barbareños* continued to doff their hats while passing his house for years after his death in 1858.[2]

The youngest of his seven sons, thirty-seven-year-old Antonio María de la Guerra, is generally regarded by most writers as somewhat irresponsible and less competent than his father. They point out that the younger de la Guerra's mismanagement had exacerbated an already terrible situation, and most of the family's vast holdings had been lost since Don José's passing. In fairness, even a more capable individual would have had difficulty coping with the catastrophes of the early 1860s, given that the family wealth was almost entirely in land and cattle.

In his own time, however, Antonio was still a powerful and respected leader in the community. He had followed his brothers into public office, having served on the city council and in the state senate. He also upheld his father's military legacy, holding the rank of colonel in the California militia and briefly serving as assistant adjutant general.

Major William Reynolds, who had become acquainted with Antonio as a militia officer, had by this time taken an active personal interest in the progress of the Native Cavalry and suggested de la Guerra for a commission. In April 1864, with the major's encouragement, he assumed responsibility for raising a company of Native Cavalry recruits, quickly attracting more than eighty men, a group consisting almost entirely of Spanish-surnamed rancheros native to the Santa Barbara area. De la Guerra's success was attributed to his energy and influence, though the ruin of the ranching economy that left many Californios without work was likely a factor.

The story of one recruit provides an idea of the sort of men who made up the new company. A native of Santa Barbara, Private Ramón "Nini" Ayala was a vaquero and rancher who had worked on Santa Cruz Island and in the Cuyama Valley in the rugged backcountry above San Buenaventura. He had a reputation for being "expert as a horseman" and as a hunter of bears, having "taken hundreds of them, always with the lasso." Often, according to one account, Ayala would face a bear alone and "had many thrilling experiences with fierce grizzlies."[3]

The Californio company was very much a family business. Its two lieutenants, Santiago de la Guerra and Porfirio Jimeno, were the captain's nephews. Juan José de la Guerra, age nineteen, was among the ranks along with more than a few other nephews and cousins.[4]

The new recruits bivouacked on the grounds of the de la Guerra family compound and on the adjacent plaza, the new captain having contracted with local saloon owner José Lobero to provide food, while awaiting formal induction into the army. The machinations of his family's political rivals delayed this for weeks, forcing the volunteers to languish while the captain used his own funds to keep them fed, a hardship given his family's situation that required him to go into further debt.[5] By late May it was reported that de la Guerra's company was "getting tired of waiting."[6]

Chief among the sources of the delay were doubts regarding de la Guerra's qualifications as an officer and about his Union loyalties. Former lieutenant governor Pablo de la Guerra, the captain's older brother, blamed these rumors on his family's political opponents, who had "done all in their power to prevent the company being raised." He went on to say that, failing in this, these "certain parties" were trying to "prevent the men who raised the company from being its officers."[7]

With regard to the captain's loyalties, the charges were not entirely baseless. Like many prominent Californios, the de la Guerras had allied themselves with the pro-Southern "Chivalry" wing of the Democratic Party. In fairness, however, as was the case with other Native Californians, this alliance appears to have been a simple political convenience and not reflective of any deeply held sympathy for the South. Other critics interpreted statements made by de la Guerra family members criticizing the treatment of Californios under U.S. rule as reflective of anti-Union sentiment, a charge that seems absurd in retrospect.[8]

One vocal critic, State Senator Ramón Hill, a Native Californian who was elected as a Unionist over a rival backed by the de la Guerra dominated Democratic machine, criticized the slate of officers, except for 2nd Lieutenant Jimeno, as inadequate. He charged that 1st Lieutenant Santiago de la Guerra, despite being "an experienced horseman," knew "not one word of English," could "not even write fluently in his own language," and was unable to perform simple arithmetic. Of Captain de la Guerra, Hill dismissed him as "not one of the best of men" to command the company but conceded, "the men will not be kept together with any other for Captain."[9]

The complaints of other detractors, members of the town's small Anglo-American community, reflected continuing mistrust of the Californio majority. Some later alleged in a letter to General McDowell that a number of the recruits were bandits. These correspondents further claimed to be "credibly informed that in that Company there are seventeen men who are known to have committed murders!" Someone, perhaps Captain de la Guerra himself, appended a scrawl at the bottom of the page that declared the writers "alarmist, weak-minded cowards, provocateurs and distortionists of veracity."[10]

Appeals by Pablo de la Guerra and Major Reynolds eventually broke the impasse. On June 2, 1864, Antonio de la Guerra formally received his commission, and by the end of July, his ninety recruits were mustered in as Company C, with the captain's nineteen-year-old nephew Juan José being sworn in as first sergeant. This company would be the only one in the battalion that inducted with the proper minimum number of privates.[11]

The company was ordered to Drum Barracks and started south along the Coast Route on August 25.[12] Though the Californios had a longstanding reputation for being "unable to go from one house to another without riding a horse," the recruits were not yet mounted, so they would make the 112-mile journey on foot. Likewise, they were without

Casa de la Guerra, the de la Guerra family compound in Santa Barbara.
From a postcard in the author's collection.

uniforms or arms, but they nonetheless received praise for their discipline and military bearing.[13]

As with the other companies, a handful of the new recruits had fought the *yanqui* invaders during the war of 1846–47. Among these was forty-year-old Francisco Lugo, a ranchero who had worked in the de la Guerra household as a servant for a time. Lugo was called "old man," likely for his prematurely gray hair as he was not the oldest trooper in the unit. He was old enough, however, to have ridden with the irregular lancers organized by General Pico during the war of 1846, though it is unclear if he was present at San Pasqual.

One night the little column stopped to camp at Cahuenga Pass in the hills above Los Angeles. Here, Lugo took Sergeant de la Guerra aside and led him away from the campfires of the Barbareños to a large tree next to an old adobe. "I came here with your father, seventeen years ago," Lugo told him, "and here on this very spot I saw them sign the documents that ended the war between the Americans and the Californians. Here sat your father, here sat Don Andrés Pico, and here sat General Fremont."[14]

After a week on the march, on September 2 Company C arrived at Drum Barracks, where they joined Company D from Los Angeles, the last of the battalion's four companies.[15]

CHAPTER 6

Company D: Los Angeles

The habitual employment of the young men of this Lower Country has been herding and ranching stock; owing to the drought and consequent extermination of the Herds that occupation is gone and there is really no mode for them to obtain an honest livelihood.

COLONEL JAMES F. CURTIS

At Drum Barracks, Company C joined the last of the battalion's three other units. Company D had been raised in Los Angeles, which was then a ramshackle adobe town of less than five thousand residents, mostly Spanish-speaking people, with a substantial Anglo-American minority composed largely of men with ties to the Southern states. The community and the surrounding county had a rough and lawless reputation and was generally regarded as a center of pro-Confederate sentiment.[1]

As the war began, officials scrambled to address reports of unrest in the area. Confederate sympathizers were said to be well organized and so bold as to display the rebel flag in public. Outright violence, while by no means common, was not unheard of. In November 1863 an effort to raise soldiers was met with such hostility that two companies of infantry were dispatched to put down a potential riot.[2]

A permanent army presence was established not only to maintain law and order but also to discourage local secessionists while emboldening the pro-Union minority. Naturally, many residents resented living under a state of de-facto martial law, and the poor local economy only exacerbated these ill feelings. Even Confederate sympathizers generally respected the money spent by the Federal army, but soldiers and contractors were paid in legal-tender notes, which California residents grown accustomed to doing business in gold were often reluctant to take. This was particularly true in Los Angeles, already economically devastated by the trifecta of devastating floods (1862), a smallpox epidemic (1862–63), and a drought (1863–65), where these notes were sometimes worth at little as 35 percent of their face value. Amid such a depression, maintaining even the most tenuous Union hold on the community would remain a challenge throughout the war.

Much of the town's Mexican American majority remained ambivalent about secession. Nonetheless, the community was divided politically between a Unionist faction, who rallied around young attorney Francisco P. Ramirez, and a Democratic Party machine organized under Sheriff Tomas Sanchez, "a true son of chivalry who had wielded a good lance at San Pasqual." Prior to the rebellion, Sanchez had thrown in with the Southern-leaning "Chivalry" faction of the party. As sectional war loomed, he allied with local secessionists as well.

In February 1861 Sanchez was involved in organizing the Los Angeles Mounted Rifles, a militia company with secessionist associations in which he served as a lieutenant. The following June, with the help of the sheriff's office, the company absconded from California to join the Confederate army in Texas as an escort for Brigadier General Johnston, taking dozens of state-issued pistols, rifles, and sabers with them. Some of these arms ended up in the hands of the rebel forces who briefly occupied Arizona.[3]

In the end, however, the sheriff's Confederate sympathies were situational at best. Sanchez did not leave with the mounted rifles but stayed in Los Angeles, eventually winning a contract to supply beef to local Union forces.[4] The sheriff would remain in office until 1867, though his political power would wane considerably as the war progressed.

José Antonio Sanchez, a thirty-three-year-old carpenter, had long partnered with his older and more prominent cousin in politics and in the militia. He had helped organize the Los Angeles Mounted Rifles, but like his *primo,* he did not join his comrades as they stole away across the desert. His feelings about secession must have been even more ambivalent than those of the sheriff, for late in 1863 he came forward with an offer to raise a Native Cavalry company in Los Angeles.

The younger Sanchez began what turned out to be the difficult task of recruiting by January 1864. As with the other companies, the effort would be entirely at his own expense. But he also faced little support, and perhaps even hostility, from local residents, who "largely preponderated with the secession element."[5] Major Reynolds reported that another company raised in Los Angeles at around the same time by a citizen named Juan J. Moreno had "dispersed," the men choosing to seek their fortune in the mines rather than languishing through delays caused by political interference and a general lack of support.[6] Similarly, Sanchez later reported that he had "recruited at different times some two hundred and fifty men," most of whom did not stick around long enough to be enrolled, much less officially mustered in.[7] Finally, on March 3 eighty-two recruits were mustered in as Company D, and Sanchez was made captain. His lieutenants were José Redona, a twenty-eight-year-old *Angelino* laborer, and J. Clement Cox, a thirty-year-old building tradesman whose work made him familiar with "Sonora Town," the Mexican district of Los Angeles. Cox was described as a "sound and reliable union man" from Pennsylvania who assisted Sanchez in organizing the company.[8]

Despite the difficulties encountered by Sanchez, officials believed that the shattered ranching economy of the region was helpful to recruitment. But unlike Company C, which was raised under similar economic circumstances, a significant number of Company D's recruits were not otherwise unemployed stockmen. Only thirty-two listed their occupations as "vaquero" or "ranchero," while thirty-four were identified as "laborers." The remaining one-fifth were from various skilled trades, including a schoolteacher and a gambler. Nearly two-thirds of the initial recruits were from Sonora or other parts of Mexico, while the rest were natives of California, except for two volunteers from South America.[9]

For the time being, Company D would be posted to Drum Barracks, which would become the battalion's home. The post was established in 1862 on the sandy coastal flats twenty-five miles due south of Los Angeles. As the district headquarters, Drum Barracks served not only as the base for army activity in Southern California but also a supply point for the interior as far away as New Mexico. It was a modern post consisting of about two dozen neat, white, wood-frame buildings around a parade ground. The associated Wilmington Depot, which sat at the waterfront a mile down the road, was a small compound composed of a barn, warehouses, and various workshops intended to store a year's worth of supplies for eight companies. Though these accommodations were doubtless impressive, some criticized the site as damp and muddy.

Wilmington Depot, Drum Barracks.
The presence of the camel indicates that this photo was probably taken in 1862 or 1863. *Courtesy Drum Barracks Civil War Museum, Wilmington, Calif. Used with permission.*

One Native Cavalry officer posted there described the place as "sad and ugly" and "full of dust and fleas."[10]

The supply depot was two hours by stage from Los Angeles, the nearest civilian settlement save the adjacent waterfront community of Wilmington. Until fairly recently, the town had been called New San Pedro, but its name was changed to honor the Delaware birthplace of its leading businessman, Phineas Banning. Wilmington's economy was entirely tied to the army, and it was very much a company town, for Banning had a financial interest in nearly every business there. Indeed, Drum Barracks and the depot sat on land that Banning himself had sold to the government. Well before the Native Cavalry's arrival, his domination of local affairs was described in a Los Angeles newspaper by a jaded California volunteer who called himself "Sancho Panza":

> The town consists of Mr. Banning's residence and Mr. Banning's blacksmith shop where Government mules are shod and Government wagons repaired; Banning's soap and tallow factory where Uncle Sam buys soap for us soldiers; Banning's jerked beefery where Uncle Sam buys jerked beef for Drum

Wilmington, California.
From Browne, "A Tour through Arizona," pt. 1.

> Barracks to feed the Sanchos on the desert and in the mountains and desolate places where no man or beast is; and Mr. Banning's wharf and warehouses and road; and the whole is covered with Mr. Banning's heavens and rests on Mr. Banning's earth and sea.

As for Drum Barracks itself, the garrison during the Native Cavalry's time there numbered between 350 and 700 officers and men. The post commander was Colonel James F. Curtis, whose 4th California Infantry was headquartered there. Curtis had earned a tough reputation as a leader in the San Francisco Committee of Vigilance, for his brief stint as a police chief in the city, and for his active service as an officer in the state militia. His background was well suited for a posting that was largely about enforcing law and order. Yet for the men of the Native Cavalry, attitudes that he maintained from his vigilante days would prove troublesome. The colonel was clearly bigoted against the Californio soldiers, writing, "first class troops must not be expected from such personnel," that such men were best employed at "relieving the other troops of much of the fatigue and drudgery of camp."

Shortly after the unit's mustering in March, Captain Sanchez asked Major Reynolds to come to Drum Barracks to train Company D in "the evolutions of their particular arm of the service." Reynolds reported rapid progress, but after only a few weeks he found that the colonel had other plans for the unit. Instead of military duties, Curtis put them to work on one of Banning's construction projects, a seven-mile-long system of flumes known as the San Gabriel Ditch, intended to divert fresh water from the San Gabriel River to Wilmington for irrigation. Banning supervised construction and purchased some 100,000 board feet of lumber for the project, with free labor provided by the army. Work began in April and continued through the end of the summer.[11]

Curtis condescendingly praised the Native Cavalry troopers for their "good service with pick and shovel," and some accounts state that the soldiers preferred the labor to camp routine. But the matter was not without controversy. Criticism came most prominently from Major Reynolds, who complained that it was taking the soldiers away from "all the benefit of drill and instruction possible." Alluding to the obvious fact that Banning's investments in Wilmington would benefit most from the troops' labor, he said that the project was "really to favor private interests more than public." Anxious to expand the battalion to a full regiment of ten companies, Reynolds expressed concern that word of the troops' use as mere laborers would "prevent any [others] enlisting for the Battn in this section of the country."[12] These assertions were supported by Major Vallejo, who also later reported that Company D had not been properly drilled nor even been under his "immediate superintendence" for the duration of the construction project.[13]

Yet Vallejo himself bore at least some of the blame for this neglect. The major did not even report to Wilmington Depot until October, but his presence apparently changed the situation little. Colonel Curtis, who in fairness was not entirely unbiased in his opinion, later reported that Vallejo did "not even pretend to appear upon parade or at any exercise of his troops."[14]

There were other complaints regarding Vallejo as well. At the end of May, a frustrated Captain Sanchez resigned. It was reported at the time that he was overwhelmed by the company paperwork, but he later maintained that he was "forced" to leave the service because of the debts he accumulated in maintaining his unit. Sanchez complained that the absent major responded to his efforts to receive reimbursement from the recruiting fund by saying "that he would be at Drum Barracks in a few days" to give the captain the money, but weeks passed and Vallejo never arrived. Finally, to his great regret, Sanchez tendered his resignation so he could focus on retiring his debt, chiefly by liquidating the "few horses and cattle" left to him after the drought. He would continue to press his claims for the next several months, which would eventually create trouble for Major Vallejo.[15]

Shortly thereafter, Lieutenant Redona followed Sanchez resigning, citing his "inability to read and write" and his "ignorance of the English language." Curtis, who believed that only Anglo officers could "be made effective," recommended a few of his friends for the new vacancies in the company, but these were not well received.[16] When 2nd Lieutenant Cox was promoted to Redona's place, 1st Sergeant Francisco Guirado, a farmer from a well-established Californio family of Los Angeles whose brother was the only Mexican American officer in the California Column, was appointed second lieutenant. But Guirado soon after fell ill and was never commissioned. The post would remain vacant, though another Guirado brother, Leandro, a twenty-one-year-old corporal, remained in the company.[17] As for the vacancy left by Sanchez's resignation, it was soon filled by another Native Californian, Edward Bale, who was promoted from Company B and reported to Drum Barracks at the end of June.

Despite the problems with officers and what must have been backbreaking labor, morale among the men of Company D seems to have remained good, and they were rated well in regular inspection reports. There were some discipline problems, and a handful of soldiers had deserted, but overall the company fared much better than others in the battalion. The assertion that these men preferred digging ditches to garrison duties may have been true to some extent; at the very least the work prevented the sort of idleness that encouraged misbehavior.

Regardless, the bulk of the San Gabriel Ditch was done by the end of August. When Company D was joined at Drum Barracks by Company C from Santa Barbara in September, the lancers were ready for a new duty: maintaining an uneasy peace in California's troublesome southern counties.

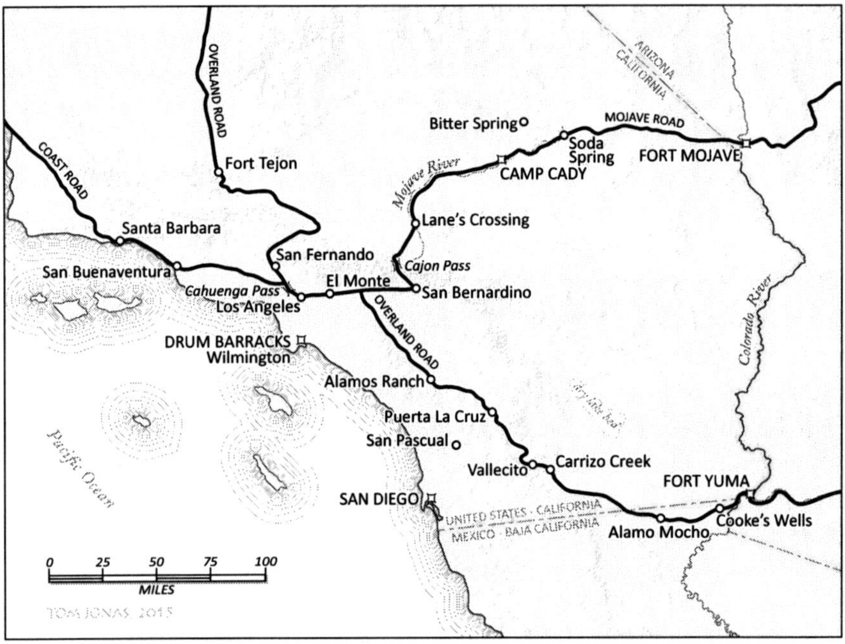

Native Cavalry operations in Southern California, 1864–1866.
Map by Tom Jonas. Copyright © 2015 by the University of Oklahoma Press.

CHAPTER 7

Service in the Southern Counties

A young man by the name of Gomez, belonging to Major Vallejo's battalion of native cavalry, lost his life last week at a dance house near Drum Barracks, in consequence of being in the course of a ball, which one female caused to be projected from a pistol in her possession, in hopes that it might make a lodgment in the person of another female. Moral: keep out of bad company.

ALTA CALIFORNIA

I am instructed to say that your letter dated 28th ultimo, addressed to Captain Swasey, A.Q.M. has just been laid before the Colonel Commanding, who directs that you be reprimanded for the use of its satirical and unofficer-like language, and you are hereby reprimanded.

LIEUTENANT ORLANDO H. LEE
(TO CAPTAIN A. M. DE LA GUERRA)

Throughout 1864, Colonel Curtis maintained doubts as to the effectiveness of the Californio troopers under his command. In addition to his low opinion of the officers and the men's ability, he also believed that the native troopers were largely thieves and that their mere presence was bad "for the morale and discipline" of the whole garrison at Drum Barracks. He wanted them sent away, perhaps to San Diego, Fort Yuma, or even New Mexico. At one point he even suggested that they be sent to garrison the sparsely populated San Fernando Valley without horses and armed only with lances and sabers, though he provided no details as to how dismounted cavalrymen could make effective use of, or even easily carry, a nine-foot-long weapon. Though Curtis argued for the importance of posting troops in the valley because "two great highways of travel" from the north to the south passed through it to merge at Cahuehga Pass, department headquarters saw no particular strategic value in the location. The colonel admitted that its value was chiefly in its isolation and because "nothing in the vicinity" would be "subject to the thieving of the native troops."[1]

After at least four similar letters, department officials finally lost patience with Curtis's bigotry and generally negative attitude:

> You report most unfavorably of the companies of the Native Cavalry under your command, and yet, instead of wishing to have them under your own eye, where you can best see to their improvement and their better discipline, you propose to place them in charge of your extreme outposts.
>
> The General expects to see, from the tone of your remarks and indisposition on your part to try and improve the character of these troops. You seem only disposed to get rid of them. The government has thought fit to include these men into its service, and they must be made into as good troops as possible, whether it be agreeable labor to do so or not. The General does not admit that they cannot be made good soldiers; on the contrary, he knows they can, and he expects you to take the necessary steps to discipline and instruct them. The military system is amply sufficient for all purposes and if it is aptly and persistently applied it will produce the proper results. You will at once see to the arming, equipment and mounting of these troops, and report monthly the progress made in discipline and instruction.[2]

With work on the San Gabriel Ditch completed in August, Company C arriving from Santa Barbara in September, and his requests for more soldiers and even artillery denied, the chastised colonel might now, however begrudgingly, employ the Native Cavalry in the unruly southern counties under his purview.[3] As the autumn election season approached, authorities became increasingly concerned about reports of "thoroughly organized and very active" secessionists in the Los Angeles area.[4] The closing months of the war promised to be a busier time for the lancers of Companies C and D.

Colonel Curtis had actually made some limited use of the Native Cavalry as early as May 1864. Reacting to rumors about secessionist sympathizers having established a colony in Baja California, he sent Captain Sanchez, then still in command of Company D, across the border to investigate. Sanchez returned to report that "some 50 men" and their families had settled south of the line in an effort to avoid a potential draft. Curtis filed this information away until August, when he wrote to department headquarters about the potential danger of Baja California becoming a "rendezvous" for secessionists. Rumors of designs on the peninsula by such men, as part of a possible alliance with Emperor Maximilian's forces, persisted through the end of 1864, so authorities remained watchful.[5]

Curtis was similarly concerned about matters much closer to home. He passed along reports that the pro-Southern element in Los Angeles was "unusually busy in overhauling and repairing its fire-arms" and that "two strangers . . . who evidently were emissaries of the Confederacy" had visited a number of communities. The colonel admitted having "no indications of intended hostilities," but he pointed out that there were "many points" in his district where belligerents could "be provoked."[6]

On Monday, October 31, a mounted detachment of Company D, "armed with lances and sabers," was ordered to ride a circuit around the county, its line of march including Los Angeles, Mission San Gabriel, El Monte, Santa Ana, and Anaheim, before returning to Drum Barracks the following Friday.[7] Two days later, in time for the November 8 election, two mixed-arms detachments of men from Company D and the 4th California Infantry moved through the county in an effort "to preserve order, to insure the loyal element in all its privileges, and as auxiliary to the civil authority." One, commanded by Captain Patrick Munday of the 4th California Infantry and consisting of his company, Lieutenant Cox, and forty mounted lancers of Company D, was ordered to camp for the week at El Monte, a community regarded as a hotbed of secessionist sentiment. Meanwhile, the 4th's Captain Benjamin West led a second column, consisting of two companies of infantry, Captain Bale, Lieutenant Jimeno, and the dismounted remainder of Company D, to Los Angeles.[8] These duties had a political as well as peacekeeping purpose, and officials admitted that the presence of troops would "stir up" pro-Union elements while intimidating the opposition during the upcoming election.[9]

One abortive incident illustrates the very real potential for unrest in the outlying communities as well as the negative attitudes some held toward Spanish-speaking men wearing the uniform of the United States. Hearing that a company of Native Cavalry was due to arrive in town in advance of the election, secessionists in San Bernardino gathered up "seventy rifles" from the surrounding countryside "in order to dispose of the 'greasers.'" A confrontation was averted when the column that arrived was instead a detachment of Anglo-American soldiers of the 4th California Infantry. Despite this scare, the election passed without incident, the mobilization of soldiers around the district credited with having "disrupted plans of local Democrats to prevent Lincoln-Johnson men from getting to the polls."[10]

For the majority of the Native Cavalry men, who remained without horses, their duties would keep them closer to base. They continued the garrison routine, which included being posted as sentries at the water tanks around the post and pacing the waterfront at Wilmington to guard the depot.[11]

Eventually, soldiers from Drum Barracks were dispatched to join the hunt for the Mason-Henry gang, with the same sort of mixed results that frustrated Company B from Camp Low. In February 1865 Captain Munday and a detachment of Native Cavalry rode out from Drum Barracks and tracked the pair down to Cajon Pass. Munday called on the desperadoes to surrender, but they instead "drew their pistols and commenced shooting." When one of the two gunmen was about to shoot him at point-blank range, the captain reached out and seized the outlaw's revolver, which then discharged, the stray ball fatally striking an eleven-year-old boy who happened to be nearby. In the end one of the gunmen was killed and the other was "badly wounded" and apprehended.

On the ride back, a San Bernardino County deputy sheriff confronted Munday and the lancers with charges arising from the scrape. It had turned out that the pair they had confronted was not Mason and Henry but two men named McGee and Wilby, the latter now in custody. Munday offered his word as an officer that he would appear in San Bernardino "to answer any charge that might be brought against him," but the deputy refused to accept this and attempted to arrest him and the cavalrymen. The captain simply ignored the lawman and pressed on to Los Angeles, where Wilby, found to be wanted for "the cold blooded murder" of a "Mexican at Tejon," was turned over to civilian custody before the detail returned to Drum Barracks. Contemporary accounts do not mention if the unfortunate McGee had ever been accused of anything. Nevertheless, Mason and Henry had again eluded the army.[12]

By this time some Native Cavalry troopers had seen their first duty in Arizona. Over the previous year or two, the deserts beyond the

Cajon Pass, California, in 1864.
Courtesy Bancroft Library, University of California, Berkeley.

mountains overlooking Los Angeles had seen increasing activity on the part of miners and prospectors. Even farther east, the new territory of Arizona was organized by the summer of 1863, with its capitol at Prescott. These newly settled districts drew the army's attention eastward as traffic increased along the Mojave Road, the route that ran across the Mojave Desert to the Colorado River. This trail needed to be secured against both marauding Indians and the largely imagined designs of organized Confederate sympathizers.[13]

In April 1864 department headquarters ordered that the lancers be posted to recently reoccupied Fort Mojave on the Arizona side of the Colorado River as a base for patrols of the Mojave Road.[14] Curtis's low regard for the Native Cavalry ultimately prevented this order from being carried out, but from time to time starting in the fall of 1864, Native Cavalry detachments were sent on the three-hundred-mile march to the

Camp Cady, California, in 1864.
Courtesy Bancroft Library, University of California, Berkeley.

post for one duty or another. In October, for example, Captain Jimeno reported that a detail of ten men left for Fort Mojave on a patrol expected to last a month.[15] In February 1865 Lieutenant de la Guerra accompanied Colonel Curtis to Fort Mojave to inspect the post and to ascertain the "causes and extent of the Indian troubles" in the region. En route they heard from "settlers and travelers" along the way who reported that marauding bands of Chemehuevi numbering "a dozen to thirty" men armed with a variety of weapons, including "improved rifles and shotguns and pistols" as well as traditional bows, would come down from the mountains to "steal stock, rob houses, lay forced tribute," and even murder citizens along the road. Additionally, the colonel was concerned that local residents were "nearly all sympathizers with the rebellion."[16]

In late February, shortly after returning to Drum Barracks from this reconnaissance, Curtis ordered Captain Bale and Company D to relieve a detachment of the 4th California Infantry at Camp Cady, a forsaken adobe blockhouse on an otherwise desolate stretch of the Mojave Road where the hidden waters of the Mojave River briefly rose above the sands. One contemporary traveler referred to the post as the "meanest" he "ever saw" and as a "deserted Botany Bay of a place" whose garrison "manage[d] to exist in some unexplained way in mud and brush hovels."[17] Curtis directed that a guard of fifteen men always remain behind to maintain the post while detachments of mounted lancers were kept constantly in the field. Their principal duty would be to patrol the road between Lane's Crossing and Soda Springs, "keeping it clear of Indians" and giving special attention to forcing them "away from the watering places."[18]

Bale's company, along with Lieutenant de la Guerra, a six-mule team, and a wagon with tents and forty days of supplies, left Drum Barracks for their new post on March 1. The duty must have been brutal.[19] The constant movement of troops, however, seems to have been effective, for the Native Cavalry's service at Camp Cady, which lasted a little over a month, largely passed without incident. The only apparent excitement came at reveille on March 30, when Lieutenant Cox, a sergeant, a corporal, and eight lancers rode out with a civilian guide named Griffith Williams toward Bitter Springs in pursuit of Indians who had reportedly abducted a San Bernardino citizen.[20] Existing records do not mention any hostile encounters with the Chimehuevis.[21]

The troopers of Company C had largely remained at Drum Barracks during this time. Even though Colonel Curtis had been chastised for his attitude toward the Native Cavalry, the relative idleness of garrison duty continued to exacerbate latent hostilities among the rank-and-file soldiers. One soldier would later testify that there were "no good feelings" between the "Mexican" cavalrymen and the Anglo-American infantrymen.[22]

One evening in late February, Captain de la Guerra gave permission for six of his men to leave the post to play a serenade at a dance house in Wilmington. At some point late that night, Corporal Lugo exchanged strong words with 4th California Infantry musician Richard Anderson. Close to midnight, Anderson left the hall and met two of his comrades, Privates Cooper and Rodney Stetson, and warned them, "Mexicans are after me." At about that time, the six barbareños were starting back for Drum Barracks when Bugler Ysmael Soto asked them to wait while he relieved himself.[23] Anderson turned back toward the hall with the other infantrymen and ran into Soto. What followed is not entirely clear.

At this point Soto and Anderson also exchanged words. Later testimony implies that the bugler of Company C spoke little or no English, while the musician of the 4th Infantry was likewise ignorant of Spanish, so the conversation overall probably was mutually unintelligible though nonetheless discernably hostile in tone. According to Anderson, Soto said something to him in Spanish, to which he replied, "You have nothing against me that you should be following me out." Then the bugler reached behind him and drew a knife. Soto testified that the infantryman had asked him what the Californio soldiers were saying about him, to which he answered that he did not know, but he never admitted to pulling a knife on Anderson. Nevertheless, both accounts agree on what happened next: someone shot Soto in the face, the ball tearing through his cheeks and nose.

The other Company C soldiers had been walking toward the post when they heard the pistol shot. They turned and ran back to find Soto struggling to rise to his feet. Privates Horatio Robinson and Pedro Bermudez carried the wounded bugler to Drum Barracks.[24] Cooper had already run back to inform Captain Munday of what had happened.

Stetson was arrested for the incident and charged with assault with intent to kill, though in the subsequent court-martial neither Soto nor Anderson were able to identify the shooter. As a result, Stetson was found guilty only of being absent without leave, his punishment being a fine for ten dollars, the better part of a month's salary. As for Soto, he was returned to duty by the end of March. Within a year he began to go deaf, which was later blamed on his injury.[25]

This was probably not the first such trouble, though it seems to be the earliest to call for a court-martial. Months later Stetson and ten soldiers of the 1st California Cavalry left Drum Barracks without permission and went on a rampage in Wilmington, kicking and beating anyone in their path. One trooper, Private Samuel Shear, loudly declared himself "the great American Chief" and threatened "to whip all soldiers or citizens who did not belong to his company," firing his pistol randomly in the streets. Bursting into a civilian house, Shearer found Corporal Lugo, grabbed him, shoved him outside, and shot at him, shouting "here is one of the damned greasers." This time the court-martial found Stetson and the others guilty, sentencing each to hard labor at Fort Alcatraz with a heavy ball chained to a leg.[26] Fortunately for Lugo and the other men of the Native Cavalry, they would soon be leaving Drum Barracks behind.

Meanwhile, morale remained high for Company C despite the dullness of the duties and the ethnic strife at the post. The barbareños were still eager to be sent east to fight, though. Sergeant de la Guerra later recounted to a newspaper that the Californios believed themselves "the best cavalry outfit in the whole country." One night in April 1865 the sergeant "set his military cap at a jaunty angle, stepped smartly along with a brace of pistols at his hips and went off to the Plaza for a dance" with some of his comrades. "De veras!" remembered de la Guerra, "we were popular that night!"[27] But the next morning a rider brought a telegram that had arrived in Los Angeles the previous day:

> Sacramento, April 10, 1865
>
> To Colonel James E. Curtis,
> Drum Barracks
>
> Lee, with his whole army, has surrendered to Grant.
>
> F. F. Low, Governor[28]

De la Guerra lamented, "We never even started."[29]

Despite the sergeant's disappointment, the soldiers at Drum Barracks reacted to this news with great enthusiasm. Colonel Curtis led the entire garrison, including the Native Cavalry, on a parade through the streets to the square at the center of Wilmington, where he called for three cheers, to which the men responded with "cheer after cheer." Then the men countermarched back to the post, "where they spent the day rejoicing."[30]

The good feeling did not last, for it was only a few days later that word of Lincoln's assassination arrived. Curtis reacted immediately, writing to San Francisco to ask for more troops, fearful that the news would "hasten the preparations of secessionists" in the southern counties who had "been organized for months to oppose the Government of the United States by force." Though his plea for additional men was ultimately refused, the colonel dispatched Captain Munday and a force of 120 men, including twenty lancers of Company D, to San Bernardino "to silence opposition and to protect Unionists."[31] The presence of even such a small number of soldiers in the field seems to have been enough to quell any unrest, and the feared guerilla war never materialized. The Native troopers who stayed behind, still largely dismounted, participated in commemorative funeral ceremonies for the president in Wilmington and Los Angeles.[32]

Though the Civil War was over, there was still much activity ahead for the lancers. Department headquarters had plans that would send them out of the state for duty on the frontier. The other two companies had already been ordered south to join Companies C and D at Drum Barracks. Once these four units were together as a battalion, the Native Cavalry would march for another posting hundreds of miles away.

CHAPTER 8

Assembling the Battalion

I had command of a battalion of cavalry—four hundred men—excellent, brave fellows, but sadly demoralized by relaxed discipline under their former Major. I soon rectified mistakes, and taught them a lesson or two, which they have not forgotten to this day.

MAJOR JOHN C. CREMONY

By the beginning of 1865, it was well known that the Native Cavalry would be part of a force being assembled to campaign against the Apaches in Arizona. Appointed commander of the newly organized District of Arizona, Brigadier General John S. Mason had other duties that prevented him from immediately assuming command. These responsibilities not only delayed his own departure but also otherwise dragged out affairs.[1] Finally, on April 11 he along with a guard of a dozen Native Cavalry lancers from Company B boarded the southbound steamer *Senator* at San Francisco to begin their journey to Prescott.[2]

At first Mason recommended that the Native Cavalry "should be kept constantly on the move against the Apaches in the northern and middle portion of the district." Believing that proximity to Mexico would present a temptation for desertion, he suggested that the border region be "occupied by reliable American troops."[3] But by the time the battalion was ready to depart California, he had changed his mind as the conflict in Mexico threatened to spread northward, thus calling for the deployment of mounted troops in southern Arizona.[4]

In the time that passed between the announcement of the battalion's new assignment and its march to Arizona, there were significant changes in the unit's leadership. It was not unheard of for the officers who recruited a volunteer organization to be replaced before active service, and this may have been at least partly the case with the Native Cavalry. But in regard to Major Vallejo, there were serious problems as well.

There were many longstanding issues with the major's leadership of the battalion. Colonel Curtis clearly had little respect for Vallejo. In charge of the post and the district, Curtis was ultimately responsible for the training of the men under his command, and he had promised the department to do all in his power to "render the Native Battalion a success." He blamed any shortcomings in this regard on "the inefficiency and utter worthlessness of its commander." His criticism of Vallejo echoed his earlier contempt for the Native Cavalry's officers and men: "Of all troops in the service of the United States, these perhaps require the most efficient officers, and actually possess the poorest. Ignorance of the English language, of itself, in my humble opinion, unfits the Major for a Command, he neither reads, writes, speaks, or understands it when spoken." Vallejo, according to Curtis, had not participated in the drill or training of his troopers, citing his "inability to command in English" as his reason for not doing so. The colonel had other criticisms that echoed complaints against other Californio officers. He cited "numerous complaints, charging larceny and other offences," including the burglary of a civilian house in Wilmington, by Native Cavalry soldiers that the major ignored. Curtis went on to say that his own efforts in "maintaining discipline" were undermined by Vallejo.[5]

It may be tempting to dismiss at least some of these complaints in light of the colonel's record of derision toward the Californio soldiers, but some of the battalion's officers had very serious issues with Vallejo as well. After his resignation as captain of Company D, José Sanchez continued to pursue his complaint against the major in his effort to recover what he had spent in raising the company. By January 1865 his grievances finally received attention from the right people. At the direction of department headquarters, Colonel Curtis ordered his adjutant, Lieutenant Orlando Lee, to investigate. Vallejo responded to the inquiry by saying that he had distributed the eighteen hundred dollars he had received from the state for recruiting the battalion among the captains of Companies A, B, and C as well as three unauthorized companies supposedly raised by Manuel Torres, Guadalupe Soberanes, and José Fitch. In response

Captain de la Guerra, who like Sanchez had gone into debt to raise his command, indignantly complained that neither he nor his lieutenants had "ever received any thing *especially* money from said Major."[6]

Curtis excused Vallejo from duty in mid-January 1865 and asked General McDowell to have him "mustered out of the service as worthless." Ahead of further inquiry about battalion finances, the major resigned on February 8. Years later, in his rambling and bitter memoir, the famously crusty Vallejo would only describe his time in the Federal service as "devoid of interest."[7] He was replaced by John C. Cremony, who transferred from the 2nd California Cavalry in late March and was at Camp Low with Company B a few weeks later.[8]

The roster of the battalion's field and staff officers saw other changes as well. Dr. Vincent Gelcich, a Croatian immigrant, veteran of the revolutionary army of Giuseppe Garibaldi, and brother-in-law of Captain Pico, had held a commission as assistant surgeon since June 1864.[9] Despite the family connection, Gelcich does not seem to have had much direct involvement with the Native Cavalry, and his commission may have been a means to put him on staff at Drum Barracks. In April, at the time it became clear that the battalion would be sent to Arizona, Dr. Gelcich transferred to the 4th California Infantry, which would remain in the state, with a promotion to surgeon.[10]

Fortunately, an eager candidate was available for the newly vacant medical position. Dr. George B. Tolman, a longtime California resident and veteran of the Mexican-American War, had attempted to raise a volunteer company at the quicksilver mines of New Almaden in 1864, but he was frustrated by the interference of local secessionists. Failing in this, Tolman instead secured a commission as an assistant surgeon in the 6th California Infantry in January 1865. After it became clear that the Native Cavalry would be sent to Arizona, Dr. Tolman, in his enthusiasm for more-active service than could be found in garrison at Benicia Barracks, requested a transfer. Arriving by the steamer *Pacific* from San Francisco, he joined the battalion as assistant surgeon at Drum Barracks on May 22.[11]

Drastic changes would also occur in Company D. It is not clear if this was something of a housecleaning, but the circumstances make it seem likely. At the end of April, shortly after returning to Drum Barracks from Camp Cady, Captain Bale, citing "urgent private affairs requiring his superindendance [*sic*]," resigned.[12] If he was forced out, the exact reasons remain unclear. Though he seems to have been an indifferent and disinterested officer, any specific problems with his leadership are lost to history. Perhaps now that his uncle, Major Vallejo, was no longer in command, his shortcomings came into greater focus, or maybe he simply lost interest in the service.

Regardless of the reasons, Bale's replacement, Captain Thomas A. Young, who took command at the end of May, was a longtime veteran of both the regular army and the California Volunteers whose experience in Arizona and New Mexico would prove valuable for the duty ahead. A month later Lieutenant J. Clement Cox similarly resigned and was replaced by another veteran soldier, Lieutenant Edmund Codington. The ambitious new subaltern had initially joined the 2nd California Cavalry and served in the Apacheria as a private before a brief stint as a second lieutenant in Captain de la Guerra's Company C.

To the north, with proceedings against Captain Pico at Benicia having ended, Company A could finally start south to join the battalion. The line of march once again took them to Pico's hometown of San Jose, where they made camp on the east side of Washington Square on May 28.[13] When the troops departed the next day, they did so without Lieutenant Soto. That officer could not take his wife and children with him to the Arizona wilderness and requested time to find a "suitable place" for them in town. He rejoined the company without his family after seven days' leave and what was doubtless a tearful farewell.[14]

Company A arrived at San Juan Bautista to join Company B two days later. The two Native Cavalry companies and the 6th California Infantry company also posted there numbered some 175 men. They gave the town "quite a milty [*sic*] appearance" as the soldiers busied themselves in preparation for the very long march ahead.[15]

Among the practical preparations, there were some administrative changes that had to be made as well. General McDowell may have put a stop to the legal proceedings against Captain Pico, but the issues brought about by his behavior was still leading to problems in Company A. It was clear that he and Lieutenant Jimenez did not get along, which was probably the reason why Major Cremony, shortly after taking command, assigned the lieutenant to detached duties with Company B. Jimenez would spend the remainder of his service detailed to one of the battalion's other companies.

The other piece of unfinished business involved Private Federico de la Noix, who wrote to the post commander at Benicia in May to charge that Captain Pico owed thirty-four dollars to his wife, who served as a company laundress, for work dating back to February 1864. This was a substantial sum, and the soldier wrote that his family depended "upon the money thus earned by hard labor and has no other resources to exist." Pico, he said, continued to refuse to settle the debt and kept putting off de la Noix until the next payday. The captain, of course, disputed the bill and the private's story.

In June, two weeks after he took command at San Juan, Cremony ordered that de la Noix be transferred to Company B. It is not clear if this move had to do with the dispute, but given what Company A had already been through and McDowell's expressed desire to get the battalion on the march, it seems likely that the major saw this as a way to restore peace. For his own part, de la Noix would ultimately not accompany the battalion to Arizona, serving instead with a detachment consisting of a corporal, a bugler, and nine lancers of Company B assigned to stay behind at San Juan Bautista.

The departure of the two companies was delayed when two of the men arrested for "rejoicing" in the wake of Lincoln's assassination escaped from Camp Low's improvised guardhouse. For years afterward, local lore held that "filthy lucre had passed the palms" of the soldiers posted as guards allowing the prisoners to slip away while the sentries slept. Major Cremony "immediately detailed his entire force and scoured the country in search of them," but one resident later reported that "after the soldiers searched two or three houses they quit." The fugitives were never caught.[16]

Cremony and Companies A and B finally left San Juan Bautista on the morning of June 16, leading an impressive train that included "14 fine mule teams and some 300 horses." Moving at a "leisurely" pace "down the coast," the column expected to arrive at Wilmington on or around July 10.[17] More than 350 miles to the south at Drum Barracks, preparations continued for the full battalion's march to Arizona. In April Pío Pico had delivered a "fine lot of California horses," totaling about a hundred head, to Drum Barracks under contract with the army at a price of eighty-five dollars each in gold, enabling more of the Californio soldiers to be mounted.[18] Otherwise, they patiently waited for their comrades to arrive from San Juan, expecting their arrival on July 1.[19]

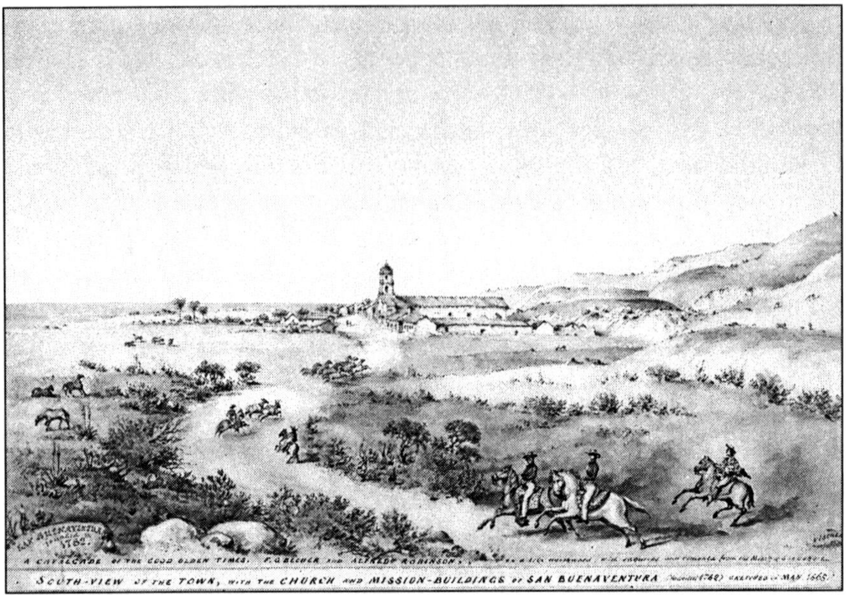

San Buenaventura (now Ventura), California, as it appeared in 1865.
Courtesy Bancroft Library, University of California, Berkeley.

Beyond these preparations, the routine at Drum Barracks remained the same. Independence Day festivities at Wilmington were delayed until the afternoon by rain. At 3:00 P.M. a procession finally assembled that included Companies C and D, a detachment of "Mounted Lancers" led by Dr. Tolman, and a "Liberty Car containing 36 school children representing the states." But the parade was regarded as a disappointment, a circumstance blamed on the poor weather and the fact that the other two Native Cavalry companies had yet to arrive.[20]

Companies A and B were actually dozens of miles up the coast, enjoying more pleasant weather and having a "lively time" with local civilians. The southbound progress of Cremony's command was no doubt slowed significantly by the sizeable train of stock that accompanied it, but a prevailing casual attitude may have been a factor as well. On July 1 the companies were camped not at Drum Barracks but rather on the plaza in Santa Barbara, remaining there for two more days. On the fourth they camped on the outskirts of San Buenaventura, where the appearance of so many soldiers was a cause for excitement. There the cavalrymen took the day off to visit with residents, including many friends and family, and to celebrate the national anniversary in true Californio style by attending a "Bull and Bear" fight at a "grand arena" in town.[21]

Finally, the two companies, which "did not appear to be fatigued after their long march," arrived at Los Angeles on July 8 and proceeded into Drum Barracks at noon the next day.[22] For the first time during the war, the battalion was assembled in one place.

Alamo Mocho, Baja California, one of the campsites on the overland road visited by the Native Cavalry en route to Fort Yuma.
From Marcy, *Prairie Traveler.*

CHAPTER 9

The March to Arizona

Hemos tenido un lindo viaje de Drum Barracks a este punto, "via hell" alias "Carisso Creek." For heaven's sake never come this way if you can help it, you will surely melt.

CAPTAIN PORFIRIO JIMENO

Bound for Arizona, the Native Cavalry companies were sent across the desert individually at intervals of a few days. This was done to conserve water and forage at the established campsites along the route, a standard practice since the "throwing forward" of the California Column a few years earlier. Company A departed Drum Barracks on July 13, and Company B left two days later. Company C, still awaiting horses, and Major Cremony would remain behind for the time being, while Company D finally set out on the nineteenth.[1]

The march of Company D was later described in a letter to the *Los Angeles Tri-Weekly News* by 1st Sergeant Juan Robarts.[2] Born in England but nonetheless fluent in Spanish, he initially enlisted under his given name of John Robarts but so thoroughly assimilated with the native troopers that even the official records would soon Hispanicize his name.[3] Of the troopers' departure, Robarts wrote, "We left Drum Barracks . . . some gay, some who had made the acquaintance of the merry God, pretty drunk, the most part very somber and very sad."[4]

Their destination would be Tubac, an old Spanish presidio in the Santa Cruz Valley of southern Arizona, nearly twenty miles north of the international boundary. In recent years the place had been reoccupied by California soldiers as a base for campaigning against the Apaches and as a sort of listening post where the U.S. Army could, in the words of one correspondent, "watch Maximillian's [*sic*] frontier."[5] The exact destination would change somewhat as the Native Cavalry was on the march, but the battalion's ultimate mission would remain the same.

The journey would happen in two parts, with the first leg taking the men to Fort Yuma on the Colorado River. Along the way the three companies were scattered over as much as one hundred miles along the old Butterfield Overland Road.[6] The route was by now well traveled, and the logistical considerations were all accounted for, but nothing about such a journey could be considered routine. Even though by most reports the route was blessed with "plenty of good water and pasture," the product of ample rains over the previous few months, the column suffered from the hazards of travel in the Colorado Desert at the height of an unusually hot summer. At Cooke's Wells, for example, a civilian teamster accompanying Company A died from the effects of the heat.[7]

In a letter to his *padrino* in Santa Barbara, Captain Jimeno probably spoke for many of the men of the battalion. He began writing in English, but when that language seemed insufficient to describe the scene, Jimeno switched to his native Spanish. He first called the campsite at the abandoned stage station of Carrizo Creek "Hell," then went on to describe conditions on the route to Fort Yuma: "Thermometer every day in the shade 113 to 116, wind none. Scorpions thick as molasses, flies, still worse, and when we want to drink cool water we have to boil it and drink it immediately or else it will get hotter. Es imposible dar una descripcion de este punto."[8]

Given the circumstances and the battalion's record so far, it should come as no surprise that a number of the troopers tried to desert. At Puerta de la Cruz, where the line of march reached the crest of the mountains and began a rugged descent into the low desert, a handful of men from Company B attempted to flee. Two of them were quickly recaptured, but this was only the beginning.[9] During the march to Tubac, the battalion lost nearly thirty men to desertion. As later events would indicate, many of these errant soldiers made their way south into Mexico.

It took about two weeks for each of the companies to reach Fort Yuma. Set among a barren but spectacular landscape, the post sat atop an imposing bluff that commanded a critical crossing of the Colorado River. On the opposite bank was a loose cluster of warehouses and workshops where the army maintained six-month stores of arms, clothing, food, and other supplies for posts as far away as Texas.

Fort Yuma, California.
From Browne, "A Tour through Arizona," pt. 1.

The lush greenery, with bosques of cottonwood, mesquite, and willow that covered the bottomlands below the fort along the Colorado and Gila Rivers, was in abrupt contrast to the surrounding desert. The post itself also presented a respite from the hardships of the adjacent wilderness. A modern installation, well supplied by river steamers, it boasted facilities comparable in many ways to what the cavalrymen had known at Drum Barracks. Though the heat that Captain Jimeno and numerous others complained of was a real problem, sometimes making the normal routine of garrison life almost impossible, conditions at the post were relatively comfortable compared to what the battalion would experience later. The troopers, however, were only to stay for a few days to rest and otherwise prepare for the second leg of their march. They departed for Tubac again by company. Company A was ferried across the Colorado to the Arizona side on August 4, with Company B following two days later.[10]

Company D, the last to arrive at Yuma, remained there for five additional days, leaving on August 9 and escorting a wagon train "laden with 'grub' for Uncle Sam's boys in Arizona." Sergeant Robarts reported that the unit followed the Gila River from the fort until the well-worn route turned away from its banks at Gila Bend, striking out along a forty-mile waterless cutoff toward the stagecoach stop at Maricopa Wells. Covering

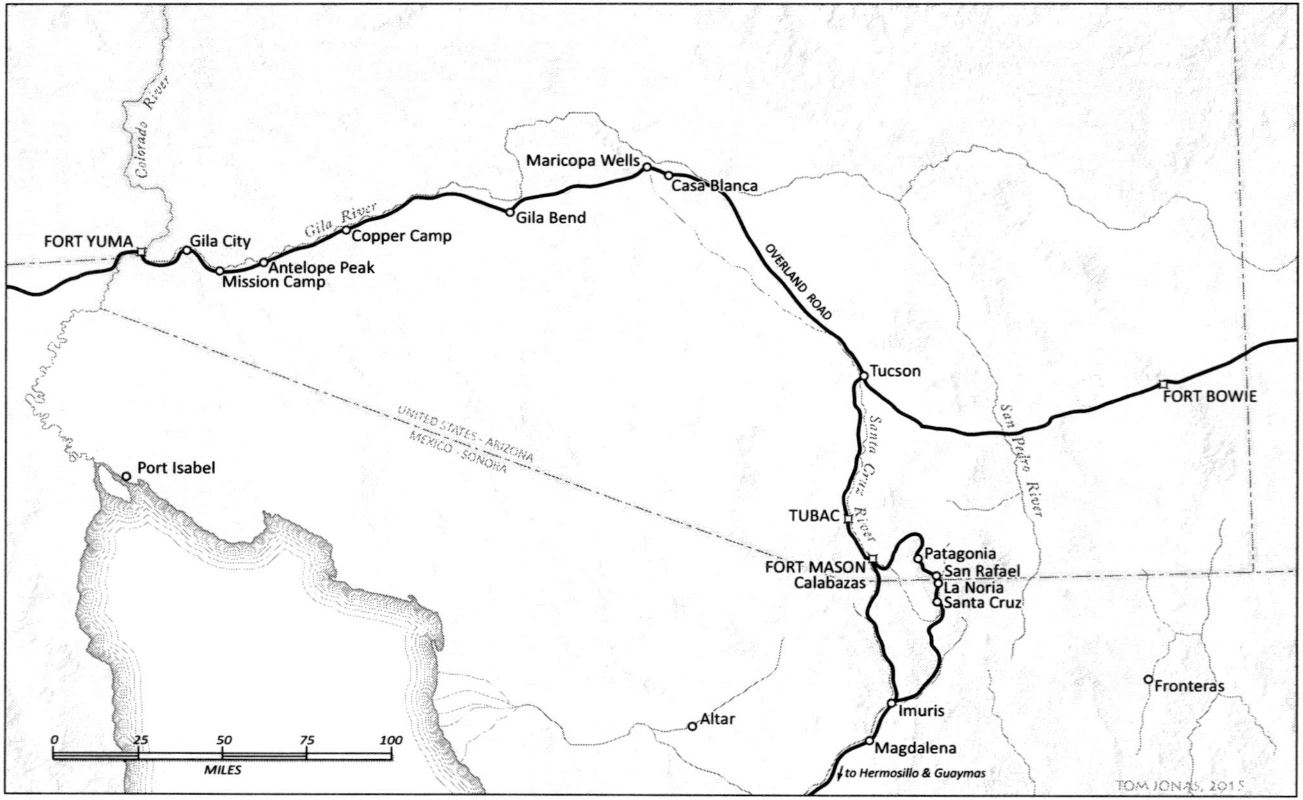

Native Cavalry operations in Arizona Territory and Sonora, 1865–1866.
Map by Tom Jonas. Copyright © 2015 by the University of Oklahoma Press.

the initial part of this journey by marching all night, the lancers of Company D arrived in the morning at the villages of the Pima and Maricopa Indians, whose "well fenced and watered" farms extended for what Robarts estimated to be "upwards of fifteen miles" along the river. At Maricopa Wells they found an encampment of California volunteers organizing a company of local recruits and otherwise preparing for a campaign against the Apaches in the Tonto Basin.[11]

Seeing plentiful melons, which were "just ripening" in the fields, was too great a temptation for the Native troopers. Unfortunately for them, the Maricopas and Pimas were not content to simply give these away. Since the lancers were, for the most part, broke, they bartered their "shirts, drawers and other articles of apparel" in exchange for the fruit. By Robarts's estimation, the Indians "got the best of every trade that was made."[12]

Company D continued east along the Butterfield Road, stopping to camp at Casa Blanca, the site of a well-known flour mill and trading post. The next day's march took them south and away from the Gila River. On August 30 the company arrived in what Robarts sarcastically described as the "flourishing and extensive city of Tucson." The adobe community of a little more than fifteen hundred mostly Mexican American residents was the first sizeable civilian settlement they had encountered since leaving Los Angeles. Robarts, however, found that the town did not live up to its reputation and derided the ramshackle adobe pueblo for "the weeds that" grew "on the tops of the houses and the 'burros' that parade[d in] the streets." The company "laid over" in Tucson for a day, then resumed the march for Tubac on the first.[13]

On the night of September 3, as the troops camped along the Santa Cruz River some eight miles north of Tubac, a soldier on watch reported spotting Apaches. This turned out to be eight or ten individuals who "did not come near enough to harm anything," only "to see if they could find a horse or mule loose."[14]

The Los Angeles company arrived at the old presidio of Tubac to find the post all but abandoned save for a quartermaster's guard left behind to deal with the remaining army property. The entire garrison, including the two Native Cavalry companies that had arrived a few days earlier, had moved twelve miles south to a site called Calabazas. Company D would soon follow.

Sergeant Robarts took pen and paper in hand and quickly wrote a note in Spanish to let the lancers' loved ones know that they had made

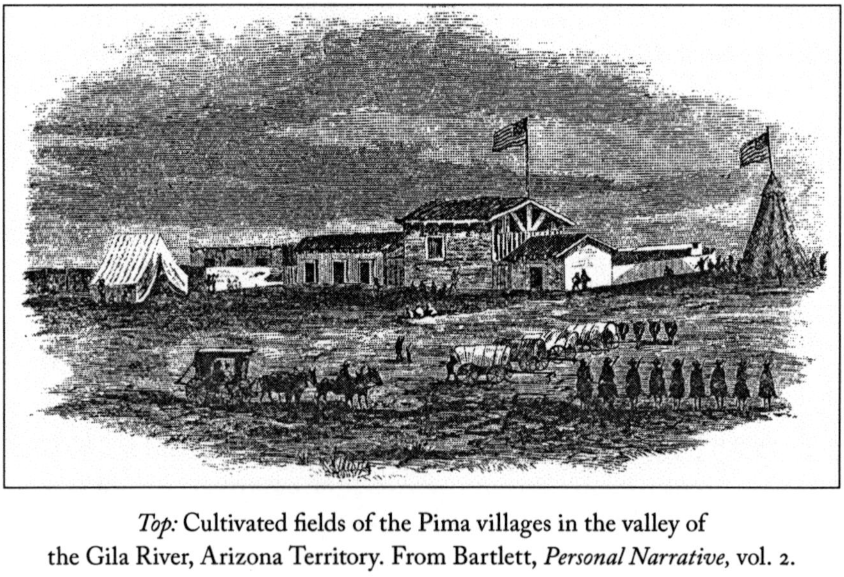

Top: Cultivated fields of the Pima villages in the valley of the Gila River, Arizona Territory. From Bartlett, *Personal Narrative*, vol. 2.

Bottom: Casa Blanca, Arizona Territory. From Browne, "A Tour through Arizona," pt. 2.

Tubac, Arizona Territory.
From Browne, "A Tour through Arizona," pt. 3.

it safely across the desert. He finished it in time to hand it to a departing express rider. Nearly a month later it was printed, untranslated, in a Los Angeles newspaper:

> Aviso—La Compania de Caballeria de Nativos Californias de Los Angeles Llegó a este punto el dia 4 Setiembre, 1865, y va mañana, dia 5 por Calabasas a la frontera. Los hombres de la compania Mandan saludas a sus parientes y amigos en Los Angeles. Todas va bien.
>
> J. R.
> Tubac, A.T., 4 Setiembre, 1865[15]

Company D continued its march the next day and arrived safely at their new post, ending a journey of more than 620 miles that took forty-seven days.[16]

Calabazas, Arizona Territory.
The post of Fort Mason would have sat in the bottomlands below the mesa, generally to the right of the ranch buildings in this lithograph.
From Gray, *Survey of a Route for the Southern Pacific R.R.*

CHAPTER 10

Watching Maximilian's Frontier

Este es un pais triste, feo y casi sin gente civilizada.

CAPTAIN PORFIRIO JIMENO

The battalion's new post, dubbed Fort Mason in honor of the district commander, was at a site briefly occupied by a Camp Moore in the previous decade.[1] A description of that camp, written by a traveler in 1857, seems consistent with accounts of Fort Mason as well:

> If you will portray in your imagination a bottom covered with tall, golden colored grass, hedged by mountains whose sands glitter like metal, divided by a meandering stream a dozen yards wide and as many inches deep [the Santa Cruz River], this shaded by cotton-woods, willows, and musquites [*sic*], then a few hundred yards higher up another stream, a creek with less volume [Portrero Creek] pouring in from the right, and in the fork an elevated rolling surface, you will have a view of Calabasas. . . . Then picture in your mind's-eye this bottom dotted with shanties of straw and cloth, and the fork covered with military tents.[2]

Calabazas itself was a substantial adobe ranch, abandoned but in good repair, which was originally built as a Franciscan mission in the eighteenth century. It sat on a low mesa that commanded "the whole country in every direction." Seven miles north of the border, the site was strategically important because it controlled the "only practicable routes into Sonora" and offered an abundance of fuel wood, grass, and water as well as limestone for construction.[3]

In addition to the Native Cavalry, Fort Mason's garrison included the men who had previously been at Tubac, among them the headquarters, staff, and three companies of the 7th California Infantry, later known as the "Hungry Seventh" for the privations they suffered in Arizona. The regiment's commander, Lieutenant Colonel Charles M. Lewis, a calm and decisive veteran of the war with Mexico, had charge of the post. Detachments of the 7th had already been in more than a few skirmishes with Apaches.[4]

They also joined the recently mustered Company E, 1st Arizona Volunteer Infantry. Recruited largely in Sonora, these soldiers were, like the Native Cavalry, mostly Spanish speaking. Lacking adequate uniforms and accoutrements, the Arizona troops were in a "sickly and ragged condition" and quickly became "the laughing stock of their countrymen far and near." These shortages limited them mostly to "making adobies" and other fatigue duties, though they eventually would be sent on a few scouts of the countryside. In early December Company E was ordered north to the Río Verde, where the Arizonans had significantly more opportunity to distinguish themselves in active service.[5]

General Mason had ordered that the new post be constructed from stone and adobe. But the men were still living in tents and shelters of "grass and brush" when the Native Cavalry arrived, and they would largely continue to do so for the next few months. It had rained "every day" following a year of unusually wet weather, and the valley was full of weeds and grass taller than "a man on horseback" and harbored so many "flies and gnats" that it was "almost impossible to do any writing in the day for the annoyance."[6] This gave rise to an insect-borne malarial-fever epidemic that hit most of the officers and men at one time or another, rendering between one-third and one-half the garrison ineffective at its height while being responsible for thirty deaths. Captain Hiram S. Washburn of the Arizona Volunteers complained that there were days that some of the California companies at the post could only muster "seven to eleven men at roll-call" and that he had to serve as officer of the day every other day for over a week because he was one of the few who remained healthy. This reality, coupled with seemingly perennial supply problems, slowed construction and other activities at the post.[7]

Captain Jimeno spoke for most of the men at Fort Mason when he described the place as "sad, ugly and almost without civilized people." He went on: "One speaks of nothing but 'Apaches, Apaches.' Of fever, almost each day someone dies. Truly, it makes one mad."[8]

Within a day or so of Jimeno's arrival, word reached Fort Mason that about fifteen men of the Native Cavalry who had deserted en route, taking with them "30 head of fine horses, numerous carbines, pistols and sabres, and all of their equipments," were being held by Mexican imperial authorities in Magdalena, Sonora, some fifty miles beyond the border. Colonel Lewis sent Captains Pico and Jimeno with thirty troopers, along with Lieutenant William Emery, a trusted officer from his own regiment who served as post adjutant, south in an effort to recover the absconders and the stolen Federal property.[9]

By this time imperial forces had "full possession of Sonora."[10] Backed by a French naval squadron at the port of Guaymas, partisans loyal to Maximilian had scattered the poorly organized republican forces in a series of victories over the previous six months and were now consolidating their power, having organized the frontier state into four military departments. The forces in and around Magdalena were commanded by Prefect José Moreno Bustamante, who had at his disposal a reported 250 to 400 men, including infantry and cavalry. Lieutenant Emery disparaged these troops as "poorly armed . . . with no uniforms of any kind" and "no flag amongst them whatever."[11]

Nevertheless, the little column from Fort Mason was entering hostile territory when it crossed the international border. Riding for two days through a "beautiful country" with "hills covered with ash and oak," the cavalrymen halted upon arrival at the outskirts of Magdalena, a town of some fifteen hundred people consisting of low adobes clustered around a dirt plaza dominated by an impressive whitewashed mission church. Here, Lieutenant Emery rode ahead of the formation to deliver the Americans' demands in writing. Captain Pico, however, quickly became impatient and charged into the town with eight to ten of his men, brandishing sabers and pistols and stopping in front of the prefect's headquarters on the plaza.[12]

Pico and Emery demanded that the deserters and the stolen property be returned. Moreno scolded the Californio captain for his "warlike manner," to which "Pico replied that the United States did not recognize the Imperial Government," only the republic under President Benito Juarez. Believing that the "U.S. troops had come there on purpose to fight," Moreno ordered a detachment of cavalry to form on the plaza and sent a courier to alert infantrymen camped four or five miles

José Moreno Bustamante, imperial prefect of the military district that included Altar and Magdalena, Sonora. From Browne, "A Tour through Arizona," pt. 4.

away. Pico, for his part, dispatched a messenger to Captain Jimeno, who remained with his lancers outside of town, asking him to be ready in case of trouble.[13]

"A single gun fired at this time would have started a general fight," wrote Emery later. The imperialists, evoking Moreno's own heroic stand against a band of American filibusters nearly a decade earlier, threatened to take the Californians prisoner and shoot them "as they did Crabb's party," while Pico boasted that his men would die fighting. During a particularly tense moment in the colloquy, an old man in the crowd, doubtless speaking for the many republican sympathizers in the town, shouted, "Viva los Americanos!"[14]

"After the excitement had somewhat subsided," wrote Emery, Moreno agreed to allow the officers to remain in Magdalena with an escort of six men while he waited for instructions from authorities in Hermosillo.

Magdalena, Sonora.
From Browne, "A Tour through Arizona," pt. 4.

Moreno demanded that Jimeno and the rest of the troopers, though, return to the United States. Riding back into Fort Mason on September 9, Jimeno reported on the situation to Colonel Lewis.[15]

It took eight days for word to arrive from Hermosillo. In the meantime Pico, Emery, and the Native Cavalry detachment were accommodated by republican sympathizers in Magdalena who treated them to "three fine dinners." Emery reported that the "better class of citizens" in Sonora were opposed to Maximilian and that "their greatest wish" was "to have the United States side with them against the French."[16]

The reply from Hermosillo ordered that Captain Pico and his troopers return to the United States within forty-eight hours without the deserters or the property. Thus, the Americans rode north empty handed. On the way back they spotted a small band of Apaches in the hills about fifteen miles south of Fort Mason. Pico led his party in pursuit, but the terrain was too "steep and rocky" for the chase to be sustained, Lieutenant Emery nearly breaking his leg when he fell with his horse. Captain Pico likewise fell with his mount and was shot through the thigh when his pistol accidentally discharged.[17] The injury required him to spend much of the next few months on sick leave in Tubac and Tucson, certainly a particularly humiliating situation for a man considered one of the best horsemen in California.[18]

The party returned to Fort Mason on September 15 to find that much had changed in their absence. The day after the column's departure, a Mexican officer, Colonel Federick A. Ronstadt, arrived with the news that Ignacio Pesquiera, the governor of Sonora, was about three miles away and seeking permission to camp in the vicinity. Defeated by the French-backed imperialists, the governor had all but disbanded his demoralized, ragtag army and crossed the border north of Santa Cruz to seek the safety of American arms. Colonel Lewis "offered him the hospitality and protection of the post." When the garrison rose for revile the next morning, they were surprised to find the mesa populated by Pesquiera's substantial train of livestock, which included "1000 head of cattle and 100 head of horses, mules and donkeys" and "some sheep and goats."[19] Meanwhile, the governor made quarters for himself, his family, and a small band of followers in the old ranch house of Calabazas, which quickly became Sonora's capitol-in-exile.[20]

Word soon arrived that the Native Cavalry deserters had been released and that the arms and equipment they had carried away had been sold at public auction. At the same time, imperial officials demanded an apology for "the insult offered them at Magdalena." Adding to the tense climate was a rumor that Moreno intended to cross the border with a large force in an attempt to take Pesquiera. The normally restrained Colonel Lewis replied, "Let him come and try it." Lieutenant Emery likewise expressed the sentiments of the restless men of Fort Mason when he wrote, "If only we could have a little fight with the French it would be something worth while."[21] Lewis dispatched Captain Young with twenty lancers of Company D to patrol the border and sent another detachment of ten lancers of Company B under Captain Jimeno to watch the road through the Patagonia Mountains to the Sonoran town of Santa Cruz. They were ordered to take care to not cross the border but merely to serve as pickets and to notify the colonel of any trouble. For the time being, nothing came of Moreno's threat.[22]

Despite this excitement, service at Fort Mason remained miserable. Heavy rains continued for most of September, and the fever continued taking a toll. On October 16 Lieutenant Crisanto Soto of Company A,

Hacienda of Patagonia, Arizona Territory.
From Browne, "A Tour through Arizona," pt. 5.

described by Jimeno as a "true friend," died at the Patagonia Mines, where a makeshift convalescent camp had been established in the drier mountain air.[23] At this point a reported 185 of the 418 enlisted men, and nine of the eleven officers at the post, were too sick for duty. Even Governor Pesquiera's wife succumbed to the disease. In December Captain Young became yet another casualty of the epidemic. By this time a third surgeon had been detailed to the post to cope with the outbreak as Fort Mason's two surgeons had both fallen ill, but the worst of it was largely over.[24]

Major Cremony and Captain de la Guerra's Company C joined their comrades at Fort Mason on November 1. Finally fully mounted and equipped, they had left Drum Barracks in late August but were delayed at Fort Yuma for over three weeks waiting for flooding on the Colorado River to subside enough for crossing. Joined en route by Captain Jimeno and the post band, they were greeted on their arrival by soldiers lined

San Rafael Valley, Arizona Territory.
From Bartlett, *Personal Narrative,* vol. 1.

up on either side of the road who saluted the Santa Barbara men and asked after their families in California.[25]

Once at Fort Mason, Cremony briefly assumed command from the ill Lewis.[26] Then the major issued a simple set of instructions for the governance of his battalion:

1st No government horses will be used for any other than government business.

2nd No government horse will be ridden faster than a trot except in the necessary duty of herding.

3rd No enlisted man will ride his horse across the parade ground except by the regular wagon roads.

4th All firing of revolver arms with in or out [*sic*] of the Garrison is strictly prohibited except in cases of actual necessity.

One can only speculate as to the behavior that prompted this order. Suffice it to say, it would not have been necessary for a slightly less unruly set of volunteers.[27]

Late on the night of November 24, word arrived from pickets at the Patagonia Mines that a large force from Sonora, consisting of about 350 Ópata volunteers under the command of Colonel Refugio Tanori, a tribal leader commissioned in the Imperial Army, had crossed the border and attacked the ranching community of San Rafael, leaving an American citizen wounded.[28] Believing the raid was an attempt to capture either Pesquiera or the republican general Jesús García Morales, who was camped just on the other side of the border at La Noria, Major Cremony quickly assembled a detachment from Companies C and D. The men rode all night along the well-worn but nonetheless rugged and difficult wagon road winding through the Patagonia Mountains, reaching San Rafael early the next morning.[29]

Once there, Cremony left battalion surgeon Tolman to tend to the wounded American before crossing the border to the town of Santa Cruz, where he learned that Tanori's command had retreated even farther south. The major sent ahead Lieutenant Edmund W. Codington of Company D and ten troopers to make contact with the imperialist colonel. After a nine-hour forty-mile chase, the lancers reached Ímuris, a small town in the Magdalena Valley, only to find that Tanori and his fleet-footed irregulars had melted into the countryside. The command remained at Santa Cruz for a few days to guard against the possibility of Tanori's return. Cremony used the opportunity to renew his acquaintance with Inez Gonzalez, a woman he helped rescue from Apache captivity as a girl many years earlier and now happily married to the local alcalde. On November 30 the major and the lancers returned to Fort Mason.[30]

By the time of Tanori's raid, French forces in Sonora's interior had fallen back to Guaymas as part of the first phase of an eventual withdrawal from Mexico. Pesquiera and his officers had used his time at Calabazas to rebuild his broken army. By December republican partisans were once again able to take the fight to the imperialists. By March 1866 the governor had returned to Sonora to personally lead the resistance in that state.[31] Though the fight against Maximilian would continue for well over a year, the empire and its French backers had long since ceased to be a threat to the frontier. By then the men of Fort Mason had turned their attention to other enemies.

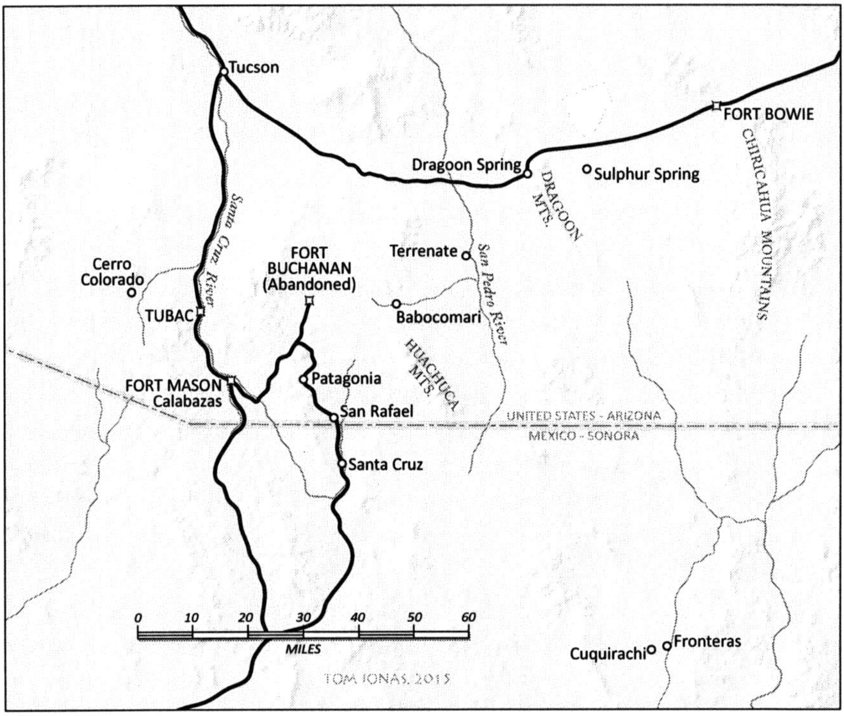

The winter campaign of 1865–1866.
Map by Tom Jonas. Copyright © 2015 by the University of Oklahoma Press.

CHAPTER 11

Campaigning against Apaches

Lo que se habla nomas, es Apaches, Apaches.

CAPTAIN PORFIRIO JIMENO

Temporarily in command of Fort Mason at the end of 1865, Major Cremony wrote to district headquarters in Prescott to complain that the post remained "in wretched destitute condition." Referring to the "fearful epidemic" that had swept the garrison a few months earlier, he wrote that "over two hundred" of the men were still "in a woebegone emaciated and delicate state of health." Cremony went on to say that his own Native Cavalry battalion was "rendered almost inert" for want of nearly everything and accused officials at the supply depot at Tucson of ignoring multiple requisitions and hoarding necessary commodities.[1]

Though Cremony was clearly engaging in at least a little hyperbole, conditions at Fort Mason were bad enough to curtail most activities against the Apaches until the end of 1865. By this time, in response to the increased U.S. military presence in Arizona Territory, the Chiricahua Apaches had largely been on the defensive for several months.[2] Nonetheless, Native Cavalry troopers had participated in a few short patrols from the post, and in response to trouble they were occasionally sent to nearby settlements such as the Cerro Colorado Mine. In October 1865 Captain Jimeno wrote to relatives in Santa Barbara to tell them about a fight with Apaches about "60 leagues" (twenty to twenty-four miles) from the post, and another soldier later reported being wounded while fighting Apaches in the mountains west of Fort Mason.[3] Private

José María García of Company C wrote home to say that though the Apaches ventured "in the neighborhood of the fort every day," they "had no courage to fight" and were "great cowards." He further stated that the troopers would ride out into the surrounding countryside in pursuit of them nearly every day, but the enemy would "disappear quickly."[4] While there were doubtless numerous such forays, the major offensive envisioned by General Mason had not yet materialized.

Finally, at the end of October 1865, having completed a tour of the territory and returned to Prescott, Mason drew up an elaborate plan for a campaign against the Apaches. It involved using soldiers from nearly every post in Arizona, including the Native Cavalry. The general called for a series of extensive scouting parties from posts in the highlands of central Arizona along with constant patrols from Fort Mason and Fort Bowie in an effort to deny the Apaches an escape route into Mexico. Mason believed the pressure exerted from such a campaign, which he ordered to begin on November 25, would force the Apaches to surrender.[5]

Criticism of this plan quickly came from many quarters, both military and civilian. Even Lieutenant General Ulysses S. Grant wrote from Washington, D.C., that the plan was "too extended" and ordered Mason to abandon it in favor of a series of more-modest operations only as "absolutely necessary to keep peace and quiet" in the territory.[6] Back in Arizona, a correspondent to the *Alta California* wrote that the general consensus among civilians was that the effort would be a "great failure" given that the volunteer troops were ill supplied and otherwise unprepared for lengthy operations in the field.[7]

For his part, Major Cremony agreed. Echoing similar sentiments as the newspaper correspondent, he believed that even his own Native Cavalry troopers were inadequate to the task. The major wrote that it "would be not only ridiculous but criminal" if he were "to send the cavalry out hunting Apaches through deep cañons and over mountain heights and armed only with pistols and lances."[8]

Grant's orders to scale back the proposed operation did not arrive in time to stop the campaign. Colonel Lewis thus proceeded as planned, though nearly three weeks after Mason's ordered starting date. On December 13 a column of 160 men, composed of elements of the Native Cavalry and the colonel's own "Hungry Seventh," departed Fort Mason for the mountains to the east. The command was divided into three detachments: the first composed of soldiers of the 7th California Infantry, the second of forty-two Native Cavalry troopers from Companies B and D (commanded by Captain Jimeno and Lieutenant Lafferty), and the third, commanded directly by Colonel Lewis, of forty-three lancers of Company C (under Lieutenants Feeks and Codington).[9]

Outfitting the expedition all but exhausted the meager supplies at Fort Mason. One hundred head of cattle and sheep were ordered slaughtered and the meat jerked "for the use of troops on scout," leaving little for those who remained at the post. Also, in order to augment the lancer's arms, a number of carbines, muskets, and rifles were requisitioned from among serviceable weapons still in storage and even from other soldiers. This left the remaining garrison nearly unable to respond to any trouble that might occur closer to base. Receiving reports of Apache raids at the Patagonia Mines during Lewis's absence, Cremony attempted to assemble a detachment under Lieutenant Jimenez to search for the offenders, but after coming up short of pack mules, clothing, and firearms, he called off the sortie.[10]

On campaign, Lewis and the detachment of Company C, taking the rugged Santa Cruz wagon road over the Patagonia Mountains, made camp at San Rafael. From there, Lieutenant Codington was dispatched across the border to Santa Cruz to roust up Antonio and Marcial, two errant civilian scouts who had been absent without leave from Fort Mason. Once reunited, the command broke camp and struck northeast across the "level valley," where progress was slowed by a "heavy growth of sacaton." At the "rocky foothills" of the Huachuca Mountains, the column took an "old but still well defined Indian trail" through a "difficult mountain pass," reaching the old Babocómari ranch the next day. The lancers made camp there on December 16 and waited for the arrival of the other two detachments.[11]

Meanwhile, serving as an escort for a pair of supply wagons, Captain Jimeno and the men from Companies B and D took the Fort Buchanan road toward the Sonoita River. Orders were to join Lewis at Babocómari, but unfamiliar with the country and lacking the services of a scout or guide, Jimeno seems to have become confused. Instead, from Fort Buchanan he struck a bit too far north toward the Whetstone Mountains. The captain and his lancers then made camp on the San Pedro River on the sixteenth and waited to be joined by the others, unaware that the colonel was waiting for them more than twenty miles to the south.[12]

Santa Cruz, Sonora.
From Browne, "A Tour through Arizona," pt. 4.

From Babocómari on the seventeenth, Lewis sent two scouting parties to look for signs of Apaches. Finding none, one instead came back with a report of a "fresh wagon track leading to the crossing of the San Pedro river."[13] The colonel correctly assumed this to be from one of Jimeno's wagons. The next day his men broke camp during a cold rain to march north to join the second detachment. Four miles out they met Captain Messenger and his infantry. Lewis then sent Lieutenant Codington and seven lancers on to contact Jimeno while the rest of the command turned back to Babocómari.

Codington reached the San Pedro Crossing in the afternoon with orders for Jimeno to take his command south to join Lewis. It was still cold and rainy when the captain and his cavalrymen broke camp at sunrise the next day and rode south across the level plain and scattered thorn bush toward Babocómari. By the time they reached the encampment early that afternoon, it was snowing sporadically.

Lewis ordered his newly reunited command to break camp at 8:00 A.M. and start toward the San Pedro River. They arrived at the site of the old presidio of Santa Cruz de Terrenate at 2:00 P.M. and made camp among

The ruined hacienda of Babocomari, Arizona Territory.
From Gray, *Survey of a Route for the Southern Pacific R.R.*

the ruins.[14] The next morning they broke camp and again divided. Messenger's infantry and Lewis's Native Cavalry detachment would march through the Dragoon Mountains via Middlemarch and South Passes, respectively, while Jimeno's lancers and the wagons would move around the range via Dragoon Springs and wait for the rest of the command to join them on the other side at Sulphur Springs.[15]

Among the cactus-and-mescal-studded "rough and broken" country on the western flank of the Dragoons, Lewis's detachment found a recently abandoned rancheria in what was later known as the West Stronghold.[16] As they proceeded on their full day's march through the pass, the men found "Indian tracks" that the scouts judged to be about ten days old. Lewis and the lancers of Company C camped at a waterhole on the eastern flank of the mountains before starting for Sulphur Springs the next morning.

When they arrived at around 11:00 A.M., the colonel received "unwelcome news." Jimeno reported that just hours before, he had met Lieutenant Alfred W. Norton and a scouting party of soldiers from the 1st California Cavalry and the 1st New Mexico Infantry from Fort Bowie.

They told the captain that the post was low on provisions and could not resupply Lewis's column as planned. Furthermore, when the soldiers of the 7th California Infantry arrived, many of them were barefoot, their shoes having worn through on the march through the mountains. Lewis thus ordered the infantry back to Fort Mason along with the two wagons and a small escort of Native Cavalry to resupply there.[17]

Jimeno and his men were left behind at Sulphur Springs. On December 24 "the cry of Indians was raised" by the detail assigned to watch the horses. The captain quickly organized twenty men for a pursuit. Giving chase to the retreating Apaches toward their stronghold in the Dragoons, the troopers engaged them in a running fight of ten miles, killing one and wounding at least two others. Unknown to them, the party they pursued was the vanguard of a larger group driving a herd of cattle. By falling back and inducing the soldiers to follow, they effectively warned the other party and allowed them to escape. The fleeing Apaches killed twenty-one head of cattle and outright abandoned six more in their retreat.

Their horses nearly spent as darkness set in, the cavalrymen returned to camp. The next day Jimeno looked over the state of his command and decided it would be unwise to renew the pursuit. Instead he moved his camp to a "little valley" nine miles to the west, where water and wood were more available than at the relatively barren Sulphur Springs. The Native Cavalry remained there, subsisting on scant rations, until December 30, when the captain decided that it would be best to move to Dragoon Springs. Learning that night of Colonel Lewis's arrival at Sulphur Springs, Jimeno and his detachment returned there the next day.

The command, along with wagons now fully laden with provisions and forage, reunited on December 31. The colonel, however, had fallen ill, so the soldiers remained camped there until January 2, 1866, when they marched for Fort Bowie along the Overland Road. With Lewis still "very sick," the column was forced to take a two-hour rest on the way. When it crossed paths with Estevan Ochoa's wagon train, loaded with supplies and also bound for the same post, Lewis, "unable to proceed on horseback," climbed aboard one of the wagons.[18]

With Jimeno in temporary command, the Native Cavalry, traveling well ahead of the colonel, arrived at Fort Bowie early that evening. The lancers found conditions at the post to be little better than what

The Chiricahua Mountains and the adjacent Sulphur Springs Valley.
From Bartlett, *Personal Narrative*, vol. 1.

they experienced at Fort Mason. The garrison, largely composed of Spanish-speaking soldiers of the 1st New Mexico Volunteer Infantry, predominantly lived in tents, brush shelters, and even "hovels" hacked out of the hillsides.[19] Nonetheless, with their horses "nearly exhausted from fatigue and want of proper food," the Native Cavalry laid over for five days to give their mounts a chance to rest and be reshod.

Before resuming the march, the column's scout, Marcial, confessed to being "ignorant" of the country ahead, so Lewis decided that he would be left behind. In his place the colonel would take Fort Bowie's resident scout, Merejildo Grijalva.[20] On January 6 Lewis and his command left Bowie, striking south from Apache Pass up the level plains and abundant grass of the Sulphur Springs Valley.

On the third day out, in the foothills of the Sierra Pedregosa some forty miles from the fort, Grijalva spotted fresh tracks while leading the column to a campsite. Then "there suddenly arose a great smoke" three miles away in the mountains to the east. Realizing that Apaches were likely at the campsite ahead and now warned of the column's approach by sentries in the hills, Lewis pressed forward "as rapidly as possible." At the campsite they found "abundant evidence that the Indians had not been long absent" and tracks that led into the adjacent mountains. Two parties of troopers were sent on foot to follow the tracks and "discover if possible the whereabouts of the enemy." They returned an hour before sunset to report finding only a "large Rancheria" that had been deserted for about two days.[21]

As these lancers were making their report, "several Indians" showed themselves on a mountaintop some two miles away. Lewis immediately sent dismounted soldiers in "various directions" to probe the flank of the mountains, figuring that the enemy numbered "some sixty or seventy." But the Apaches were "unencumbered and secure in their native mountains" and "could laugh at any efforts" by the cavalrymen "to get within shooting distance." As night set in, the colonel realized his position was surrounded and vulnerable, so he ordered the guards doubled and had the men sleep with their horses' reins in their hands. The Apaches made at least one attempt upon the camp that night, taunting the soldiers with "distant cries" until 2:00 A.M.

At daybreak the Apaches were long gone, and all signs showed they had headed south. Hoping to overtake them, Lewis pressed forward with the column through thorny brush along the base of the mountains and across the border into Sonora. After a hard ride of nearly twenty-five miles, the horses showed "signs of great distress," and the column stopped to camp.

By the second day of the pursuit, it was "painfully evident" that further efforts "would be futile." The cavalry horses "were worn out," and the men were low on provisions. Lewis decided that the prudent course would be to return to Fort Mason "by the nearest route."

Now some twenty-five miles south of the border, the column struck west across country sparse of grass until they came upon the Rio Fronteras and the road to the Presidio of Fronteras.[22] The town itself was in a rich valley that Codington described as having great agricultural

Fronteras, Sonora.
From Bartlett, *Personal Narrative*, vol. 1.

potential. Years of Apache depredations, however, had reduced the community's population from more than two thousand to fewer than five hundred. The presidio's *comandante* received Colonel Lewis and the Native Cavalry in a "cordial manner," expressing "much gratitude" for their waging war against the Apaches, who "had robbed them of everything they possessed," and gave them permission to camp on the outskirts of the town.

Breaking camp late the next morning, the Americans headed to Cuquirachi, a village six miles to the south, to obtain grain for their horses from Ochoa, who was there with his wagon train loading up with corn for Fort Bowie. After spending the night there, Lewis and his men resumed the march, taking a rugged mountain trail leading north and west toward Santa Cruz. By the time the route leveled off at the

San Pedro valley, the cavalrymen were on foot, with many of the horses "broken down" and even the mounts of the officers "little better off."

The column spotted four Apaches three miles away as they passed the flank of the Sierra San José. Lewis dispatched a few picked men whose horses were in better shape to give chase. Even though the lancers "strained every nerve" to overtake the Apaches, the enemy nonetheless "eluded pursuit" and disappeared into the mountains.

After two more days, the column crossed back into the United States at San Rafael, having left behind several broken-down horses. The bulk of the hungry, tired, and threadbare command finally shambled back into Fort Mason on January 17, 1866. Lieutenant Feeks, having been left behind at the San Pedro with a small detail, the spent horses, and no provisions, arrived with the last of the mounts three days later.

Mason's winter campaign was over. It was generally regarded as a failure, a conclusion attributed to several circumstances. These included unrest in Mexico, which limited the availability of supplies, the severity of the winter weather, a lack of enthusiasm among California soldiers close to the end of their three-year enlistments, and the difficulty of coordinating the movements of troops from so many posts. For his part, Lieutenant Codington specifically blamed the lack of results on Captain Jimeno, holding him responsible for, among other things, a two-day delay at the San Pedro River crossing that, he claimed, had deprived the expedition "the pleasure of finding the whole Chiricahua tribe of Indians at home." Given the numerous delays and logistical shortcomings of the entire venture, it seems unfair to blame Jimeno, for he and the longsuffering soldiers of the Native Cavalry seem to have performed adequately under the circumstances.[23]

CHAPTER 12

Into the Sunset

The Union American residents of Santa Barbara have seen with deepest concern that the Government has announced its intention of disbanding Co. C, Native California Cavalry. . . .

This Company, if disbanded, will return here. There is no branch of industry in which they can gain a livelihood. . . . As they are skilled in the use of arms, it is more than probable that some of them will become armed and organized banditti, and plunder and slaughter travelers on our solitary roads. . . .

We therefore most earnestly pray you to retain that Company in the service, if at all possible.

CHARLES ENOCH HUSE, S. R. I. STURGEON, AND F. W. FROST

In late October 1865, well before Colonel Lewis took the Native Cavalry into the wilderness on his fruitless hunt for Apaches, General McDowell at department headquarters in San Francisco ordered that the battalion be relieved from duty in Arizona as "soon as possible." With their three-year enlistments winding down and the rebellion long since over, the Native Cavalry along with the other California Volunteer soldiers would soon be relieved by regulars returning from the eastern states. By early December the handful of Califorino troopers who remained in California had been discharged at Drum Barracks and San Francisco.[1]

Less than a week after returning from the field, the Native Cavalry were marching west to Drum Barracks for mustering out. Just as when they arrived months before, the men departed by company, with Company A leaving Fort Mason on January 22, 1866. Captain Pico, still unable to walk or ride long distances because of his wounded leg, followed his company in an ambulance along with Hermegildo Balderamos of Company B, a farrier who suffered from three severely broken ribs after being kicked by a horse in the line of his duties a month earlier.

Companies B and D followed on the twenty-fourth and twenty-sixth, respectively. Company C and Major Cremony would not start toward California until a week later.[2] The cavalrymen endured a delay of a few weeks while waiting to cross the flooded Colorado River and camped opposite Fort Yuma. There, they briefly crossed paths with the 14th U.S. Infantry, the regulars who would take up the Native Cavalry's former posts in the interior of Arizona Territory. The troopers finally arrived at Drum Barracks with modest fanfare in March and were discharged by the end of the month. One newspaper succinctly reported that the Native Cavalry had "done good service."[3]

Major Cremony and Company C remained camped at Fort Yuma while the other three units marched on. Leaving behind their horses and lances, they joined departing soldiers of the 2nd and 7th California Infantry at dawn on March 11 and started down the Colorado by flat-bottomed steamboat. That evening the party, now numbering some 350 officers and men, camped at Port Isabel at the head of the Gulf of California and boarded the oceangoing steamer *Oregon* the next morning.[4] After an uneventful six-day voyage, the *Oregon* anchored at Cabo San Lucas to take on a shipment of sperm whale oil before heading north along the Pacific Coast. What followed was a harrowing seven days of rough seas, heavy fog, sickness, inadequate water, and diminishing rations of hard tack and salt beef. Finally on March 26, the party disembarked at the Folsom Street wharf in San Francisco.[5] There, the servicemen attracted a bit more attention than usual thanks to the presence of two officers: Captain Juan Cheveria and Lieutenant José Cabezon, Maricopa tribal leaders commissioned in the recently organized Arizona Volunteer Infantry. The local press made note of the novelty of Indians wearing the uniform of the United States.[6]

The California Volunteers, including the Native Californian troopers of Company C, were marched to the Presidio of San Francisco, where they would be billeted eight days to wait for their discharges. Once this was done, the Californios, threadbare from the rigors of frontier service, received their back pay and were reportedly "seen on every street corner" in the city, "spending their greenbacks with great liberality" in clothing stores.[7] Santa Barbara later welcomed the veterans of Company C with two days of celebration that included a parade as well as dances and bullfights.[8]

⁂ ⁂ ⁂

The service of the Native Cavalry was over. Now out of uniform, the battalion's former officers began their postwar careers.

Major Vallejo, who had resigned from the service over a year earlier, retired to Lachryma Montis, the estate of his brother, Mariano near Sonoma, where he spent his "leisure hours in reading and occasionally in painting landscapes." On occasions when he was visited by his "favorite niece Lulu," he would pick up a guitar and sing "the ancient ballads" he had learned from "the indian cantor" who taught him music while "at school in Monterey." But his retirement was not entirely idyllic. His sister-in-law, Doña Francisca Vallejo, considered him rude and objected to the way he treated his wife. She resented his presence in the household and at some point left Mariano to live with a daughter in Sonoma. The old major, who by the 1870s needed a cane to walk, remained a very bitter man. In 1874 he wrote a rambling attempt at an autobiography that gruffly dismissed his time in the service as "devoid of interest." Otherwise, his memoir is largely an inventory of the numerous wrongs perpetuated against him by various Anglo-Americans during and after the U.S. conquest. He was still arguing for redress from the government when he died in 1876.[9]

The man who had replaced Vallejo in battalion command, John C. Cremony, returned to journalism in San Francisco after his discharge. His service in Arizona, including his time with the Native Cavalry, became the basis for embellished articles he wrote for *The Overland Monthly,* a literary magazine edited by Bret Harte that also counted the major's California contemporaries J. Ross Browne and Mark Twain as contributors. Cremony wrote a book of his experiences on the frontier, *Life among the Apaches,* which was first published in 1868 and is now regarded as a classic of southwestern literature, even if accounts of his exploits are at least slightly exaggerated.

Cremony quickly assumed the role of colorful local character in San Francisco, a city well known for its eccentrics. In 1872 he was among a group of artists, journalists, and musicians who formed the Bohemian Club, a men's organization that continues to be active and whose membership over the years has included some of the nation's political elite. Cremony is credited with drafting the club's founding document, known as the Cremony Standard. The old cavalryman died in San Francisco in 1879.

Vincent Gelcich, who served as the battalion's assistant surgeon for a little over eight months before becoming surgeon of the 4th California Infantry, remained at Drum Barracks after the Native Cavalry departed for Arizona. In addition to the enhanced prestige, the promotion allowed him to better monitor his investments in the state. In February 1865 petroleum was discovered by vaqueros hunting bears in the San Fernando district of Los Angeles County, and Gelcich partnered with his wife's uncle, Andrés Pico, and others to quickly stake claims to the area. After his service he consolidated his holdings and started the company now known as Chevron.[10] He returned to private practice, eventually settling his family in Los Angeles. There, he was active in the Grand Army of the Republic (GAR) and took in Carlos Moreau, an old veteran of Company C, who he hired to work at his drugstore. Gelcich died in 1885 from the effects of an old injury he had received in 1862 "while riding from Wilmington to prevent the raising of the rebel flag." The doctor was eulogized as one of Los Angeles's most prominent boosters.[11]

The man who replaced him, Dr. George Tolman, who had been overwhelmed in trying to deal with the epidemic at Fort Mason, returned to civilian practice for a time after the war, but financial problems drove him back to the army. Assigned to the Department of the Columbia, Tolman served as an assistant surgeon at various posts in Idaho and eastern Oregon during the campaigns of Lieutenant Colonel George R. Crook. Unfortunately, a difficult marriage reportedly led him to drinking, and he was discharged. Despite his troubles, Tolman had some modest success as a druggist in San Francisco. But by the late 1880s, long since having abandoned his mentally unstable wife, he was living on a Civil War pension and remained active in the GAR. In 1912, after years of declining health, he died at the Old Soldiers Home in Yountville.

In the summer of 1866, California officials drew up plans for a new U.S. cavalry regiment that was to be composed largely of veterans of the California Volunteers and organized for service in the Southwest.[12]

José R. Pico enlisted the help of prominent friends to get himself a commission in the new regiment but to no avail, though Porfirio Jimeno and John Lafferty were recommended. A later offer by Pico to raise a company of Native Californians to fight the Modocs was likewise ignored.[13] Nevertheless, he remained active in the GAR and for the rest of his life insisted on being called "Major"; he even posed for a portrait wearing a colonel's uniform. Eventually, he was sued by a dealer of military decorations for, among other things, not having paid for the uniform and accoutrements that he often sported on public occasions.[14]

Failing in his efforts to continue his military career, Pico attempted to enter politics, but his runs for state treasurer, the legislature, and county sheriff were unsuccessful. Eventually moved to San Francisco, he worked as a realtor and was later implicated in a land-fraud scheme involving property in Baja California, though the matter went nowhere.[15]

By the 1880s Pico was in a desperate financial state and became known for frequently borrowing money from friends. Eventually, he began pursuing a claim of $8,111.25 against the state, which he alleged was still owed him for expenses incurred raising his company in 1863 and 1864. Taking his case to the legislature, Pico became a fixture at the capitol for the next several sessions until 1902, when the assembly and the governor finally agreed to the appropriation. During this quest, one newspaper lamented the irony of the situation: "During the Alcalde days the Picos made many munificent grants to the state, but the last of his race, now a broken-down pensioner, is having a hard time to collect a bill forty years old."[16]

Captain Pico died at his modest home in Alameda, with his third wife at his side, in 1905. After a long illness, an "old wound" in his left foot became infected, though it is not clear if this injury was the one he sustained in Sonora, the one he allegedly received at San Pasqual, or one from some other incident.[17] His passing was eulogized in *Sunset* magazine as the end of an era. Calling him "the last of the name" and invoking the long history of his family in California and his military service, the writer turned to a doggerel that said more about romantic notions about the Californios than about Pico's checkered career:

> Last of thy gallant race, farewell!
> When darkness on his eyelids fell
> The chain was snapped—the tale was told
> That linked the new world to the old;—

The new world of our happy day
To those brave times which fade away
In memories of flocks and fells,
Of lowing herds and mission bells.
He linked us to the times which wrote
Vallejo, Sutter, Stockton, Sloat,
Upon their banners—times which knew
The cowled Franciscan, and the gray
Old hero priest of Monterey.

In his proud eye one saw again
The chivalry of ancient Spain;
The grace of speech, the gallant air,
The readiness to do and dare.
And he was ready; and his hand
For love of this, his motherland,
Was quick to strike and strong to lead;
He served her in her hour of need
And, loving, served her as he knew,
What better proof, though unconfessed,
Than these old scars upon his breast?

Once these broad fields which slope away
Asleep in verdure, zone on zone,
With countless herds, were all his own,
Once from his white ancestral hall,
A lavish welcome ran to all,
Today the land which gave him birth
Allots him but a plot of earth—
A tomb where winter roses creep
On Santa Clara's crumbling wall;
Fit place, perhaps for one to sleep
Who knew and loved her best of all.

So ends in rest life's fitful day.
He saw an era pass away.
He touched the morning and the noon
Of that sweet time which, all too soon,
To twilight hastened when the call
Of Fremont from her mountain wall
Provoked the golden land to leap
New-vestured from her age-long sleep.

The train moves on. No hand may stay
The onward march of destiny;
But from her valleys, rich in grain,
From mountain slope and poppied plain
A sigh is heard—his deeds they tell,
And sighing, hail and call farewell.[18]

Pico's rival, Lieutenant Marcelino E. Jimenez, seems to have fared better than the captain with whom he clashed. After his discharge Jimenez relocated to San Francisco, where he was naturalized as a U.S. citizen in 1866. He worked as a clerk and translator for the courts and, at one point, the state legislature. In 1873 he moved to Ventura, where he established himself as a clerk and a notary public in the newly organized county, taking up ranching by 1876. Jimenez was still working as a clerk in 1878, after which he disappears from the historical record.

After being drummed out of the service in February 1865, Ernest Hippolyte Legross took up farming in the Sacramento Valley and eventually became a U.S. citizen. Despite his mediocre record, he received a pension and was active in veteran's organizations in later years. When his Scottish wife, Brigget, whom he married in San Francisco during his service, died in 1907, he took up residence at the Sawtelle Soldiers Home in Los Angeles. Legross died suddenly at a meeting of the local chapter of the GAR in 1909.

Zebina Streeter, whose service as a second lieutenant in Company B might be charitably characterized as brief and undistinguished, had perhaps the most colorful postbellum career of any of the Native Cavalry's officers. After his dishonorable discharge, Streeter drifted to Santa Barbara, where his estranged father was now married into an established Californio family. There, he enlisted in Company C as a private, though he did not go with them to Arizona and instead stayed behind at Drum Barracks, where he was discharged in December 1865. He later appeared in Mexico as "Don Casimiro," an officer in the republican forces of Juarez. Upon the end of that conflict, Streeter returned to the United States and worked as an interpreter and packer for the army, in which capacity he participated in the 1872 peace talks with Cochise. By 1882 he had fallen in with the Chiricahua leader Juh, participating in raids on both sides of the border and becoming known as the "White Apache." Despite this, he later joined Brigadier General Leonard Wood in the pursuit of Geronimo. Streeter was killed in 1889 in a gunfight arising from an argument over a woman in Nacozari, Sonora.[19]

John Lafferty accepted a commission as a lieutenant in the new regiment organized from former California Volunteers in 1866, which became the 8th U.S. Cavalry. After distinguishing himself in campaigns against the Paiutes in Nevada, Lafferty participated in campaigns against Apaches in Arizona. In a skirmish in the Chiricahua Mountains in October 1869, an Apache bullet carried away most of his teeth and a good part of his jaw, leaving him permanently unable to eat solid food and giving him great difficulty speaking. Lafferty nonetheless continued to serve in the army in a limited capacity and retired as a captain in 1878. He died in San Francisco in 1899.

Porfirio Jimeno turned down an offer of a commission in the regular army after the war, instead journeying to Mexico. It seems that, contrary to some reports, Jimeno did not venture south to enlist with the republican forces against Maximilian, but rather to claim property that belonged to his father, Manuel Casarin Jimeno, who had left his family in California during the conquest and died in Mexico City in 1853. Either way, Porfirio arrived too late to join the rebellion, reporting shortly after landing at Mazatlán in April 1867 that "Max" was "clearing out" and that future correspondence should "say 'Republica Mexicana' on the Envelope" as there was "no Empire."

> Digale a mi nana (pobrecita) que this city is what we call in California "*a la moda de País.*" El pueblo es Mexicano entero, el aspecto y en fin todo es verdaderamento Mexicano, la temperature buena pero al medio dia mucha calor, en fin dicen que desde los onze hasta las tres en las calles no se mas de "Beggars and dogs." I of course don't go out between those.
>
> Please tell tia Trinidad that I would send her chacuales from here but it is better to send them from the City of Mexico, as they are prettier and cheaper. Tell uncle Miguel that if he wishes to speculate on horseflesh he had better not come here because everybody rides "*burros*" I have not seen a horse since my arrival. They have many fruit trees here, cocoa-nut, banana, &c. I hardly taste it because I don't think they are healthy. . . .
>
> This is a *free* country, here if you want to cross the city limits you have to get your name recorded and get a "Passport" with about 20 signatures but the worst part is a person has to pay for it, so I don't go out of the limits and don't think I will until I have to start (day after tomorrow).[20]

Jimeno was still complaining about the weather as he always did during his service, comparing it unfavorably to Calabazas. The former captain, who spoke of nothing but misery and loneliness when he wrote home from Drum Barracks and Arizona, now seemed to remember the days of his service there fondly. He asked his stepfather to wish his ailing uncle, Captain de la Guerra, well and to "ask him if he does not recollect our *good* old times in *Arizona* & *Sonora!*"[21] From Mazatlan he went on by stage to Mexico City via San Blas, Tepic, Guanajuato, and Guadalajara. Jimeno died in the Mexican capital in 1870.[22]

Captain de la Guerra soon reentered politics, serving on the Santa Barbara County Board of Supervisors, in the state senate, and as mayor. But the captain, who had been laid up on sick call for much of his time in Arizona, was in ill health for most of his remaining life due to a "social disease" acquired during his service. Treated with injections of mercury, de la Guerra died in 1881, blind, toothless, and partially paralyzed, at the age of fifty-four.[23]

The captain's nephew fared much better. Juan José de la Guerra had enlisted in the company as a private, was promoted to sergeant, and returned from Arizona as an acting second lieutenant. He started practicing law, became chief clerk of the California assembly, and worked for many years as an interpreter for the state supreme court. Returning to Southern California, he was active in veterans organizations and was an honored guest when his hometown celebrated "Spanish Days." When de la Guerra passed away at the Sawtelle Home at the age of ninety-three in 1940, he was reported to be the last surviving Native Cavalry veteran.[24]

José Antonio Sanchez continued to seek compensation for the personal expenses he incurred as captain of Company D. As Pico would do in later years, he took his request to the legislature. But a bill to provide relief to him and José Redona, his former lieutenant, failed in two consecutive sessions. Unlike Pico, Sanchez did not have the luxury of time, dying at the age of forty-one in 1869.

As for Redona, his subsequent career was far more active than was his brief tenure as an officer in the Native Cavalry. He became a constable in his rough-and-tumble hometown of Los Angeles, and contemporary newspapers record his involvement in a number of scrapes and shootings in the pursuit of his duties. In 1874 as a deputy sheriff, he participated in the capture of the famed "social bandit" Tiburcio Vásquez at Rancho

La Brea. Redona was married to Fermina Sepulveda, the daughter of a prominent local pioneer, and was active in public affairs, including the GAR, the Democratic Party, and numerous "Spanish American" organizations. He died in 1891 at the age of fifty-five.[25]

* * *

Having been recruited from poverty and obscurity, most of the enlisted men in the battalion seem to have returned to quiet lives in California, with the passing of these veterans occasionally receiving notice in the press. Many were active in the GAR and other veterans organizations, and their service remained a source of pride for both themselves and the community. A few of them had postwar careers worth noting.

Benigno Pico, the first sergeant of Company A and who had deserted and returned under strange circumstances in the early days of the battalion, after his discharge returned to the San Luis Obispo area. His Scottish American wife, Anne, gave birth shortly thereafter, suggesting the possibility that she may have accompanied her husband in the service, perhaps as a laundress. For a time he ran a post office and a hotel at Port Harford, then moved south to become the proprietor of a hotel in San Fernando. Pico was an active member of the GAR, and by all accounts he seems to have been a reasonably successful and prominent citizen. Ironically, the old cavalry sergeant died in 1905 after being struck by an electric streetcar in Los Angeles.

Prudencio García, the sergeant of Company A who conspired with Lieutenant Jimenez to get Captain Pico removed from the army, was arrested for forging soldier's discharges in San Francisco within a few weeks of mustering out at Drum Barracks.[26] These false papers would have allowed the bearer to fraudulently collect bounties and other money due to returning soldiers, a racket that seems to have been a serious problem given the volume of California Volunteers leaving the service. The issue does not seem to have gone much further, and he returned to his civilian life in San Jose, where García was active in the GAR. He died in 1904 at the veterans home in Yountville in Napa County.[27]

After his discharge as a sergeant of Company A, José Picasso enlisted in the U.S. Marine Corps. His military career was short lived, however, as he was discharged after a matter of months for respiratory difficulties, possibly a consequence of the lingering effects of the chest wound he received in the ambush on the Trinity River in 1864. Picasso eventually returned to his native Italy.

Of the men who deserted during the battalion's service in Arizona, the fates of only two are known with certainty. Bernard Means and his younger brother, Timothy, were sergeants in Company B who deserted from Fort Mason in late September 1865. Like so many others, they fled south into Sonora, eventually reaching the French-occupied port town of Guaymas, where they rented a room above a restaurant. Eventually, the two returned to the United States, first to California and then to Michigan and Missouri. Each was able to successfully apply for a pension despite having deserted. Timothy died in Missouri in 1903; his older brother followed a year later.[28]

Bugler Pedro Miranda was among the detachment of Company B who stayed behind at San Juan Bautista when the rest of the battalion moved on to Arizona. During his service there, he married a beautiful local girl, fifteen-year-old Rita Hernández, who was described as wild and flirtatious. He returned to San Juan after his discharge and settled into a more-or-less quiet domestic life. In 1866 he was shot during an altercation at a particularly rowdy wedding, which was more action than he ever saw in the army. He soon recovered, but his fiery wife apparently tired of life with him and ran away with the Tiburcio Vasquez gang in 1871. Miranda seems to have passed away sometime before 1890. Rita later remarried.[29]

Rafael Pico, who had been a bugler in Company C, became a well-regarded musician in his native Santa Barbara. In the 1870s as a clarinet player, he was an early member of the orchestra organized by José Lobero to perform at his famed opera house, which in 2014 remains the city's premiere arts-and-culture venue. When Pico passed away in 1897, one newspaper wrote that the musician "knew nothing of the value of money: hence he died poor."[30]

Company C's other bugler, Ysmael Soto, never entirely recovered from the injuries he sustained when he was shot at the Wilmington dance hall in 1865. His nose never properly healed so that he sometimes had difficulty breathing, and his face remained horribly scarred. He married twenty-four-year-old Adelaida Ruiz in Santa Barbara in 1876, but she left him six years later, took up with a man named Barney Shoemaker, and called herself "Mrs. Shoemaker." After this Soto "became a hard drinker" and his health declined considerably. By 1885 he was suffering from vision and hearing loss, but a medical board determined that these were due to syphilis and denied him a full pension. In 1893 he reported being nearly blind and deaf, but a pension was again refused as the wounding that led to these conditions occurred while off duty. After Soto died in 1895 at age fifty-three, his wife successfully applied for a widow's pension after having barely spoken to him in years. It was revoked when reports surfaced of her "notorious adulterous cohabitation."[31]

The bear-hunting vaquero Ramón "Nini" Ayala returned to Santa Cruz Island after he was discharged from Company C. He worked in both the cattle and sheep operations there, eventually becoming a foreman. By the time he left to live on the mainland, Ayala was known as the oldest vaquero on the island. He died at Ventura (formerly San Buenaventura) in 1913.

Cleofas Ponce de León, a ranchero and native Barbareño who served in Company C, was reportedly a descendant of Juan Ponce de León, famed conquistador of Florida. After the war he briefly became "quite wealthy" as an "extensive rancher" in Santa Barbara County. A lifetime bachelor and well-liked resident of the community, he died in 1899 at the age of fifty-four.[32]

Pedro Romero, another soldier of Company C, suffered a sad fate that implies that he was never able to adjust to civilian life. A few years after returning to Santa Barbara, he was married at the mission, though his wife eventually left him. He lived alone for many years in a two-room adobe house in Montecito in the wooded hills east of Santa Barbara. One day in 1916, the seventy-three-year-old veteran told his brother "that he would kill himself, as he despaired of recovery from an illness that he had suffered for twenty-five years, but the threat had been made before, and it was paid no attention." The next morning Romero "poured kerosene oil on his bedding and all over the inside of his little dwelling and then touched a match to it, with the result that the house was quickly destroyed." By the time his brother saw the flames, it was too late to save Pedro.[33] His estranged wife was later able to collect a widow's pension.

John "Juan" Robarts, the bilingual English first sergeant of Company D, remained in Los Angeles, where he eventually became a U.S. citizen, a prominent attorney, and a member of the GAR. He was found seated in his office chair one morning in 1894, dead from a heart attack.[34]

José Victor Corona, a farmer from Sonora who served with Company D, returned to Los Angeles after his discharge. He was still suffering from the lingering effects of an illness that kept him laid up on sick call during much of his time at Fort Mason. His wife, who had followed him throughout his service, had ministered to him with traditional remedies and continued to do so in California. Corona died in 1869, never having recovered his health.[35]

At least three Native Cavalry soldiers, all from Company D, returned to Arizona after their service. Santos Avila settled in Calabazas, very near the site of Fort Mason, where he took up ranching and raised a family. He briefly returned to California to take up residency at the Sawtelle Home in 1914 before moving back to Nogales to be with his wife and her family. Avila died there in 1916. Nicolas Cordova, a native of Cumpas, Sonora, as an old man moved to the border-smelter community of Douglas, Arizona Territory, the area which the Native Cavalry scouted for Apaches in the winter of 1865–66. Presumably, he joined family there and died in 1911. Santos Laguna, also a Sonoran, eventually took his family back to Mexico to pursue work as a miner. By 1880 this had led him to the Arizona copper camp of Globe, but he moved back to Los Angeles in 1897. Laguna died at the Sawtelle Home in 1902.

Just as the individual officers and men had moved on after the war, so too did California. The Native Cavalry was not entirely forgotten, but over time the culture they represented became increasingly marginalized. By the time the bow-legged veterans began receiving federal pensions, the southern counties were no longer a stronghold for Californio culture. These long-established residents soon became outnumbered by Anglo newcomers, and even Spanish-surnamed families were increasingly more likely to be recent Mexican immigrants or their descendants rather than the sons and daughters of Alta California's founders.[36] The big ranches, to the extent that they still existed, were broken into pieces by fenced farms. Business came to be conducted almost exclusively in English, while speaking Spanish was increasingly regarded as a sign of poverty and ignorance. Sombreros, short jackets, and *calzoneras* gave way to less flamboyant dress indistinguishable from the rest of the United States. The indulgent fiestas of the past were tamed for more conservative tastes, eventually becoming mere dress-up affairs to entertain Anglo-Americans. Even the most accomplished of the old Native Californians were regarded as mere reminders of a colorful and romanticized past who, by necessity, had to politely step aside in the name of progress. A new generation of Californios, one with only a borrowed nostalgia for an unremembered past, awkwardly assimilated into a California that had become more like other places.

It would be decades before Spanish-speaking Californians would again achieve even the limited economic vitality and political clout as a community that the Californios had in the 1850s and 1860s. Meanwhile, their language and traditions had become regarded as quaint relics, just as the lances the men of the Native Cavalry had carried.

APPENDIX A

The Men of the Native Cavalry

What follows is a list of the officers and enlisted men who served in the Native California Cavalry. The list was compiled from surviving official records and augmented by the research of local historian David R. Jackson of Los Angeles, who has tirelessly worked for years to track down personal information about the individuals associated with the battalion through baptismal records, pension documents, and death notices.

The task of making this list was made difficult by the poor recordkeeping of some of the officers. This was compounded by both the fact that most Anglo-American officers were unfamiliar with Spanish, and most of the enlisted men were illiterate. As a consequence there are numerous variations of many of the names in the different places where they appear. These discrepancies were reconciled to the extent possible. In respect for traditional Spanish naming customs, which were still being followed in California in this era, an individual's full name is listed here where it could be found, though it does not appear in military records. Name variants, though not necessarily outright misspellings, are listed parenthetically.

Personal data, where available, are as listed in the muster and enlistment rolls, thus current at the time of enlistment. If an individual was not mustered out with his company, the circumstances under which he left the service are listed. Desertions are only listed if the soldier did not return to his unit.

All listed locations should be assumed to be in California unless otherwise noted.

Field and Staff

Commissioned Officers

Vallejo, José Manuel Salvador (Salvador). Major. Age 49. Commissioned by the governor of California, December 9, 1863, at San Francisco. Resigned February 28, 1865.

Cremony, John C. Major. Age 36. Transferred from 2nd Cavalry, California Volunteers, March 24, 1865, at San Francisco.

Gelcich, Dr. Vincent. Assistant Surgeon. Age 36. Born in Split, Dalmatia, Austro-Hungarian Empire. Previous military service under General Giuseppe Garibaldi in Italy. Commissioned by the governor of California, June 2, 1864, at San Francisco. Promoted to Surgeon, 4th Infantry, California Volunteers, April 22, 1865, at Drum Barracks.

Tolman, Dr. George Bowers. Assistant Surgeon. Age 39. Previous military service as a volunteer in the Mexican-American War. Transferred from 6th Infantry, California Volunteers, May 8, 1865, at San Francisco.

Company A

Initially mustered in at the Presidio of San Francisco, May 23, 1863
Mustered out at Drum Barracks, March 20, 1866

Commissioned Officers

Jimenez, Marcelino Erasmo. 2nd Lieutenant. Age 29. Commissioned by the governor of California, March 23, 1863, at San Jose.

Pico y Bernal (Pico), José María de la Natividad y Reymundo (José Ramón). Captain. Age 33. Commissioned by the governor of California, February 26, 1863, at San Francisco.

Soto y Pacheco (Soto), Crisanto de Jesús (Crisanto). 1st Lieutenant. Age 35. Commissioned by the governor of California, June 5, 1863, at San Francisco. Died of disease October 16, 1865, at Patagonia, Arizona Territory.

Enlisted

Areya (Araya), Marcos. Private. Age 25. Born in Chile. Enlisted March 16, 1863, at San Francisco.

Astorga, Ramón. Private. Age 22. Enlisted June 8, 1863, at San Francisco. Deserted October 8, 1863, at the Presidio of San Francisco.

Avalos, Bruno. Private. Age 19. Enlisted March 11, 1863, at San Francisco.

Babin, Arturo (Arthur). Private. Age 26. Enlisted August 22, 1863, at San Francisco.

Balardes (Belardos), Diciderio (Disidario). Corporal. Age 24. Enlisted April 2, 1863, at San Juan Bautista.

Baldes, Candido. Corporal. Age 27. Enlisted April 13, 1863, at San Jose.

Baldes, Joaquin. Private. Age 28. Enlisted May 5, 1863, at San Luis Obispo. Died of disease November 3, 1864, at Tubac, Arizona Territory.

Bandonado, Ygnacio. Private. Enlisted January 2, 1865, at Marysville. Deserted August 7, 1865, at Gila City, Arizona Territory.

Balencia, Francisco. Private. Age 32. Enlisted August 13 at San Jose. Died of disease while on furlough at San Rafael. No date given.[1]

Balencia, Manuel. Private. Age 30. Enlisted May 11, 1863, at Alviso. Deserted November 20, 1863, at the Presidio of San Francisco.

Barmes, Augusto (Auguste) H. Private. Age 40. Enlisted August 30, 1863, at San Jose. Deserted April 11, 1865, at Cloverdale.

Bermudes (Bermudas), Pedro. Private. Age 23. Enlisted May 16, 1863, at Watsonville.

Borques (Borgues), Ramón. Private. Age 22. Enlisted March 7, 1863, at San Jose. Deserted at the Presidio of San Francisco, September 29, 1863.

Boverdez (Boverdiz), Casimiro (Casimira). Private. Age 30. Enlisted August 30, 1863, at San Jose. Deserted October 12, 1863, at the Presidio of San Francisco.

Cadena (Caneda, Cardena), Antonio. Private. Age 24. Enlisted March 16, 1863, at San Jose.

Canido (Canedo), Narciso. Corporal. Age 29. Enlisted August 15, 1863, at San Jose.

Carillo, Casimiro. Private. Age 34. Enlisted March 14, 1863, at San Jose.

Castro, José L. Private. Age 21. Enlisted June 1, 1863, at San Jose. Deserted April 2, 1865, at Fort Wright. In confinement at Fort Wright since April 5, 1865, upon mustering out.

Covacewich (Covacewiche), Dionicio. Private. Age 22. Enlisted August 10, 1863, at San Jose.

de la Noix (Delano, Delanoix, Delanoy), Fredric (Federico). Private. Age 29. Artist. 5'10". Born in Mexico. Transferred to Company B June 14, 1865.

Delgadillo, Domingo. Private. Age 21. Enlisted March 20, 1863. Deserted April 28, 1863, at San Jose.

Deliard, Auguste. Private. Age 26. Enlisted August 14, 1863, at San Jose.

Delior (Deliar), Aldolfo (Adolpho). Private. Enlisted August 14, 1863, at San Jose. Deserted from Fort Wright, April 5, 1865.

Deltin (Deltine), José (Joseph). Corporal. Age 29. Enlisted August 8, 1863, at San Jose.

De Montreville (Demontreville), Eugene. Private. Age 25. Enlisted July 18, 1863, at Stockton. Deserted November 17, 1863, at the Presidio of San Francisco.

Díaz (Dias), José M. Private. Age 31. Enlisted April 13, 1863, at San Francisco. Deserted July 6, 1863, at the Presidio of San Francisco.

Didot (Drolet), Augustin. Private. Age 22. Enlisted August 8, 1863, at San Jose. Deserted November 23, 1863, at the Presidio of San Francisco.

Dierstefise (Dierstphise), Adolphe (Adolpho). Private. Age 26. Enlisted August 8, 1863, at San Jose.

Duarte, Reyes. Private. Age 21. Enlisted April 17, 1863, at Watsonville. Deserted May 29, 1863, at the Presidio of San Francisco.

Dumont, Henry. Bugler. Age 24. Enlisted August 8, 1863, at San Jose. Deserted April 14, 1865, at Fort Wright.

Eglize, Michael. Private. Age 21. Enlisted July 14, 1863, at Monterey. Deserted May 15, 1865, at Benicia Barracks.

Ferrera, Carlos. Private. Age 31. Enlisted August 21, 1863, at San Jose. Deserted October 2, 1863, at the Presidio of San Francisco.

Forrestier, Augusto (Auguste). Private. Age 35. Enlisted August 18, 1863, at San Jose.

Galea, Lucas. Private. Age 29. Enlisted March 7, 1863, at San Jose.

Galindo, Francisco. Private. Age 21. Enlisted March 7, 1863, at San Jose. Deserted June 30, 1863, at San Jose.

García, Jesús. Private. Age 25. Packer. Hazel eyes. Black hair. Dark complexion. 5'7". Born in Mexico. Enlisted January 2, 1865, at Marysville.

García, Prudencio (Prudencia). 1st Sergeant. Age 21. Enlisted March 1, 1863, at San Jose.

Gerard, Emilio. Private. Age 25. Enlisted August 4, 1863, at San Jose.

Gomez, José. Corporal. Age 30. Enlisted March 16, 1863, at San Jose. Resigned December 5, 1864.

Gonzales (Gansales), José M. Bugler. Age 19. Enlisted March 7, 1863, at San Jose. Deserted May 22, 1865, at Benicia Barracks.

Guerin, Adolphe, Private. Age 24. Enlisted August 22, 1863, at San Francisco. Deserted September 24, 1863, at the Presidio of San Francisco.

Guilman (Guelleman), Antonio. Private. Age 28. Enlisted July 18, 1863, at Alameda. Discharged for disability October 27, 1865, at Drum Barracks for wound in foot received in action at Green Valley, April 23, 1865.

Gutierres (Gutiero), Sebastian. Private. Age 43. Enlisted April 13, 1863, at San Jose.

Higuera, Francisco. Sergeant. Age 22. Enlisted May 25, 1863, at Santa Clara. Died of disease November 19, 1865, at Fort Mason, Arizona Territory.

Higuera, José J. Private. Age 27. Enlisted April 2 at San Juan Bautista. Deserted May 28, 1863, at San Juan Bautista.

Jolly, Francisco. Private. Age 30. Enlisted August 12, 1863, at San Francisco. Deserted April 11, 1865, at Cloverdale.

Juarez (Juares), Pedro. Private. Age 22. Enlisted May 13, 1863, at Santa Cruz. Deserted May 28, 1863, at the Presidio of San Francisco.

Laurier (Loy), Alexandro. Sergeant. Enlisted August 23, 1863, at San Jose. Deserted April 4, 1865, at Fort Wright.

LeBlond, Henry. Private. Age 21. Enlisted April 2, 1863, at San Juan Bautista. Deserted May 27, 1865, at Benicia Barracks.

Leon, Juan. Private. Age 27. Enlisted April 13, 1863, at San Francisco.

Leyva (Leyra), José R. Sergeant. Age 29. Enlisted May 9, 1863, at Santa Barbara.

Lopez (Loper), Joaquin. Private. Age 37. Enlisted March 3, 1863, at San Jose.

Loredo, Miguel. Private. Age 22. Enlisted August 3, 1863, at San Jose.

Luisano (Lorisana), Pedro P. Private. Age 21. Enlisted May 12, 1863, at Watsonville. Deserted July 5, 1865, at the Presidio of San Francisco.

Madriaga (Madraga, Maduaga), Ancieto (Ansieto). Private. Age 34. Enlisted April 11, 1863, at San Jose.

Maladano, Ignacio. Private. Age 40. Packer. Hazel eyes. Black hair. Dark complexion. 5'9¼". Born in Mexico. Enlisted January 2, 1865, at Marysville.[2]

Marchand, Prospero. Private. Age 28. Enlisted October 20, 1863, at the Presidio of San Francisco. Mustered out March 16, 1866, at the Presidio of San Francisco.

Marcos (Marcon), Leon (Leon, Marcos). Private. Age 27. Enlisted August 22, 1863, at San Jose. Deserted April 5, 1865, at Fort Wright.

Martinez (Martines), José María. Private. Age 21. Enlisted March 11, 1863, at Alviso.

Mesa, Antonio. Private. Age 24. Enlisted August 23, 1863, at San Jose. Deserted August 7, 1863, at Gila City, Arizona Territory.

Miranda (Mirando), Manuel. Private. Age 22. Enlisted July 21, 1863, at San Jose. Deserted October 8, 1863, at the Presidio of San Francisco.

Oardena, Antonio. Private. Enlisted at March 16 at San Jose. Deserted September 29, 1863, at the Presidio of San Francisco.

Obregue, Pedro. Private. Age 35. Enlisted September 7, 1863, at San Francisco. Deserted October 1, 1863, at the Presidio of San Francisco.

Orona, Antonio. Private. Age 21. Enlisted April 24, 1863, at San Jose. Discharged for disability July 25, 1865, at Drum Barracks.

Ortega, Mariano. Private. Age 23. Laborer. Black eyes. Black hair. Dark complexion. 5'3¾". Born in Santa Fe, New Mexico. Enlisted August 13, 1864, at Sacramento. Deserted August 7, 1865, at Gila City, Arizona Territory.

Oumon (Omon), Amie (Amey). Private. Age 21. Enlisted August 8, 1863, at San Jose. Deserted May 27, 1865, at Benicia Barracks.

Pacheco, Francisco. Private. Age 31. Enlisted May 11, 1863, at Alvarado.

Perceval, Carlos. Private. Age 32. Enlisted August 14, 1863, at San Jose.

Perkins, Samuel. Private. Age 18. Enlisted September 5, 1863, at San Francisco.

Picasso, José. Corporal. Age 28. Enlisted May 16, 1863, at San Jose.

Pico, Benigno. Sergeant. Age 24. Enlisted February 18, 1863, at San Jose.

Querloy, Pedro (Pierre). Private. Age 24. Enlisted August 8, 1863, at San Jose.

Quilfe, Adolfo. Private. Enlisted August 8, 1863, at San Francisco.

Rodrigues, José. Private. Enlisted. August 12, 1863, at San Francisco. Deserted November 24, 1865, at the Presidio of San Francisco.

Rodrigues, José M. Private. Age 21. Enlisted May 12, 1863, at Santa Cruz.

Rodrigues, Mariano. Private. Age 43. Enlisted March 2, 1863, at San Jose.

Rodrigues, Ygnacio. Private. Age 42. Enlisted April 25, 1863, at San Jose. Deserted November 4, 1863, at the Presidio of San Francisco.

Rojas, Miguel. Sergeant. Age 29. Enlisted April 13, 1863, at San Francisco.

Romero, José. Private. Age 26. Enlisted March 21, 1863, at Watsonville. Discharged for disability July 25, 1865, at Drum Barracks.

Romero, José M. Corporal. Age 31. Enlisted March 14, 1863, at Santa Cruz.

Ruis, José. Private. Age 21. Enlisted October 1, 1863, at San Francisco.

Sandarte (Sandarta, Sandarts), Higinio. Bugler. Age 22. Enlisted March 14, 1863, at San Jose. Deserted August 10, 1865, at Antelope Peak, Arizona Territory.

Seguin, Pedro. Private. Age 25. Enlisted July 15, 1863, at Stockton. Deserted January 28, 1865, at Fort Wright.

Stokes, Manuel. Private. Age 21. Enlisted March 18, 1863, at San Jose. Deserted May 29, 1863, at the Presidio of San Francisco.

Suñol (Sunol), Juan. Private. Age 30. Enlisted July 18, 1863, at Stockton. Deserted January 28, 1865, at Fort Wright.

Toribio (Toribia), Balardes. Private. Age 21. Enlisted April 17, 1863, at San Juan Bautista. Deserted August 9, 1865, at Gila City, Arizona Territory.

Vasques, José. Private. Age 43. Enlisted March 4, 1863, at San Jose.

Villa, José Y. Private. Age 22. Enlisted March 23, 1863, at Watsonville. Deserted August 10, 1865, at Antelope Peak, Arizona Territory.

Welsh, Guadalupe. Private. Age 19. Enlisted May 9, 1863, at Stockton. Deserted May 29, 1863, at the Presidio of San Francisco.

Willhem, José (Joseph). Private. Age 26. Enlisted July 18, 1863, at Stockton. Deserted January 28, 1865, at Fort Wright.

Ybarra (Ybana), Francisco. Private. Age 31. Enlisted April 2, 1863, at San Jose. Deserted September 29, 1865, at the Presidio of San Francisco.

Yglesias (Yglesia), Miguel. Private. Enlisted July 14, 1863, at Monterey.[3]

Company B

Initially mustered in at the Presidio of San Francisco, March 1864. Mustered out at Drum Barracks, March 15, 1866

ASTERISK (*) INDICATES A SOLDIER WHO SERVED WITH THE DETACHMENT AT CAMP REYNOLDS, ANGEL ISLAND, JULY 21–OCTOBER 1864.

DAGGER (†) INDICATES A SOLDIER WHO REMAINED BEHIND ON DETACHED SERVICE AT CAMP LOW, SAN JUAN BAUTISTA, WHILE THE BATTALION WAS POSTED TO ARIZONA.

DOUBLE DAGGER (‡) INDICATES AN OFFICER OR SOLDIER WHO PARTICIPATED IN GENERAL MASON'S WINTER CAMPAIGN, DECEMBER 1865–JANUARY 1866.

Commissioned Officers

Bale y Sobreanes, Eduardo (Bale, Edward T.). 1st Lieutenant. Age 22. Born in California. Promoted to Captain (Company D) June 29, 1864.

‡Jimeno y de la Guerra (Jimeno), Porfirio Juan de Dios (Porfirio). Captain. Promoted from Company C March 17, 1865, at Drum Barracks.

Lafferty, John. 1st Lieutenant. Age 29. Born in New York. Commissioned by the governor of California July 6, 1864, at Sacramento.

Legross, Ernest H. Captain. Commissioned by the governor of California September 29, 1863, at Sacramento. Resigned March 10, 1865.

Streeter, Zebina Nathaniel. 2nd Lieutenant. Age 24. Clerk. Gray eyes. Auburn hair. Light complexion. 5'5". Born in Genoa, New York. Commissioned by the governor of California May 9, 1864, at Sacramento. Dismissed from the service October 21, 1864, by sentence of general court-martial.

Enlisted

†Albaus, Michael. Private. Age 29. Seaman. Hazel eyes. Black hair. Copper complexion. 5'3". Born in Talcahuano, Chile. Enlisted November 17, 1864, at San Francisco. Mustered out December 5, 1865, at San Francisco.

‡Amaro, Juan. Private. Age 25. Soldier. Black eyes. Black hair. Dark complexion. 5'10". Born in Algiers. Enlisted March 20, 1865, at San Francisco.

Anativa, Carlos. Private. Age 39. Miner. Black eyes. Black hair. Dark complexion. 5'4". Born in Valparaiso, Chile. Enlisted December 1, 1864, at the Presidio of San Francisco. Deserted August 10, 1865, at Mission Camp, Arizona Territory.

Assedo (Ascedo, Assolo), Victor. Private. Age 18. Ranchero. Black eyes. Black hair. Copper complexion. 5'3½". Born in Monterey. Enlisted March 10, 1865, at Monterey. Deserted August 12, 1865, at Copper Camp, Arizona Territory.

‡Ayala, Fermin. Private. Age 19. Waiter. Black eyes. Black hair. Dark complexion. 5'4". Born in Panama, New Granada. Enlisted July 22, 1864, at San Francisco.

Bailey, John. Private. Age 31. Laborer. Gray eyes. Light hair. Fair complexion. 5'10". Born in Waterford, Ireland. Enlisted September 30, 1864, at San Francisco.

*Baker, John. Corporal. Enlisted March 7, 1864, at San Francisco.

Balderamos, Hermingildo. Farrier. Age 33. Ranchero. Hazel eyes. Black hair. Dark complexion. 5'7". Born in Chihuahua, Mexico. Enlisted February 28, 1865, at Monterey.

Bates, Henry. Farrier. Enlisted December 31, 1863, at San Francisco. Discharged for disability June 10, 1865, at the Presidio of San Francisco.

Bell, John. Sergeant. Enlisted March 25, 1864, at San Francisco.

Bonnard, Gustave. Private. Enlisted February 22, 1864, at San Francisco.

†Borunda, Francisco. Private. Age 35. Ranchero. Brown eyes. Brown hair. Fair complexion. 5'6". Born in Monterey. Enlisted December 12, 1864, at the Presidio of San Francisco. Mustered out December 5, 1865, at San Francisco.

‡Bovas (Bower), Ludvigio (Ludviga). Private. Age 20. Laborer. Gray eyes. Black hair. Brown complexion. 5'3". Born in Piedmont, Italy. Enlisted July 11, 1864, at San Francisco.

*Bradley, George. Private. Enlisted March 24, 1864, at San Francisco. Deserted October 8, 1864, at Camp Reynolds, Angel Island.

‡Cáceres (Casseras), John G. Private. Enlisted on October 22, 1864, at Sacramento.

Carrillo (Careo), Jesús. Private. Age 22. Laborer. Black eyes. Black hair. Copper complexion. 5'4½". Born in Acapulco, Mexico. Enlisted March 17, 1865, at San Juan Bautista. Discharged for disability July 25, 1865, at Drum Barracks.

†Carrillo (Cario), Juan (John). Private. Age 24. Herder. Dark eyes. Black hair. Dark complexion. 5'4". Born in San Luis Obispo. Enlisted March 14, 1865, at San Juan Bautista.

Casteyon, Crisarte (Crisarto). Private. Age 19. Laborer. Brown eyes. Black hair. Dark complexion. 5'8". Born in Ta Pac, Mexico. Enlisted February 2, 1865, at San Francisco. Deserted July 11, 1865, at Antelope Peak, Arizona Territory.

‡Castillo (Castello), Jesús. Private. Enlisted July 22, 1864.

Castro, Jesús. Private. Age 23. Laborer. Brown eyes. Dark hair. Dark complexion. 5'5". Born in San Pablo. Enlisted February 2, 1865. Deserted August 10, 1865, at Mission Camp, Arizona Territory.

Castro, John Joseph. Private. Age 27. Vaquero. Hazel eyes. Auburn hair. Dark complexion. 5'6½". Born in Valparaiso, Chile. Enlisted March 21, 1864, at Placerville.

Castro, José. Private. Age 24. Laborer. Gray eyes. Black hair. Dark complexion. 5'6". Born in San Pablo. Enlisted January 27, 1865, at San Francisco. Deserted August 12, 1865, at Copper Camp, Arizona Territory.

†Castro, Juan. Private. Age 30. Miner. Brown eyes. Black hair. Dark complexion. 5'3". Born in San Jose. Enlisted January 19, 1865, at Camp Low. Mustered out December 5, 1865, at San Francisco.

Chicot, Guillaume. Sergeant. Enlisted August 11, 1865, at San Francisco. Discharged for disability April 7, 1865, at Camp Low.

Clement, Auguste. Bugler. Age 28. Baker. Brown eyes. Black hair. Dark complexion. 5'6". Born in Valogne, France. Enlisted August 25, 1864, at San Francisco. Deserted March 15, 1865 at Camp Low.

Clermont, Aime. Private. Enlisted February 19, 1864, at San Francisco. Deserted May 30, 1864, at the Presidio of San Francisco.

*Coyne, Patrick. Private. Enlisted March 14, 1864, at San Francisco. Deserted October 8, 1864, at Camp Reynolds, Angel Island.

Cunningham, John W. Corporal. Enlisted February 26, 1864, at San Francisco. Died of disease November 13, 1865, at Fort Mason, Arizona Territory.

Curo, Joseph Angel. Private. Enlisted March 12, 1864, at San Francisco.

*de la Mothe, Gaston. Bugler. Enlisted February 20, 1864, at San Francisco. Deserted August 12, 1865, at Copper Camp, Arizona Territory.

†de la Noix (Delano, Delanoix, Delanoy), Fredric (Federico). Private. Age 29. Artist. 5'10". Born in Mexico. Transferred June 14, 1865, from Company A. Mustered out December 5, 1865, at San Francisco.

†de la Osa (Delaojo), Feliciano. Private. Age 30. Vaquero. Dark eyes. Black hair. Dark complexion. 5'5½". Born in Los Angeles. Enlisted November 12, 1864, at San Francisco. Mustered out December 5, 1865, at San Francisco.

Demoffe, Victor. Private. Enlisted December 30, 1863, at San Francisco. Deserted May 30, 1864, at the Presidio of San Francisco.

Desere, Chalefour. Private. Enlisted March 26, 1864, at San Francisco.

Dirks, Henry. 1st Sergeant. Enlisted February 4, 1864, at San Francisco.

†Diversion, Eugene. Private. Age 31. Enlisted January 21, 1864, at San Francisco. Mustered out December 5, 1865, at San Francisco.

*‡Dock, Michael. Private. Enlisted January 11, 1864, at San Francisco.

Dudan, Auguste. Private. Age 20. Jeweler. Brown eyes. Brown hair. Fair complexion. 5'3". Born in Paris, France. Enlisted June 9, 1864, at the Presidio of San Francisco.

Esmer (Esner), Alexis. Private. Age 33. Shoemaker. Blue eyes. Light hair. Fair complexion. 5'7". Born in Manche, France. Enlisted May 26, 1864, at San Francisco. Deserted September 29, 1864, at the Presidio of San Francisco.

Estrada (Estrado), Francisco (Francis). Private. Age 19. Laborer. Black eyes. Black hair. Dark complexion. 5'5½". Born in Mazatlan, Mexico. Enlisted December 27, 1864, at San Francisco.

Estrado, Demetro (Demetris). Private. Age 30. Miner. Black eyes. Black hair. Dark complexion. 5'7". Born in San Andreas. Enlisted December 9, 1864, at the Presidio of San Francisco.

Falkenberg, William. Corporal. Enlisted February 8, 1864, at San Francisco.

Fournair (Furnier), John (Jean). Enlisted March 9, 1864. Deserted May 18, 1864, at the Presidio of San Francisco.

Freunde, Auguste. Private. Age 34. Gardener. Blue eyes. Brown hair. Fair complexion. 5'4". Born in Loraine, France. Enlisted October 10, 1864, at San Francisco. Deserted October 8, 1864, at Camp Reynolds, Angel Island.

*Galliard, Louis (Luis). Private. Enlisted March 8, 1864, at San Francisco. Deserted March 15, 1865, at Camp Low.

Gandel (Gandell), Pierre. Enlisted 12, 1864, at San Francisco. Deserted May 14, 1864, at the Presidio of San Francisco.

Gascon, Leopoldo (Paul Leon). Private. Enlisted November 1, 1863, at Monterey. Deserted May 18, 1864, at the Presidio of San Francisco.

Gimie, Francois. Private. Age 21. Laborer. Gray eyes. Brown hair. Dark complexion. 5'6". Born in Lauguedoc, France. Enlisted March 6, 1865, at San Francisco.

Golphe (Golphu), Oscar. Private. Age 28. Carpenter. Gray eyes. Dark hair. Fair complexion. 5'6". Born in Bordeaux, France. Enlisted September 25, 1864, at San Francisco. Deserted March 15, 1865, at Camp Low.

†Gonzales, José. Private. Age 36. Miner. Black eyes. Black hair. Dark complexion. 5'7". Born in Valparaiso, Chile. Enlisted December 1, 1864, at the Presidio of San Francisco. Mustered out December 5, 1865, at San Francisco.

Green, Joseph. Private. Age 21. Painter. Gray eyes. Black hair. Dark complexion. 5'5". Born in Monterey. Enlisted January 27, 1865, at San Francisco. Deserted August 9, 1865, at Gila City, Arizona Territory.

*Grow, Ambrose. Private. Enlisted July 22, 1864, at San Francisco.

*Guerre, Francisco. Sergeant. Enlisted July 29, 1864, at San Francisco. Deserted August 11, 1865, at Antelope Peak, Arizona Territory.

Hill (Hil), Tavitimo. Private. Age 29. Laborer. Hazel eyes. Black hair. Dark complexion. 5'3". Born in Santa Fe, New Mexico. Enlisted at December 8, 1864, at San Francisco. Deserted August 11, 1865, at Antelope Peak, Arizona Territory.

Hotanick, Joseph. Enlisted March 27, 1864, at San Francisco. Deserted October 20, 1864, at the Presidio of San Francisco.

Huil, Eugene. Private. Enlisted December 30, 1863, at San Francisco. Deserted May 18, 1864, at the Presidio of San Francisco.

Ibarra (Ybarra), Francisco. Private. Enlisted May, 1863, at San Jose. Dishonorably discharged February 23, 1865, at Camp Low.

Ibarra (Ybarra), Franco. Private. Age 18. Ranchero. Black eyes. Black hair. Dark complexion. 5'4". Born in Mexico. Enlisted on August 13, 1864, at the Presidio of San Francisco. Deserted September 27, 1865, at Fort Mason, Arizona Territory.

*Keyes, Benjamin. Private. Enlisted March 4, 1864, at San Francisco. Deserted October 8, 1864, at Camp Reynolds, Angel Island.

King, John B. Private. Age 16. Waiter. Hazel eyes. Black hair. Dark complexion. 5'3¾". Enlisted November 18, 1864, at San Francisco.

Kness, Adam. Private. Enlisted February 13, 1864, at San Francisco. Deserted September 27, 1865, at Fort Mason, Arizona Territory.

Laborde, Louis. Private. Enlisted December 30, 1865, at San Francisco.

Lazarraga, Santos. Private. Age 31. Carpenter. Dark eyes. Dark hair. Dark complexion. 5'5". Born in Cazala, Mexico. Enlisted February 6, 1865, at San Francisco.

Lecerf, Victor. Private. Enlisted March 24, 1864, at San Francisco.

LeFebre, Edward. Private. Enlisted March 13, 1864, at San Francisco. Deserted August 10, 1865, at Mission Camp, Arizona Territory.

*Leflock, Felix. Private. Enlisted March 24, 1864, at San Francisco.

Limereux (Limererel), John. Private. Age 40. Cook. Brown eyes. Light hair. Fair complexion. 5'5". Born in Picardis, France. Enlisted October 24, 1864, at the Presidio of San Francisco. Deserted March 17, 1865, at Camp Low.

Lottelier, Adolph. Private. Enlisted January 11, 1864, at San Francisco. Deserted May 11, 1864, at the Presidio of San Francisco.

Luis (Louis), Pedro. Private. Age 28. Soldier. Black hair. Black eyes. Dark complexion. 5'3½". Born in Algiers. Enlisted March 20, 1865, at San Francisco. In confinement by civil authorities from April 4, 1865, to muster out of company.[4]

Malet (Malot), Francois. Private. Enlisted November 1, 1863, at Monterey.

‡Manjanes (Manjares), Carlos. Private. Age 31. Ranchero. Black eyes. Black hair. Dark complexion. 5'7". Born in Monterey. Enlisted October 18, 1864, at San Francisco.

Marstrand. Charles. Private. Enlisted November 15, 1863, at San Jose.

Means, Bernard. Farrier Sergeant. Enlisted February 26, 1864, at San Francisco. Deserted September 27, 1865, at Fort Mason, Arizona Territory.

*Means, Timothy. Sergeant. Enlisted February 26, 1864, at San Francisco. Deserted September 27, 1865, at Fort Mason, Arizona Territory.

Mehrand, Louis. Private. Enlisted November 15, 1863, at San Jose.

*Mendes, Besento. Private. Age 33. Vaquero. Dark eyes. Black hair. Dark complexion. 5'8½". Born in Sinaloa, Mexico. Enlisted March 14, 1864, at Placerville. Deserted August 12, 1865, at Copper Camp, Arizona Territory.

Mentro, Susafe. Private. Age 21. Soldier. Black eyes. Black hair. Dark complexion. 5'10". Born in Languedoc, France. Enlisted March 20, 1865, at San Francisco.

*†Miranda (Meranda, Mirando), Pedro. Bugler. Age 21. Enlisted February 25, 1864, at San Francisco. Mustered out December 5, 1865, at San Francisco.

Moraga, Agustin. Private. Age 35. Shoemaker. Black eyes. Black hair. Dark complexion. 5'8". Born in Chile. Enlisted May 16, 1864, at Placerville. Deserted August 11, 1865, at Antelope Peak, Arizona Territory.

Moreno, Antonio. Private. Age 30. Laborer. Black eyes. Black hair. Dark complexion. 5'6". Born in Sonora, California. Enlisted December 1, 1864, at the Presidio of San Francisco. Deserted August 9, 1865, at Gila City, Arizona Territory.

Mota, José. Corporal. Enlisted December 30, 1863, at San Francisco. Deserted September 1, 1864, at the Presidio of San Francisco.

Moxant, Charles. Private. Enlisted March 25, 1864, at San Francisco.

Moya (Moga), Dolph. Private. Age 29. Tailor. Blue eyes. Brown hair. Ruddy complexion. 5'5". Born in Sella, France. Enlisted March 11, 1865, at San Juan Bautista. Deserted July 3, 1865 near Santa Barbara.

Namate, Luis. Private. Age 35. Soldier. Dark eyes. Black hair. Dark complexion. 5'8". Born in Algiers. Enlisted March 20, 1865, at San Francisco.

Nelson, Peter. Private. Enlisted March 24, 1864, at San Francisco. Deserted March 22, 1865, at Camp Low.

Newell, Joseph J. J. Corporal. Enlisted March 4, 1864, at San Francisco. Deserted March 22, 1865, at Camp Low.

‡Padilla, Juan (John). Private. Age 19. Waiter. Dark eyes. Black hair. Dark complexion. 5'2". Born in Mazatlan, Mexico. Enlisted November 12, 1864, at San Francisco.

*Paris, Alexander. Corporal. Enlisted March 7, 1864, at San Francisco.

‡Parra, José Anselmo. Age 30. Miner. Black eyes. Black hair. Dark complexion. 5'3". Born in San Felipe de Concoqua, Chile. Enlisted December 1, 1864, at the Presidio of San Francisco.

Peraza, Ventura (Peraza Ventura). Private. Age 33. Laborer. Black eyes. Dark hair. Dark complexion. 5'3". Born in Mexico. Enlisted January 16, 1865, at San Francisco.

*Perras, Juan (John). Private. Enlisted March 9, 1864, at San Francisco.

Deserted December 2, 1865 from the guardhouse at Fort Mason, Arizona Territory, after being sentenced to death for murder.

‡Pierre, Renauld (Renault). Private. Age 20. Sailor. Gray eyes. Light hair. Fair complexion. 5'5". Born in Charante Inferiene, France. Enlisted September 30, 1864, at San Francisco.

Provost, Francis. Private. Enlisted March 25, 1864, at San Francisco.

Pulgavin, John. Private. Age 29. Miner. Black eyes. Black hair. Dark complexion. 5'6". Born in Guayaquil, Columbia. Enlisted December 1, 1864, at the Presidio of San Francisco. Deserted August 12, 1865, at Copper Camp, Arizona Territory.

Remond (Remont), Motte. Private. Age 37. Laborer. Brown eyes. Dark hair. Dark eyes. 5'6". Born in Paris, France. Enlisted August 3, 1864, at San Francisco.

Roche, Louis. Private. Enlisted December 30, 1864, at San Francisco. Deserted May 18, 1864, at the Presidio of San Francisco.

Rodriguez (Rodrigues), José. Private. Age 35. Carpenter. Brown eyes. Black hair. Dark complexion. 5'7". Born in Havana, Cuba. Enlisted February 20, 1865, at San Francisco. Deserted August 12, 1865, at Copper Camp, Arizona Territory.

Rowan, James R. Private. Enlisted December 30, 1863, at San Francisco. Held by civilian authorities at San Francisco from February 16, 1864.

Ruault, Eugene. Private. Age 27. Laborer. Gray eyes. Light hair. Fair complexion. 5'7". Born in Cote de Mar, France. Enlisted September 26, 1864, at San Francisco.

Salazar, Alfego. Private. Age 21. Soldier. Brown eyes. Brown hair. Dark complexion. 6'0". Born in Toluca, Mexico. Enlisted February 21, 1865, at San Francisco.

‡Salisbury, Alexander. Commissary Sergeant. Enlisted March 9, 1864, at San Francisco.

Samora, Santiago (Santiga). Private. Age 28. Laborer. Brown eyes. Black hair. Dark complexion. 5'8". Born in New Granada. Enlisted February 2, 1865, at San Francisco. Deserted August 12, 1865, at Copper Camp, Arizona Territory.

*†Segobia, Manuel. Corporal. Age 39. Laborer. Black eyes. Black hair. Dark complexion. 5'9". Born in Chile. Enlisted March 28, 1864, at Sacramento. Mustered out December 5, 1865, at San Francisco.

Sentenae, Hippolyte. Private. Enlisted January 9, 1864, at San Francisco. Deserted May 11, 1864, at the Presidio of San Francisco.

*Solesara (Salasara, Sallesara), Francisco. Private. Age 23. Laborer. Black eyes. Black hair. Dark complexion. 5'7". Born in San José, Central America. Enlisted March 11, 1864, at Placerville. Died August 8, 1865, at Gila City, Arizona Territory.

Spaniola, John. Private. Age 24. Sailor. Hazel eyes. Black hair. Dark complexion. 5'5". Born in Rigo, Italy. Enlisted April 14, 1865, at San Francisco. Deserted September 1, 1864, at the Presidio of San Francisco.

*Spinks, Frank. Private. Enlisted December 30, 1863, at San Francisco.

*‡Swan, Robert. Sergeant. Enlisted March 9, 1864, at San Francisco.

Tapia (Topia, Topin), Francito (Froncito, Franszita). Private. Age 31. Laborer. Black eyes. Black hair. Dark complexion. 5'3½". Born in Chile. Enlisted March 28, 1864, at Sacramento. Deserted August 10, 1865, at Mission Camp, Arizona Territory.

‡Torios, Miguel. Private. Enlisted December 31, 1864, at San Francisco.

Torres, Juan. Corporal. Enlisted December 29, 1863, at San Francisco. Deserted October 15, 1864, at the Presidio of San Francisco.

Tournis (Tourmie), Juan. Private. Age 23. Gardener. Brown eyes. Black hair. Dark complexion. Born in Asasjen, France. Enlisted February 21, 1865, at San Francisco. Discharged for disability July 25, 1865, at Drum Barracks.

Touzets (Touzet), Julio Gustave. Private. Age 40. Painter. Brown eyes. Dark hair. Dark complexion. 5'8". Born in Paris, France. Enlisted September 22, 1864, at San Francisco.

Trujillo (Truylio), Ricardo. Private. Age 23. Laborer. Black eyes. Black hair. Dark complexion. 5'6". Born in Mazatlan, Mexico. Enlisted March 3, 1865, at San Francisco. Deserted August 12, 1865, at Copper Camp, Arizona Territory.

*Unger, McKelvie J. Sergeant. Previous service as 2nd lieutenant, Company D, 2nd Cavalry, California Volunteers.[5] Enlisted February 5, 1864, at San Francisco.

Valenzuela, Pablo. Private. Age 24. Saddler. Hazel eyes. Black hair. Dark complexion. 5'4¾". Born in Alamos, Sonora. Enlisted November 19, 1864, at San Francisco. Deserted July 21, 1865, at Puerto Las Cruces.

Vargas, Luis. Private. Age 19. Carpenter. Brown eyes. Brown hair. Fair complexion. 5'6". Born in Guaymas, Sonora. Enlisted February 8, 1865, at San Francisco.

Victor, Christian. Enlisted April 30, 1864, at San Francisco. Deserted June 23, 1864, at the Presidio of San Francisco.

†Vidal, Guadalupe. Private. Age 26. Enlisted December 23, 1863, at San Francisco. Mustered out December 5, 1865, at San Francisco.

Will, George. Private. Age 23. Laborer. Black eyes. Black hair. Dark complexion. 5'3½". Born in Sacramento. Enlisted May 3, 1864, at Sacramento.

Woods, William. Corporal. Enlisted February 2, 1864, at San Francisco. Deserted September 27, 1865, at Fort Mason.

Yllioren, Andres. Private. Age 20. Trader. Brown eyes. Black hair. Dark complexion. 5'5". Born in Chilapa, Mexico. Enlisted February 20, 1865, at San Francisco.

Company C

Initially mustered in at Santa Barbara, July 25, 1864.
Mustered out at the Presidio of San Francisco, April 2, 1866.

DOUBLE DAGGER (‡) INDICATES AN OFFICER OR SOLDIER WHO PARTICIPATED IN GENERAL MASON'S WINTER CAMPAIGN, DECEMBER 1865–JANUARY 1866.

Commissioned Officers

Codington, Edmund Whipple. 2nd Lieutenant. Age 24. Promoted from the ranks of Company B, 2nd Cavalry, California Volunteers by a commission from the governor of California, March 10, 1865, at San Francisco. Promoted to 1st lieutenant (Company D) July 25, 1865, at Drum Barracks.

de la Guerra y Carillo (de la Guerra), Antonio María de Alta Gracia Francisco Remigio (Antonio María). Captain. Age 37. Born in Santa Barbara. Commissioned by the governor of California June 2, 1864, at Santa Barbara.

de la Guerra y Lorenzana (de la Guerra), Felipe Santiago (Santiago). 1st Lieutenant. Age 27. Born in Santa Barbara. Commissioned by the governor of California June 2, 1864, at Santa Barbara.

‡Feeks, Julius John. 2nd Lieutenant. Age 19. Promoted from the ranks of Company B, 2nd Cavalry, California Volunteers by a commission from the governor of California, September 7, 1865, at Sacramento.

Jimeno y de la Guerra (Jimeno), Porfirio Juan de Dios (Porfirio). 2nd Lieutenant. Age 23. Born in Monterey. Commissioned by the governor of California June 2, 1864, at Santa Barbara. Promoted to Company B March 17, 1865, at Drum Barracks.

Enlisted Men

Arellanes, José de la Luz. Private. Age 19. Ranchero. Gray eyes. Black hair. Dark complexion. 5'5". Born in Santa Barbara. Enlisted July 25, 1864, at Santa Barbara.

Arellanes y Sánchez, José Vicente Julian. Private. Age 25. Ranchero. Black eyes. Black hair. Dark complexion. 5'7". Born in Santa Barbara. Enlisted July 25, 1864, at Santa Barbara.

Ayala, José. Private. Age 27. Ranchero. Black eyes. Black hair. Light complexion. 5'4". Born in Santa Barbara. Enlisted July 25, 1864, at Santa Barbara.

‡Ayala, Juan José Ramón de los Santos (Ayala, Ramón). Corporal. Age 25. Ranchero. Black eyes. Black hair. Light complexion. 5'7½". Born in Santa Barbara. Enlisted July 25, 1864, at Santa Barbara.

Ayala y Lugo (Ayala), Abram de Jesús (Abram). Private. Age 23. Ranchero. Gray eyes. Black hair. Light complexion. 5'7". Born in Santa Barbara. Enlisted July 25, 1864, at Santa Barbara.

Badillo, Felipe. Private. Age 28. Ranchero. Gray eyes. Black hair. Light complexion. 5'7½". Born in Santa Barbara. Enlisted July 25, 1864, at Santa Barbara.

Badillo, Felipe de Jesús. Private. Age 19. Ranchero. Black eyes. Black hair. Light complexion. 5'5". Born in Santa Barbara. Enlisted July 25, 1864, at Santa Barbara.

Belderrain, Guillermo (William). Private. Age 22. Ranchero. Gray eyes. Auburn hair. Light complexion. 5'7½" Born in Los Angeles. Enlisted at July 25, 1864, at Santa Barbara. Deserted September 7, 1865, at Rancho Buena Vista.

Bermudez, Pedro. Private. Age 26. Ranchero. Gray eyes. Black hair. Dark complexion. 5'5". Born in Santa Barbara. Enlisted at July 25, 1864, at Santa Barbara.

‡Bickmore, Isaac Danford (J. D.). Sergeant. Age 26. Blacksmith. Gray eyes. Auburn hair. Light complexion. 5'5". Born in Brown County, Illinois. Enlisted December 4, 1864, at Drum Barracks.

‡Calderón y Zurita (Calderón), José de Jesús (José de Jesús). Corporal. Age 29. Black eyes. Black hair. Dark complexion. 5'10". Born in Santa Barbara. Enlisted July 25, 1864, at Santa Barbara.

‡Cantúa y Lorenzana (Cantúa), Santiago Esteban (Santiago). Corporal. Age 24. Ranchero. Black eyes. Black hair. Dark complexion. 5'8½". Born in Santa Barbara. Enlisted July 25, 1864, at Santa Barbara.

Carrillo y Castro (Carrillo), José Gertrudis Carmelo (José).[6] Sergeant. Age 45. Ranchero. Gray eyes. Gray hair. Light complexion. 5'7". Born in Santa Barbara. Enlisted July 25, 1864, at Santa Barbara. Discharged for disability June 9, 1865, at Drum Barracks.

‡Carrillo y Ortega (Carillo), Juan José (Juan).[7] Sergeant. Age 25. Ranchero. Black eyes. Black hair. Dark complexion. 5'7". Born in Santa Barbara. Enlisted July 25, 1864, at Santa Barbara.

Cordero, Francisco. Private. Age 44. Ranchero. Gray eyes. Gray hair. Dark complexion. 5'6". Born in Santa Barbara. Enlisted July 25, 1864, at Santa Barbara.

‡Cordero, José Antonio. Private. Age 22. Ranchero. Black eyes. Black hair. Dark complexion. 5'7". Born in Santa Barbara. Enlisted July 25, 1864, at Santa Barbara.

Cordero, José de Jesús. Private. Age 33. Ranchero. Black eyes. Black hair. Dark complexion. 5'8". Born in Santa Barbara. Enlisted July 25, 1864, at Santa Barbara.

‡Cordero, Juan de Jesús. Private. Age 32. Ranchero. Gray eyes. Black hair. Dark complexion. 5'8". Born in Santa Barbara. Enlisted July 25, 1864, at Santa Barbara.

Cordero, Manuel. Private. Age 22. Ranchero. Gray eyes. Black hair. Dark complexion. 5'7". Born in Santa Barbara. Enlisted July 25, 1864, at Santa Barbara. Deserted September 27, 1865, at Fort Yuma.

Cordero, Romualdo. Private. Age 23. Ranchero. Gray eyes. Black hair. Light complexion. 5'8½". Born in Santa Barbara. Enlisted July 25, 1864, at Santa Barbara.

Corrales, Loreto. Private. Age 42. Ranchero. Gray eyes. Gray hair. Dark complexion. 5'8½". Born in San José, Mexico. Enlisted July 26, 1864, at Santa Barbara.

Cota (Costa), Ignacio. Private. Age 19. Ranchero. Gray eyes. Black hair. Dark complexion. 5'11". Born in Santa Barbara. Enlisted September 7, 1864, at Drum Barracks.

Cota, Miguel. Private. Age 22. Ranchero. Gray hair. Black eyes. Light complexion. 5'7". Born in Santa Barbara. Enlisted July 25, 1864, at Santa Barbara.

‡Cota y Olivera (Cota), Pedro María (Pedro). Sergeant. Age 26. Ranchero. Black eyes. Black hair. Light complexion. 5'8". Born in Santa Barbara. Enlisted July 25, 1864, at Santa Barbara.

de la Guerra y Sepúlveda (de la Guerra), Juan José (Juan José). 1st Sergeant. Age 19. Ranchero. Gray eyes. Auburn hair. Light complexion. 5'5". Born in Santa Barbara. Enlisted July 25, 1864, at Santa Barbara.

Durazo, Ramón. Private. Age 36. Ranchero. Black eyes. Black hair. Dark complexion. 6'2". Born in Santa Barbara. Enlisted July 25, 1864, at Santa Barbara.

‡Elizade, Francisco (Elizada). Private. Age 29. Ranchero. Black eyes. Black hair. Dark complexion. 5'7½". Born in Santa Barbara. Enlisted July 25, 1864, at Santa Barbara.

Espinoza, Clemente. Private. Age 44. Ranchero. Black eyes. Gray hair. Dark complexion. 5'6". Born in Santa Barbara. Enlisted July 25, 1864, at Santa Barbara. Discharged for disability June 9, 1865, at Drum Barracks.

Espinoza, Joaquin. Private. Age 19. Ranchero. Black eyes. Black hair. Dark complexion. 5'8½". Born in Santa Barbara. Enlisted July 25, 1864, at Santa Barbara.

Games, Antonio. Private. Age 39. Ranchero. Black eyes. Black hair. Dark complexion. 5'8½". Born in Santa Barbara. Enlisted July 25, 1864, at Santa Barbara.

García, Francisco. Private. Age 40. Ranchero. Gray eyes. Black hair. Dark complexion. 5'5". Born in Santa Barbara. Enlisted July 25, 1864, at Santa Barbara.

García, José de J. Private. Age 19. Ranchero. Black eyes. Black hair. Light complexion. 5'7½". Born in Santa Barbara. Enlisted July 25, 1864, at Santa Barbara. Deserted September 27, 1865, at Fort Yuma.

García, José Dolores. Private. Age 43. Ranchero. Gray eyes. Black hair. Dark complexion. 5'6". Born in Santa Barbara. Enlisted July 25, 1864, at Santa Barbara.

García, José María. Private. Age 28. Ranchero. Gray eyes. Black hair. Dark complexion. 6'0". Born in Santa Barbara. Enlisted July 25, 1864, at Santa Barbara.

García, Liberato de Jesús. Private. Age 20. Ranchero. Gray eyes. Black hair. Dark complexion. 5'5". Born in Santa Barbara. Enlisted August 1, 1865, at Santa Barbara. Deserted September 27, 1865, at Fort Yuma.

García, Manuel. Private. Age 24. Ranchero. Gray eyes. Black hair. Dark complexion. 5'5". Born in Santa Barbara. Enlisted July 25, 1864, at Santa Barbara.

García, Manuel Francisco. Age 22. Ranchero. Gray eyes. Black hair. Dark complexion. 5'6". Born in Santa Barbara. Enlisted July 25, 1864, at Santa Barbara.

García, Vicente. Sergeant. Age 44. Ranchero. Black eyes. Black hair. Light complexion. 5'6½". Born in Santa Barbara. Enlisted July 25, 1864, at Santa Barbara.

German, Manuel. Private. Age 30. Ranchero. Black eyes. Black hair. Dark complexion. 5'10". Born in Santa Barbara. Enlisted July 25, 1864, at Santa Barbara.

Gilber, Luis. Private. Age 34. Ranchero. Gray eyes. Black hair. Light complexion. 6'0". Born in Santa Barbara. Enlisted July 25, 1864, at Santa Barbara. Discharged for disability June 9, 1865, at Drum Barracks.

Gilber, Miguel. Private. Age 30. Ranchero. Gray eyes. Auburn hair. Light complexion. 5'9". Born in Santa Barbara. Enlisted July 25, 1864, at Santa Barbara.

Gomez, Antonio. Private. Age 19. Ranchero. Hazel eyes. Black hair. Dark complexion. 5'4". Born in San Jose. Enlisted July 25, 1864, at Santa Barbara. Deserted December 1, 1864, at Drum Barracks.

Gutiérrez, Catarino E. Sergeant. Age 30. Schoolmaster. Black eyes. Black hair. Dark complexion. 5'5". Born in Guadalajara, Jalisco, Mexico. Enlisted January 20, 1864, at Los Angeles. Transferred from Company D October 31, 1864. Deserted September 3, 1865, at Rancho los Alamitos.

Gutierrez, Diego. Private. Age 27. Ranchero. Gray eyes. Black hair. Dark complexion. 5'6". Born in Guadalajara, Jalisco, Mexico. Enlisted July 25, 1864, at Santa Barbara.

Juarez, Francisco. Private. Age 19. Ranchero. Gray eyes. Black hair. Dark complexion. 5'8". Born in Santa Barbara. Enlisted July 25, 1864, at Santa Barbara.

Lara, Matias. Private. Age 36. Ranchero. Gray eyes. Auburn hair. Light complexion. 5'8". Born in Santa Barbara. Enlisted July 25, 1864, at Santa Barbara.

Lean, Guillermo. Private. Age 19. Farmer. Gray eyes. Auburn hair. Light complexion. 5'5". Born in New York City. Enlisted March 30, 1865, at Drum Barracks.

Lopez, Bernadino. Private. Age 43. Ranchero. Black eyes. Black hair. Dark complexion. 5'11". Born in Santa Barbara. Enlisted July 25, 1864, at Santa Barbara.

Lopez, Ermengildo. Private. Age 41. Ranchero. Gray eyes. Black hair. Dark complexion. 5'9". Born in Mexico. Enlisted July 25, 1864, at Santa Barbara.

Lugo, Francisco. Private. Age 37. Ranchero. Gray eyes. Gray hair. Light complexion. 5'7". Born in Santa Barbara. Enlisted July 25, 1864, at Santa Barbara.

Lugo, José. Private. Age 29. Ranchero. Black eyes. Black hair. Dark complexion. 5'8". Born in Santa Barbara. Enlisted July 25, 1864, at Santa Barbara.

Madrueno, Jesús. Private. Age 37. Blacksmith. Gray eyes. Black hair. Dark complexion. 5'5". Born in Santa Barbara. Enlisted July 25, 1864, at Santa Barbara.

Moreau, Carlos. Private. Age 18. Clerk. Black eyes. Light hair. Light complexion. 5'5". Born in Zacatecas, Mexico.[8] Enlisted July 25, 1864, at Santa Barbara.

Moreno, José. Private. Age 27. Ranchero. Black eyes. Black hair. Dark complexion. 5'6". Born in Santa Barbara. Enlisted July 25, 1864, at Santa Barbara. Discharged for disability July 25, 1865, at Drum Barracks.

Moreno, Pío. Private. Age 26. Ranchero. Black eyes. Black hair. Dark complexion. 5'6½". Born in Los Angeles. Enlisted July 25, 1864, at Santa Barbara.

Ojeda, Florencio. Corporal. Age 44. Ranchero. Gray eyes. Gray hair. Light complexion. 5'9½". Born in Santa Barbara. Enlisted July 26, 1864, at Santa Barbara.

Olivas, Felipe. Private. Age 20. Ranchero. Black eyes. Black hair. Dark complexion. 5'7". Born in Santa Barbara. Enlisted July 28, 1864, at Santa Barbara.

Olivas, José Antonio. Private. Age 35. Ranchero. Black eyes. Black hair. Dark complexion. 5'9½". Born in Santa Barbara. Enlisted July 25, 1864, at Santa Barbara.

Olivas, Pablo. Private. Age 19. Ranchero. Black eyes. Black hair. Dark complexion. 5'7½". Born in Santa Barbara. Enlisted July 25, 1864, at Santa Barbara. Died of consumption December 26, 1864, at Drum Barracks.

Olivas, Victorino. Private. Age 23. Ranchero. Gray eyes. Black hair. Dark complexion. 5'7". Born in Santa Barbara. Enlisted July 25, 1864, at Santa Barbara.

Olivera, Santiago. Private. Age 33. Ranchero. Black eyes. Black hair. Dark complexion. 5'8". Born in Los Angeles. Enlisted February 14, 1865, at Drum Barracks.

Ordaz, Luis Vicente. Commissary Sergeant. Age 29. Ranchero. Gray eyes. Black hair. Light complexion. 5'6". Born in Santa Barbara. Enlisted July 25, 1864, at Santa Barbara.

Orellana, Nicolas. Private. Age 40. Ranchero. Gray eyes. Black hair. Light complexion. 5'8". Born in Estrella, Chile. Enlisted July 25, 1864, at Santa Barbara.

‡Ortega, Vicente. Private. Age 29. Ranchero. Gray eyes. Gray hair. Light complexion. 5'8". Born in Santa Barbara. Enlisted July 27, 1864, at Santa Barbara.

Pico, José Ramón de la Concepción (Ramón). Corporal. Age 26. Ranchero. Gray eyes. Auburn hair. Light complexion. 5'10". Born in Santa Barbara. Enlisted July 25, 1864, at Santa Barbara.

Pico, Miguel. Corporal. Age 24. Ranchero. Black eyes. Black hair. Dark complexion. 5'7½". Born in Santa Barbara. Enlisted July 25, 1864, at Santa Barbara.

Pico y Ruíz (Pico), José Rafael de los Ángeles de Alta Gracia (Rafael). Bugler. Age 34. Musician. Black eyes. Black hair. Dark complexion. 5'5". Born in Santa Barbara. Enlisted July 25, 1864, at Santa Barbara.

‡Ponce de León y Solórzano (Ponce de León), José Cleofás de Altagracia (Cleofas).[9] Private. Age 19. Ranchero. Black eyes. Black hair. Dark complexion. 5'6". Born in Santa Barbara. Enlisted August 1, 1864, at Santa Barbara.

‡Ríos y Alvarado (Ríos), Miguel de los Angeles (Miguel). Sergeant. Age 18. Carpenter. Gray eyes. Auburn hair. Light complexion. 5'8". Born in Los Angeles. Enlisted March 30, 1865, at Drum Barracks.

Robinson, Horatio. Private. Age 36. Farrier. Black eyes. Gray hair. Light complexion. 5'9". Born in Santa Barbara. Enlisted at July 25, 1864, at Santa Barbara. Mustered out March 20, 1866, at Drum Barracks.

Rodriguez, Antonio. Corporal. Age 44. Ranchero. Black eyes. Black hair. Dark complexion. 5'7½". Born in Santa Barbara. Enlisted July 25, 1864, at Santa Barbara.

Rodriguez, José. Quartermaster Sergeant. Age 36. Ranchero. Gray eyes. Gray hair. Light complexion. 5'4". Born in Santa Barbara. Enlisted July 25, 1864, at Santa Barbara.

Rodriguez, José de Jesús. Private. Age 29. Ranchero. Black eyes. Black hair. Dark complexion. 5'8". Born in Santa Barbara. Enlisted July 25, 1864, at Santa Barbara.

Rodriguez, Pedro. Private. Age 32. Ranchero. Black eyes. Black hair. Dark complexion. 5'6". Born in Santa Barbara. Enlisted August 1, 1864, at Santa Barbara.

Romero, José Antonio. Private. Age 20. Ranchero. Gray eyes. Black hair. Dark complexion. 5'4". Born in Santa Barbara. Enlisted July 25, 1864, at Santa Barbara.

Romero, Pedro. Private. Age 19. Ranchero. Gray eyes. Black hair. Dark complexion. 5'4". Born in Santa Barbara. Enlisted July 25, 1864, at Santa Barbara.

Ruiz, Juan de la Cruz. Private. Age 40. Ranchero. Gray eyes. Black hair. Light complexion. 5'10". Born in Santa Barbara. Enlisted July 25, 1864, at Santa Barbara.

Samane, Roman. Private. Age 19. Ranchero. Black eyes. Black hair. Dark complexion. 5'6½". Born in Santa Barbara. Enlisted July 26, 1864, at Santa Barbara.

‡Saragosa (Zaragosa), Francisco. Age 25. Ranchero. Black eyes. Black hair. Dark complexion. 5'8". Born in Mexico. Enlisted July 25, 1864, at Santa Barbara.

Sierra, Guadalupe. Private. Age 22. Ranchero. Black eyes. Black hair. Dark complexion. 5'4". Born in Sonora, Mexico. Enlisted July 26, 1864, at Santa Barbara. Deserted June 29, 1865, at Drum Barracks.

Smith, Philip. Farrier. Age 36. Farmer. Blue eyes. Gray hair. Light complexion. 5'8". Born in Cavan, Ireland. Enlisted April 6, 1865, at Drum Barracks. Mustered out March 20, 1866, at Drum Barracks.

Soto, Antonio. Sergeant. Age 29. Ranchero. Gray eyes. Black hair. Light complexion. 5'8". Born in Santa Barbara. Enlisted July 25, 1864, at Santa Barbara. Discharged for disability June 9, 1865, at Drum Barracks.

Soto, Jesús María Luisano (Jesús). Corporal. Age 30. Ranchero. Black eyes. Black hair. Dark complexion. 5'10". Born in Santa Barbara. Enlisted July 25, 1864, at Santa Barbara.

Soto, Juan. Private. Age 26. Ranchero. Black eyes. Black hair. Dark complexion. 5'8". Born in Santa Barbara. Enlisted July 25, 1864.

Soto, Ysmael Jacobo. Bugler. Age 23. Ranchero. Gray eyes. Auburn hair. Light complexion. 5'10". Born in Santa Barbara. Enlisted July 25, 1864, at Santa Barbara.

Streeter, Zebina Nathaniel. Private. Age 26. Clerk. Gray eyes. Auburn hair. Light complexion. 5'5". Born in Genoa, New York. Previously served as 2nd lieutenant, Company B. Enlisted December 5, 1864, at Drum Barracks. Mustered out December 5, 1865, at San Francisco.

Torres (Torrez), Dionisio. Private. Age 42. Ranchero. Black eyes. Black hair. Dark complexion. 5'10". Born in Belen, New Mexico. Enlisted July 25, 1864, at Santa Barbara. Died of heart disease August 1, 1864, at Santa Barbara.

‡Valdez, José Salvador. Private. Age 29. Ranchero. Black eyes. Black hair. Light complexion. 5'7". Born in Santa Barbara. Enlisted July 25, 1864, at Santa Barbara.

Valencia, Felipe. Private. Age 26. Ranchero. Gray eyes. Auburn hair. Light complexion. 5'7½". Born in Santa Barbara. Enlisted July 25, 1864, at Santa Barbara. Deserted March 6, 1865, at Drum Barracks.

Valencia, Juan Ignacio de Altagracia. Private. Age 37. Ranchero. Gray eyes. Black hair. Dark complexion. 5'6". Born in Santa Barbara. Enlisted at July 25, 1864, at Santa Barbara. Discharged for disability July 25, 1865, at Drum Barracks.

Valencia, Narciso. Private. Age 21. Ranchero. Black eyes. Black hair. Dark complexion. 5'9". Born in Santa Barbara. Enlisted July 25, 1864, at Santa Barbara.

Valencia, Pablo. Private. Age 42. Ranchero. Gray eyes. Gray hair. Dark complexion. 5'8". Born in Santa Barbara. Enlisted July 25, 1864, at Santa Barbara.

Valenzuela, Clodoveo. Corporal. Age 36. Ranchero. Black eyes. Black hair. Light complexion. 5'8". Born in Santa Barbara. Enlisted July 25, 1864, at Santa Barbara. Deserted September 3, 1865, at Rancho los Alamitos.

Valenzuela, José María. Private. Age 26. Ranchero. Black eyes. Black hair. Dark complexion. 5'8". Born in Santa Barbara. Enlisted July 25, 1864, at Santa Barbara.

Valenzuela, Juan Ignacio. Private. Age 34. Ranchero. Gray eyes. Black hair. Light complexion. 5'8". Born in Santa Barbara. Enlisted July 25, 1864, at Santa Barbara.

Yell, Pilott. Private. Age 38. Saddler. Blue eyes. Auburn hair. White complexion. 6'0". Born in Henderson, Kentucky. Enlisted January 14, 1865, at Drum Barracks. Discharged for disability June 9, 1865, at Drum Barracks.

Company D

Initially mustered in at Drum Barracks March 3, 1864.
Mustered out at Drum Barracks March 20, 1866.

DOUBLE DAGGER (‡) INDICATES AN OFFICER OR SOLDIER WHO PARTICIPATED IN GENERAL MASON'S WINTER CAMPAIGN, DECEMBER 1865–JANUARY 1866.

Commissioned Officers

Bale y Sobreanes, Eduardo (Bale, Edward T.). 1st Lieutenant. Age 22. Born in California. Promoted from Company B June 29, 1864.

‡Codington, Edmund W. 1st Lieutenant. Age 24. Miner and Clerk. Born in New York. Promoted from Company C August 28, 1865, at Drum Barracks.

Cox, Jeremiah Clement. 1st Lieutenant. Tradesman. Gray eyes. Light hair. Light complexion. Promoted to 2nd lieutenant from the ranks March 11, 1864, at Drum Barracks. Promoted to 1st lieutenant September 19, 1864. Resigned July 22, 1865.

Redona, José. 1st Lieutenant. Age 28. Constable. Black eyes. Brown hair. Dark complexion. Born in Mexico. Commissioned February 10, 1864, at Los Angeles.

Sanchez, José Antonio. Captain. Age 33. Carpenter. Gray eyes. Black hair. Light complexion. 5'11". Born in Los Angeles. Previously served as a private in the Los Angeles Mounted Rifles, California State Militia. Commissioned February 10, 1864, at Los Angeles.

Young, Thomas A. Captain. Age 33. Born in New York. Previously captain of Company G, 5th Infantry, California Volunteers. Died of disease December 3, 1865, at Fort Mason, Arizona Territory.

Enlisted Men

Abila y Rosas (Avila), Santos. Private. Age 21. Vaquero. Black eyes. Black hair. Dark complexion. 5'3½". Born in Los Angeles. Enlisted January 13, 1864, at Los Angeles.

Abril, Francisco. Private. Age 21. Laborer. Black eyes. Black hair. Dark complexion. 5'6½". Born in Los Angeles. Enlisted January 13, 1864. Deserted July 3, 1864, at Drum Barracks.

Aguayo, Antonio. Private. Age 23. Weaver. Hazel eyes. Black hair. Dark complexion. 5'7½". Born in Sonora, Mexico. Enlisted January 13, 1864, at Los Angeles.

‡Aguilar, Rafael. Private. Age 28. Laborer. Black eyes. Black hair. Dark complexion. 6'0". Born in Sonora, Mexico. Enlisted January 13, 1864, at Los Angeles.

Altamirano y Mesa (Altamirano), Isidro de la Resurrección (Isidro). Private. Age 23. Vaquero. Hazel eyes. Black hair. Light complexion. 5'9". Born in Los Angeles. Enlisted February 25, 1864, at Los Angeles. Deserted August 8, 1865, at Fort Yuma.

‡Alvarado, Esteban. Private. Age 25. Vaquero. Black eyes. Black hair. Dark complexion. 5'9½". Born in Monterey. Enlisted January 13, 1864, at Los Angeles.

Armenta (Aramento), Tomás (Thomas). Private. Age 27. Gambler. Hazel eyes. Black hair. Dark complexion. 5'3½". Born in Sonora, Mexico. Enlisted January 13, 1864, at Los Angeles. In confinement at Drum Barracks for murder from June 1865. Dishonorably discharged July 2, 1866.

‡Arrezaga (Arzaga), Laureano. Private. Age 33. Plasterer. Black eyes. Black hair. Dark complexion. 5'7½". Enlisted January 14, 1864, at Los Angeles. Enlisted January 14, 1864, at Los Angeles.

Barreras (Barrevas), Julián. Private. Age 19. Laborer. Hazel eyes. Black hair. Dark complexion. 5'7". Born in Los Angeles. Enlisted February 1, 1864, at Los Angeles.

Bennett, Michael (Miguel). Sergeant. Age 35. Saddler. Black eyes. Black hair. Dark complexion. 5'8". Born in Poland. Enlisted December 26, 1865, at Los Angeles.

Bernal (Vernal, Peña), Dolores (José Dolores). Bugler. Age 18. Ranchero. Black eyes. Black hair. Dark complexion. 5'4". Born in California. Enlisted January 13, 1864, at Los Angeles. Died December 4, 1865, at Fort Mason, Arizona Territory.

Bojórquez (Bojorguez), Luís. Private. Age 23. Vaquero. Black eyes. Black hair. Dark complexion. 5'7½". Born in Sonora, Mexico. Enlisted January 13, 1864, at Los Angeles. Deserted October 7, 1864, at Drum Barracks.

Borbón, Romualdo D. Private. Age 23. Vaquero. Hazel eyes. Black hair. Dark complexion. 5'6". Born in Sonora, Mexico. Enlisted January 13, 1864, at Los Angeles. Deserted October 7, 1864, at Drum Barracks.

Buelna y Valencia (Buelna), José Teodosio del Refugio (Teodosio). Private. Age 18. Vaquero. Black hair. Black eyes. Dark complexion. 5'7½". Born in Los Angeles. Enlisted March 24, 1864, at Los Angeles. Deserted at Drum Barracks, June 17, 1864.

Bufanda (Bujanda), Jesús. Private. Age 22. Laborer. Gray eyes. Brown hair. Dark complexion. 5'8". Born in Sonora, Mexico. Enlisted May 4, 1864, at Drum Barracks. Deserted December 23, 1865, while confined to the guardhouse at Fort Mason, Arizona Territory.

Camacho, Lorenzo. Commissary Sergeant. Laborer. Age 29. Hazel eyes, Black hair, Dark complexion. 5'8". Born in Sonora, Mexico. Enlisted January 14, 1864, at Los Angeles.

Campo (O'Campo, Ocampo), Camilo. Private. Teamster. Age 23. Hazel eyes. Black hair. Dark complexion. 5'6". Born in Popayan, New Granada. Enlisted January 25, 1864, at Los Angeles.

‡Caravajales, Sebastián (Sylvester). Private. Age 20. Laborer. Black eyes. Black hair. Dark complexion. 5'3". Born in Banámichi, Sonora. Enlisted January 15, 1865, at Los Angeles.

‡Carrasco, Juan. Private. Age 18. Vaquero. Black eyes. Black hair. Black complexion. 5'6". Born in Mexico. Enlisted January 13, 1864, at Los Angeles.

Carrillo (Corello), Francisco. Private. Age 23. Vaquero. Black eyes. Black hair. Dark complexion. 5'5". Born in Sonora, Mexico. Enlisted January 13, 1864, at Los Angeles. Deserted November 15, 1864, at Drum Barracks.

Castillo, Refugio. Sergeant. Mechanic. Age 29. Black eyes. Black hair. Dark complexion. 5'7". Born in Sonora, Mexico. Enlisted January 14, 1864, at Los Angeles.

‡Chávez (Chaveo), Jesús. Corporal. Laborer. Age 33. Black eyes. Black hair. Dark complexion. 5'6". Born in Sonora, Mexico. Enlisted March 5, 1864, at Los Angeles.

Conoció (Colocio), Severino. Private. Age 22. Laborer. Black eyes. Black hair. Dark complexion. 5'4¾". Born in Sonora, Mexico. Enlisted March 24, 1864, at Los Angeles.

Cordova, Nicolás. Private. Age 33. Laborer. Black eyes. Black hair. Dark complexion. 5'9". Born in Sonora, Mexico. Enlisted January 20, 1864, at Los Angeles.

Cordova, Santiago. Private. Age 26. Laborer. Black eyes. Black hair. Dark complexion. 5'8½". Born in Sonora, Mexico. Enlisted January 13, 1864, at Los Angeles.

‡Corona, José María. Sergeant. Laborer. Age 21. Hazel eyes. Brown hair. Light complexion. 5'0". Born in Magdalena, Sonora. Enlisted February 23, 1864, at Los Angeles.

Corona, José Victor (Joseph). Corporal. Farmer. Age 26. Black eyes. Black hair. Light complexion. 5'7½". Born in Magdalena, Sonora. Enlisted February 23, 1864, at Los Angeles.

Corona, Teodosio. Enlisted November 18, 1864, at Drum Barracks. Not mustered in on account of disability.

Cuevas (Curoas), Ruperto. Private. Age 24. Miner. Hazel eyes. Black hair. Dark complexion. 5'6". Born in Sonora, Mexico. Enlisted January 14, 1864, at Los Angeles. Deserted July 19, 1864, at Drum Barracks.

‡Domingo, José. Private. Age 23. Laborer. Black eyes. Back hair. Dark complexion. 5'8". Born in Mexico. Enlisted January 13 1864 in Los Angeles.

‡Domínguez, José A. Private. Age 21. Vaquero. Black eyes. Black hair. Dark complexion. 5'10". Born in Los Angeles. Enlisted November 11, 1864, at Drum Barracks.

Domínguez y Avila, José María. Private. Age 20. Vaquero. Black eyes. Black hair. Fair complexion. 5'9". Born in Los Angeles. Enlisted February 12, 1865, at Drum Barracks.

Dominguez y Castelo (Dominguez), Dolores Casildo (Dolores). Private. Age 20. Vaquero. Hazel eyes. Brown hair. Light complexion. 5'10". Born in Los Angeles. Enlisted January 13, 1864, at Los Angeles. Deserted August 8, 1865, at Fort Yuma.

Domínguez y Várelas, Eduardo Cayetano. Private. Age 18. Vaquero. Black eyes. Black hair. Dark complexion. 5'7". Born in Santa Barbara. Enlisted January 13, 1864, at Los Angeles.

Duarte, Francisco. Private. Age 26. Vaquero. Black eyes. Black hair.

Dark complexion. 5'6½". Born in Los Angeles. Enlisted February 23, 1864, at Los Angeles. Murdered October 23, 1865, at Fort Mason, Arizona Territory.[10]

Elizade y Ruiz (Elizade), José Diego Vidal (Diego). Private. Age 19. Vaquero. Hazel eyes. Black hair. Dark complexion. 5'9". Born in Los Angeles. Enlisted January 20, 1864, at Los Angeles.

Elizalde y Ruiz (Elizade), José de los Dolores (Dolores). Private. Age 23. Vaquero. Gray eyes. Black hair. Dark complexion. 5'9". Born in Los Angeles. Enlisted January 13, 1864, at Los Angeles.

Enríquez, Martín. Private. Age 19. Laborer. Gray eyes. Black hair. Dark complexion. 5'7". Born in Sonora, Mexico. Enlisted April 7, 1864, at Los Angeles. Deserted December 22, 1864, at Drum Barracks.

‡Estrada, Francisco. Private. Age 45. Laborer. Hazel eyes. Black hair. Dark complexion. 6'0". Born in Sonora, Mexico. Enlisted February 23, 1864, at Los Angeles.

Estrada, Manuel. Private. Age 21. Laborer. Gray eyes. Brown hair. Dark complexion. 5'7". Born in Sonora, Mexico. Enlisted January 27, 1864, at Los Angeles. Deserted July 9, 1864, at Drum Barracks.

Feliz, Francisco. Private. Age 18. Black eyes. Black hair. Dark complexion. 5'4". Laborer. Born in Sonora, Mexico. Enlisted March 18, 1864, at Los Angeles. Deserted June 17, 1864, at Drum Barracks.

Fimbres, Nicolás. Private. Age 24. Laborer. Gray eyes. Dark hair. Light complexion. 5'5". Born in Sonora, Mexico. Enlisted April 6, 1864, at Los Angeles. Discharged for disability July 1, 1864, at Drum Barracks.

‡Flores, Amado. Corporal. Age 33. Laborer. Black eyes. Black hair. Dark complexion. 5'8". Born in Chihuahua, Mexico. Enlisted on January 20, 1864.

García, Antonio. Private. Age 25. Blacksmith. Hazel eyes. Black hair. Dark complexion. 5'6". Born in Sonora, Mexico. Enlisted February 5, 1864, at Los Angeles.

García, Dionosio. Farrier. Age 24. Blacksmith. Hazel eyes. Black hair. Dark complexion. 5'6". Born in Sonora, Mexico. Enlisted January 20, 1864, at Los Angeles. Discharged for disability July 25, 1865, at Drum Barracks.

García, Francisco. Private. Age 34. Vaquero. Black eyes. Black hair. Dark complexion. 5'9". Born in California. Enlisted January 14, 1864, at Los Angeles.

García, Tomás. Private. Age 18. Black eyes. Black hair. Dark complexion. 5'7½". Born in Sonora, Mexico. Enlisted March 15, 1864. Deserted December 1, 1864, at Drum Barracks.

Garnica, Yginio (Hignigo). Private. Age 28. Laborer. Black eyes. Black hair. Dark complexion. 5'9". Born in Sonora, Mexico. Enlisted February 23, 1864, at Los Angeles.

Gomez, Francisco. Sergeant. Age 36. Hazel eyes. Black hair. Dark complexion. 5'9". Born in Sonora, Mexico. Enlisted February 7, 1864, at Los Angeles. Died October 16, 1864, at Drum Barracks.

González, Jesús. Private. Age 18. Laborer. Hazel eyes. Black hair. Dark complexion. 5'6". Born in Sonora, Mexico. Enlisted January 30, 1864, at Los Angeles. Deserted February 10, 1865, at Drum Barracks.

Guirado y Urquides (Guirado), Francisco de Paula (Francisco). 1st Sergeant. Age 23. Clerk and Farmer. Gray eyes. Black hair. Dark complexion. 5'7½". Born in Los Angeles. Enlisted March 21, 1864, at Los Angeles. Declined a commission as 2nd lieutenant. Discharged for disability May 9, 1865, at Drum Barracks.

Guirado y Urquides (Guirado), José María Leandro (Leandro). Corporal. Age 19. Vaquero. Hazel eyes. Black hair. Brown complexion. 5'8". Born in Los Angeles. Enlisted January 14, 1864, at Los Angeles.

‡Gustamante, José. Private. Age 23. Baker. Black eyes. Black hair. Light complexion. 5'9½". Born in Sonora, Mexico. Enlisted December 12, 1864, at Drum Barracks.

Gutiérrez, Catarino E. Private. Age 30. Schoolmaster. Black eyes. Black hair. Dark complexion. 5'5". Born in Guadalajara, Jalisco. Enlisted January 20, 1864, at Los Angeles. Transferred to Company C October 31, 1864.

Herrera (Cañedo), José J (José). Recruit. Enlisted January 16, 1864, at Los Angeles. Never mustered. Died March 1, 1864, at Drum Barracks.

Herrera (Hierra), Ramón. Private. Age 36. Laborer. Hazel eyes. Black hair. Dark complexion. 5'5". Born in Valparaiso, Chile. Enlisted February 28, 1864, at Los Angeles.

‡Jara, Domingo. Private. Age 30. Laborer. Hazel eyes. Black hair. Dark complexion. 5'5". Born in Sonora, Mexico. Enlisted January 13, 1864, at Los Angeles.

‡King y Juarez (King), José Vicente Roberto (José). Private. Age 19. Laborer. Gray eyes. Dark hair. Light complexion. 5'4". Born in Santa Cruz. Enlisted April 14, 1865, at Drum Barracks.

Laguna, Santos. Private. Age 22. Shoemaker. Black eyes. Black hair. Dark complexion. 5'6½". Born in Sonora, Mexico. Enlisted January 15, 1864, at Los Angeles.

López y Vasquez (López), José Antonio del Refugio (José A.). Private. Age 18. Black eyes. Black hair. Fair complexion. 6'0". Born in Los Angeles. Enlisted February 27, 1865, at Drum Barracks.

López, Jesús. Private. Age 21. Vaquero. Hazel eyes. Black hair. Dark complexion. 5'7". Born in Los Angeles. Enlisted February 1, 1864, at Los Angeles.

‡Marrón (Manon), Gabriel. Private. Age 22. Laborer. Black eyes. Black hair. Dark complexion. 5'10½". Born in San Diego. Enlisted January 13, 1864, at Los Angeles.

Marrón, Jesús M. Private. Age 20. Shoemaker. Hazel eyes. Black hair. Dark complexion. 6'0". Born in Sonora, Mexico. Enlisted January 25, 1864, at Los Angeles.

Marrón, José del R. Private. Age 23. Dark eyes. Black hair. Dark complexion. 5'8". Born in Mexico. Enlisted April 18, 1864, at Drum Barracks. Deserted June 22, 1864, at Drum Barracks.

Martínez, Francisco. Private. Age 35. Black eyes. Black hair. Dark complexion. 5'5". Born in Sonora, Mexico. Enlisted January 13, 1864, at Los Angeles. Deserted November 30, 1864, at Drum Barracks.

Martínez, Rafael. Private. Age 23. Vaquero. Hazel eyes. Black hair. Dark complexion. 5'10". Born in California. Enlisted January 14, 1864, at Los Angeles. Deserted July 3, 1864, at Drum Barracks.

Mazon, Abel. Sergeant. Age 20. Carpenter. Blue eyes. Brown hair. Light complexion. 5'5". Born in Sonora, Mexico. Enlisted January 30, 1864, at Los Angeles.

Mendibles, Angel. Private. Age 22. Laborer. Hazel eyes. Brown hair. Dark complexion. 5'8½". Born in Sonora, Mexico. Enlisted February 26, 1864, at Los Angeles.

Mendibles, Trinidad. Private. Age 33. Laborer. Hazel eyes. Brown hair. Dark complexion. 5'7½". Born in Sonora, Mexico. Enlisted February 26, 1864, at Los Angeles.

‡Moreno, José Maria. Private. Age 25. Vaquero. Black eyes. Black hair. Dark complexion. 5'8". Born in Los Angeles. Enlisted February 26, 1864, at Los Angeles.

Moreno, José Maria. Private. Age 19. Vaquero. Black eyes. Black hair.

Dark complexion. 5'8". Born in Los Angeles. Enlisted February 26, 1864, at Los Angeles.

Moreno y Feliz (Moreno), Jesús María (Jesús M.). Private. Age 20. Bookmaker. Hazel eyes. Black hair. Dark complexion. 6'0". Born in Hermosillo, Sonora. Enlisted January 23, 1864, at Los Angeles. Deserted July 3, 1864, at Drum Barracks.

Nuñez (Nimez), Valentín. Private. Age 21. Farrier. Hazel eyes. Black hair. Dark complexion. 5'6". Born in Sonora, Mexico. Enlisted January 20, 1864, at Los Angeles. Discharged for disability April 30, 1865, at Drum Barracks.

‡Ocaña y Ruiz (Ocaña), José Francisco Gregorio (Francisco). Private. Age 23. Vaquero. Black eyes. Black hair. Dark complexion. 5'6½". Born in Los Angeles. Enlisted January 13, 1864, at Los Angeles.

Olivas y Pico (Olivas), Blas (Blas). Private. Age 21. Vaquero. Black eyes. Black hair. Dark complexion. 5'10". Born in Santa Bárbara. Enlisted January 30 1864, at Los Angeles.

Oyos (Oyas), Jesús. Private. Age 21. Vaquero. Gray eyes. Brown hair. Dark complexion. 5'5". Born in Sonora, Mexico. Enlisted January 18, 1864, at Los Angeles.

Padilla, José. Private. Enlisted July 12, 1864, at Los Angeles. Deserted December 22, 1864, at Drum Barracks.

Padilla, Perdió. Private. Age 21. Laborer. Black eyes. Black hair. Dark complexion. 5'10". Born in Ures, Sonora. Enlisted September 5, 1864, at Drum Barracks.

Palacios y Lara (Palacios), José Salvador (Salvador). Private. Laborer. Hazel eyes, Black hair. 5'5". Light complexion. Born in Los Angeles. Enlisted February 20, 1864, at Los Angeles.

‡Quinteros, Dolores. Private. Age 28. Laborer. Hazel eyes. Black hair. Light complexion. 5'9". Born in Los Angeles. Enlisted January 20, 1864, at Los Angeles.

Ramírez, Francisco. Private. Age 28. Vaquero. Black eyes. Black hair. Dark complexion. 5'8½". Born in Sonora, Mexico. Enlisted April 15, 1865, at Drum Barracks. Deserted August 8, 1865, at Fort Yuma.

Ramirez y Várelas, Antonio María. Quartermaster Sergeant. Age 21. Tin Maker. Hazel eyes. Black hair. Dark complexion. 5'8". Born in Los Angeles. Enlisted January 25, 1864, at Los Angeles.

Reyes y Villavicencio, José Antonio Eusebio (José Antonio Reyes).

Corporal. Age 23. Vaquero. Hazel eyes. Black hair. Dark complexion. 5'8". Born in Los Angeles. Enlisted January 13, 1864, at Los Angeles.

‡Rivas, José Francisco. Private. Age 20. Vaquero. Dark eyes. Black hair. Dark complexion. 5'3". Born in Los Angeles. Enlisted March 9, 1864, at Los Angeles.

Rivera, Fernando. Private. Age 23. Laborer. Hazel eyes. Black hair. Dark complexion. 5'8". Born in Mexico. Enlisted January 13, 1864, at Los Angeles. Deserted November 15, 1864, at Drum Barracks.

Rivera, José M. Private. Age 19. Vaquero. Black eyes. Black hair. Dark complexion. 5'10". Born in Sonora, Mexico. Enlisted January 13, 1864, at Los Angeles.

Rivera, Ramón. Private. Age 25. Vaquero. Black eyes. Black hair. Dark complexion. 5'8". Born in Los Angeles. Enlisted January 20, 1864, at Los Angeles.

‡Rivera y Ruiz (Rivera), Felipe de Jesús (Felipe). Corporal. Age 20. Vaquero. Hazel eyes. Black hair. Dark complexion. 6'0". Born in Los Angeles. Enlisted January 13, 1864, at Los Angeles.

Rivera y Ruiz, José Ramon Porfirio. Private. Age 25. Vaquero. Black eyes. Black hair. Dark complexion. 5'8". Born in Los Angeles. Enlisted January 20, 1864, at Los Angeles.

Robarts, John (Juan). 1st Sergeant. Age 21. Miner. Gray eyes. Light hair. Light complexion. 5'8". Born in Somerset, England. Enlisted September 20, 1864, at Drum Barracks.

Robbins y Carillo (Robinson), Juan José (Juan). Private. Age 20. Painter. Hazel eyes. Black hair. Dark complexion. 5'1". Born in California. Enlisted January 13, 1864, at Los Angeles.

Rodríguez, Félix (Felis). Private. Age 22. Vaquero. Black hair. Black eyes. Dark complexion. 5'6". Born in Los Angeles. Enlisted January 16, 1864, at Los Angeles.

‡Rodríguez, Ramón. Private. Age 24. Laborer. Black eyes. Black hair. Dark complexion. 5'11". Born in Sonora, Mexico. Enlisted March 18, 1864, at Los Angeles.

Rojas, Juan. Private. Age 34. Laborer. Hazel eyes. Black hair. Dark complexion. 5'8". Born in Sonora, Mexico. Enlisted January 25, 1864, at Los Angeles.

Romero, Hilario (Ylario). Private. Age 19. Laborer. Gray eyes. Black hair. 5'4". Born in Los Angeles. Enlisted May 19, 1864, at Los Angeles.

Ruiz (Ruis), José María. Corporal. Age 45. Vaquero. Enlisted February 15, 1864. Hazel eyes. Black hair. Light complexion. 6'0". Born in Sonora, Mexico. Enlisted February 15, 1864, at Los Angeles.

‡Salazar, Dolores. Private. Age 25. Laborer. Black eyes. Black hair. Dark complexion. 5'5½". Born in Sonora, Mexico. Enlisted January 13, 1864, at Los Angeles.

‡Santa Cruz, Pablo. Private. Age 26. Ranchero. Black eyes. Black hair. Dark complexion. 5'4½". Born in Sonora, Mexico. Enlisted January 13, 1864, at Los Angeles.

‡Sauceda, Feliz. Private. Age 32. Black eyes. Black hair. Dark complexion. 5'8½". Born in Sonora, Mexico. Enlisted January 13, 1864, at Los Angeles.

‡Silvas, José Antonio. Corporal. Age 28. Vaquero. Black eyes. Black hair. Light complexion. 5'9". Born in Los Angeles. Enlisted February 23, 1864, at Los Angeles.

‡Sortillón, Jesús. Private. Age 21. Black eyes. Black hair. Dark complexion. 5'10". Born in Sonora, Mexico. Enlisted January 13, 1864, at Los Angeles.

Soto, Miguel. Private. Age 32. Vaquero. Hazel eyes. Black hair. Dark complexion. 5'9". Born in Los Angeles. Enlisted January 26, 1864, at Los Angeles.

Stales, José María. Private. Age 26. Hazel eyes. Black hair. Dark complexion. 5'7". Born in Sonora, Mexico. Enlisted January 23, 1864, at Los Angeles.

‡Tapia, Juan. Private. Age 22. Laborer. Gray eyes. Black hair. Dark complexion. 5'10". Born in Sonora, Mexico. Enlisted April 7, 1864, at Los Angeles.

Torres, Gregorio. Private. Age 25. Laborer. Hazel eyes. Black hair. Dark complexion. 5'8". Born in Sonora, Mexico. Enlisted February 4, 1864, at Los Angeles. Died March 4, 1864, at Drum Barracks.

Valenzuela, Ignacio. Private. Age 25. Vaquero. Hazel eyes. Black eyes. Dark complexion. 6'2". Born in Sonora, Mexico. Enlisted January 30, 1864, at Los Angeles. Deserted December 22, 1864, at Drum Barracks.

Verdugo, Andrés. Private. Age 18. Laborer. Hazel eyes. Black hair. Dark complexion. 5'7". Born in Los Angeles. Enlisted February 1, 1864, at Los Angeles. Deserted July 9, 1864, at Drum Barracks.

Verdugo, Donaciano (Feliciano). Private. Age 19. Vaquero. Hazel eyes.

Black hair. Dark complexion. 5'5". Born in Los Angeles. Enlisted January 13, 1864, at Los Angeles. Accidentally shot November 19, 1864, at Wilmington.

‡Vernal, José Antonio. Private. Age 18. Vaquero. Hazel eyes. Black hair. Dark complexion. 5'7". Born in California. Enlisted February 1, 1864, at Los Angeles.

Villalobos, José de la Luz. Private. Age 45. Laborer. Hazel eyes. Black hair. Light complexion. Born in Sonora, Mexico. Enlisted February 15, 1864, at Los Angeles.

APPENDIX B

The Women of the Native Cavalry

That women in the Civil War era followed their husbands or lovers in the service, or otherwise attached themselves to the army, is fairly well known but too little discussed. In the case of the Native Cavalry, there are only a few fleeting mentions of these women in the official records, and they are often unnamed. This is a source of some frustration for the author who wants to give these individuals their due.

Given the heritage of the soldiers, it is tempting to compare these women to the *soldaderas* of the Mexican army. Though popular imagination most associates these camp followers with the Mexican Revolution of 1910, the term "soldadera" actually dates back to the French Intervention (1862–67). In addition, women had a long-established support role (and an occasional combat role) in the army.[1] In other parts of the Spanish-speaking world, including Chile, they had a more formalized role as uniformed *cantineras* who served a similar function. While there is no evidence that the Native Cavalry directly inherited these traditions, most of the men came from cultures where it was considered acceptable for women to be with the army.

At best, the nineteenth-century U.S. Army tolerated the presence of women, but their official role was limited. Regulations provided for up to four "washer-women" or "laundresses" per company. They were required to be of certified "good character" and were subject to army discipline for "gross misconduct, drunkenness or breech of camp etiquette." They were issued regular rations like the soldiers and were paid for their work by deductions from the men's monthly salaries. Usually, these women were married to soldiers in the company as a hedge against potential trouble. The regulations left much, including whether or not there would be laundresses at all, to the discretion of company commanders.

It is not clear if the Native Cavalry had a full complement of laundresses. The identities of only two of them are known.

The wife of farrier Hermenegildo Balderamos served as a laundress in Company B during its time in California and Arizona. Balderamos was injured during his service and was carried in an ambulance to Drum Barracks with Captain Pico when the company returned to California. The records do not indicate whether Mrs. Balderamos rode with her husband or followed with the company on foot.

The wife of Private Federico de la Noix of Company A accompanied Pico's men to the Humboldt District. In the spring of 1865, the soldier wrote to the commander at Benicia Barracks to complain that the captain was withholding some thirty-four dollars that his wife was owed for washing dating back to February 1864. This seems to have been the source of some tension in the company, and de la Noix was eventually transferred to Company B. He, and presumably his wife, stayed behind with a detachment in California when the battalion departed for Arizona.

A number of wives, common law and otherwise, accompanied their husbands in the service. Doubtless at least some of them were laundresses. Others may have followed the battalion simply to support their husbands. In some cases the women may have been motivated by the same poverty that drove the men to enlist, for they (and occasionally their children) simply had nowhere else to go.

⁂ ⁂ ⁂

Bertha Bennett (nee Ettinger), the wife of Saddler Sergeant Miguel Bennett, was employed by Assistant Surgeon Tolman as a hospital matron at Fort Mason. It is unclear if the couple's three children had accompanied them as well, though this seems likely.

Maria de Calderón, wife of Corporal José de Jesús Calderón of Company C, accompanied her husband to Arizona and served as a cook.

Norinda Campo, wife of Private Camilio Campo of Company D, gave birth to a daughter, Honoria Rosa, while she was with her husband in Arizona.

Clara Duarte lived in Wilmington while her husband, Corporal José Antonio Silvas of Company D, served at Drum Barracks. There is no record of whether or not she followed him to Arizona.

María Carmen Duarte followed her husband, Corporal José Victor Corona of Company D, to all of his duty stations, including Camp Cady and Fort Mason, where as she later reported, she "was subject to fear of dangers by the attacks of the hostile Indians." At Calabazas she treated her husband with "home remedies" when he fell ill with "stomach trouble." The corporal never fully recovered and died in Los Angeles in 1869. Mrs. Corona was the sister of Private Francisco Duarte of Company D, who was murdered at Fort Mason in October 1865. Her sister, Teresa, was the common-law wife of another Company D soldier, José María Corona, José Victor's brother, and she may also have followed the Native Cavalry to Arizona.

Marta Morales Gómez lived in a *jacal* just outside of the Drum Barracks property fence with her husband, Sergeant Francisco Gómez of Company D. She did not remain with the unit after her husband died in October 1864.

Francisca de la Concepción Valencia lived in a tent on the outskirts of Drum Barracks. In 1865 she gave birth to a child, Francisco, the son she had with Corporal Bernardino López of Company C. The corporal was married to another woman at the time.

* * *

This list should not be regarded as complete, for there were without doubt numerous other women who in one capacity or another shared the privations of the service with the men of the Native Cavalry.

APPENDIX C

The Chain of Command

In the Far West, Union forces retained a geographic organization like that of the antebellum army, being organized into "departments" subdivided into "districts." The Native Cavalry spent most of its term of service under the Department of the Pacific, which was headquartered in San Francisco and included the West Coast states as well as the territories of Arizona, Nevada, Utah, and Washington.

This department was divided into as many as six districts:

District of California: Headquartered at San Francisco. This comprised all of California outside of the Districts of Humboldt and Southern California.

District of Humboldt: Headquartered at Fort Humboldt. This comprised Del Norte, Humboldt, Klamath, Mendocino, Napa, Sonoma, and Trinity Counties.

District of Oregon: Headquartered at Fort Vancouver. This comprised Idaho and Washington Territories and the state of Oregon.

District of Southern California: Headquartered at Drum Barracks. This comprised Los Angeles, San Bernardino, San Diego, San Luis Obispo, Santa Barbara, and Tulare Counties. At this time San Bernardino County included what is now Riverside County and San Diego County extended to the Colorado River, so Fort Yuma and Fort Mojave (on the New Mexico/Arizona side of the river) were included within this district.

District of Utah: Headquartered at Camp Douglas. This comprised Nevada and Utah.

District of Arizona (Added in March 1865): Headquartered at Prescott. This comprised the Territory of Arizona.

This arrangement lasted through the end of the Civil War, during which time the four companies of Native Cavalry served in three districts: California, Humboldt, and Southern California.

In July 1865, with the rebellion defeated, the U.S. Army underwent a sweeping reorganization. Forces in the Far West were now gathered into the Division of the Pacific, under the command of Major General Henry Wager Halleck. The division was subdivided into two smaller departments: the Department of the Columbia, which covered Idaho, Oregon, and Washington, and the Department of California, which included Arizona, California, and Nevada and was commanded by Major General Irvin McDowell in San Francisco. The Territory of Arizona, plus Fort Yuma on the California side of the Colorado River, remained organized as a district under the command of Brigadier General John Mason in Prescott. As a part of this reorganization, the Native Cavalry was assembled as a battalion and transferred to the District of Arizona.

Organizational charts for the region in official correspondence at the time break down forces by posts rather than battalions or regiments, as larger units were generally distributed throughout a district or department by company. Thus, in practice, a battalion or regiment was solely a bureaucratic creature as each component company would report to its post commander, who was not necessarily an officer of its own regiment.

In the case of the Native Cavalry, for example, Major Vallejo at Drum Barracks was commander of the 1st Battalion, but his duties were largely administrative, the four companies being scattered about California and no practical way for him to oversee their day-to-day affairs. In December 1864, for example, Pico's Company A reported at Fort Wright to Captain Douglas, who reported to Colonel Whipple at district headquarters at Fort Humboldt, while Company B, posted to the Presidio, answered to a different district commander altogether. Companies C and D reported to yet another chain of command under the District of Southern California.

In the American army of the era, the term "battalion" did not have the formal meaning that it did in Europe or that it does in the modern U.S. Army. Instead, it simply meant a permanent organization smaller than a full ten-company regiment. The terms "troop" and "squadron" were not in official use for cavalry in the United States, as they were elsewhere, until after the Civil War.

The basic unit of cavalry was the company. A company consisted of a captain, a first lieutenant, a second lieutenant, a first sergeant, a quartermaster sergeant, a commissary sergeant, five sergeants, eight corporals, two teamsters, two farriers, one saddler, one wagoner, two buglers, and between eighty and one hundred soldiers. Because of recruiting difficulties (explained in previous chapters) as well as the nature of the volunteer service, only Company C of the four Native Cavalry companies had its full complement of noncommissioned officers and men upon mustering. Constant attrition assured that all of these companies remained well below strength, as only Company B continued recruitment after initial mustering.

"Field and staff" refers to the battalion-level officers. This would include a major, who commanded; an assistant surgeon ("surgeon" being a regimental-level position); and two first lieutenants, one as adjutant and the other as quartermaster. In the Native Cavalry neither of the latter two positions were filled, and company-level officers were detailed at various times for these duties.

APPENDIX D

Desertions in the Native Cavalry

Desertion is an unavoidable part of the story of the Native Cavalry. Most of the published writing about the battalion makes at least some mention of the unusually large number of soldiers who absconded, and a few notable incidents make it clear that addressing the problem was at least an occasional preoccupation. The topic deserves special attention and is handled separately here so that it does not dominate the main narrative.

An estimated 278,644 soldiers deserted from the Union army during the Civil War, about 14 percent of the total force. Among the California Volunteers, 1,855 men, or about 11 percent, deserted, a number that compares favorably not only to the rate during the war but also to that in the antebellum army. The Native Cavalry blemished this otherwise fine record, accounting for nearly a tenth of these despite the fact that the battalion accounted for less than 3 percent of Federal forces from California. In total, well over a third of the soldiers in the battalion deserted, some doing so multiple times.[1]

Some official records list desertions that are not shown in others. This, along with the battalion's notoriously inadequate recordkeeping and the possibility that some absent soldiers somehow returned in a timely manner, means that the numbers available to the modern historian likely underrepresent the reality. Nonetheless, they do give a good idea of the scale of the trouble.

Desertion rates varied considerably among the four companies, which is illustrated in the accompanying table. Company C experienced only a handful of desertions, while Companies A and B each suffered rates of well over 50 percent. These numbers fail to do justice to the full extent of the problem, however. With more than eighty desertions, Company B would have been reduced beyond effectiveness had not recruitment efforts continued through the spring of 1865. By this time its rolls had turned over almost completely, and one could say that it was an entirely new unit. Ironically, Company B's last recruits, four veteran soldiers who enlisted at Monterey, were themselves deserters from the French forces occupying Mexico.

Captain Pico's Company A, which had the longest and most geographically extensive service of the four companies, did not benefit as much from additional recruiting. As a consequence, losses suffered from illness and injury combined with some fifty desertions to diminish the command to near ineffectiveness. Only thirty-three of the eighty-eight men who assembled at the Presidio in 1863 were still with the company when it mustered out in March 1866. Finally, Company D suffered a substantial, though sustainable, number of desertions that would seem excessive in any other unit.

Generally, desertion seems to have been a crime of opportunity, for there is little indication of anything more than minimal planning in any of the cases. Nearly half of desertions occurred when the companies were on the move, presumably when any precautions were necessarily lax. Few soldiers deserted in groups, which indicates that men went "over the hill" because they were presented with a chance to do so rather than as the result of an intentional plan. Conversely, desertions in all four companies diminished after their posting to Fort Mason, perhaps because those inclined to do so had already left.

Officially, the maximum penalty for desertion in wartime, even so far from the principal seat of action, was death. In practice, however, such extreme punishment was rare. The punishment for soldiers who returned, or were returned, was largely financial, with the offender's pay being withheld to make up for lost time and equipment. This relative lenience was common throughout the army as a response to manpower needs and the concerns of sympathetic officers.

This policy of forgiveness seems to have been effective since a good number, if not most, of the errant soldiers came back to the service. Many returned of their own accord, and the provost guard in California was surprisingly effective at apprehending the remaining deserters.

Some soldiers took advantage of what amounted to amnesty only to desert again. One extreme case is Private Edward LeFebre, who was

Table D.1. Desertion Incidents by Month, 1863–1866

		Company				Total
		A	B	C	D	
1863	May	6	—	—	—	6
	June	0	—	—	—	0
	July	4	—	—	—	4
	August	0	—	—	—	0
	September	4	—	—	—	4
	October	5	—	—	—	5
	November	6	—	—	—	6
	December	0	—	—	—	0
	Total	25	—	—	—	25
1864	January	0	1	—	—	1
	February	1	1	—	—	2
	March	0	4	—	—	4
	April	0	12	—	—	12
	May	0	7	—	—	7
	June	0	1	—	4	5
	July	0	12	0	8	20
	August	0	2	0	0	2
	September	0	1	0	0	1
	October	0	4	0	2	6
	November	0	1	0	3	4
	December	0	0	1	5	6
	Total	1	46	1	22	70
1865	January	2	2	0	0	4
	February	0	0	0	1	1
	March	0	7	0	0	7
	April	11	0	0	0	11
	May	5	1	0	0	6
	June	0	0	1	0	1
	July	0	2	0	0	2
	August	6	19	0	3	28
	September	0	5	6	0	11
	October	0	1	0	0	1
	November	0	0	0	0	0
	December	0	1	0	1	2
	Total	24	38	7	5	74
1866	January–March	0	0	0	0	0
	Total	0	0	0	0	0
Total		**50**	**84**	**8**	**27**	**169**
Percentage		**56%**	**57%**	**8%**	**26%**	**38%**

Mission Camp, Arizona, Territory.
From Browne, "A Tour through Arizona," pt. 2.

among the volunteers recruited by Captain Legross in San Francisco in March 1864. After only a month in the service, he deserted from the Presidio along with two other francophone lancers. He was apprehended by authorities from Camp Union near Sacramento late that summer and placed in confinement for a time at the Presidio before being returned to duty. LeFebre again deserted in January 1865, this time with Bugler Gaston de la Mothe, while the company was posted at Camp Low. The two were arrested three days later at Monterey and returned to the service. LeFebre absconded a third and final time, along with three comrades, in August at Mission Camp, Arizona Territory, where the company was briefly bivouacked en route to Tubac. He never returned.

In some cases the official record inspires some interesting questions. Private Francisco Estrada of Company B, a nineteen-year-old Mexican-born laborer, deserted en route to Fort Mason in August 1865. He returned to his company at Fort Yuma as it passed through on the way back to California in February 1866, which leaves one to wonder where he was in the meantime. Arizona was largely undeveloped and presented few opportunities to live off the land. The small population clustered about reliable sources of water, so by their very nature, settled places, with the exception of a handful of remote mining camps, were well trafficked by the army and thus poor hideouts.

It is more likely that Estrada was among the men of Companies A and B who fled to Sonora, possibly one of those later held by the imperial garrison at Magdalena. If this was the case, he was the only captive whose fate after release is known. What is certain, however, is that many of the men who deserted, both Spanish speaking and otherwise, sought sanctuary in Mexico despite the turmoil there, both in Sonora and Baja California. Two brothers in Company B, Sergeants Bernard and Timothy Means, absented themselves from Fort Mason in late September 1865 and made it all the way to Guaymas, where they resided for a time before returning to the United States. But those who crossed the border were not entirely beyond the reach of the army. At least two forays into Mexico sought to recover deserters, though in both cases the flight of those pursued was aided by a lack of cooperation from Mexican officials.

For the Californio soldiers, their proximity to family and home may have provided both a means and a motive for leaving the ranks. The example of 1st Sergeant (soon to be Private) Benigo Pico of Company A, who went absent without leave while on detached service in order to get married in January 1864, is an extreme case, but the records show that a few soldiers deserted by overstaying furloughs, and it can be assumed that there were more. The potential for this problem was recognized as early as 1862 by Colonel James Henry Carleton, who argued against using volunteers raised in Southern California for service in Los Angeles County because of the discipline problems, particularly with regard to leave, that might emerge.[2]

In the 1920s historian Ella Lonn wrote what remains one of the few comprehensive studies of the phenomenon of desertion in the Civil War. In it she makes the bigoted but all-too-common assertion that Mexican American soldiers were simply ill suited for military service and especially prone to desertion. This casual dismissal fails to tell the whole story and, in the case of the Native Cavalry, ignores the fact that large numbers of non-Spanish-surnamed volunteers deserted as well. In fairness, however, there is evidence that ethnic strife played a role here. A group of French-speaking deserters from Company A who robbed a civilian residence during their flight from Fort Gaston in early 1864 claimed that their inability to speak Spanish led to discrimination and outright abuse from their comrades and officers. There are allusions to similar tensions in Company B as well.

More than anything, however, the "disease," as Lonn calls it, seems to have been a problem of leadership. It is significant that Companies A and B, which suffered the most desertions, were also the ones led by captains who faced accusations of financial and even physical abuse, corruption, and other bad behavior. Captain Legross, who commanded Company B for much of its service in California, was clearly inadequate for the job, and both he and Captain Pico seem to have been disliked by a significant faction of the enlisted men under their command. In contrast, Company C, led by a respected and well-known pillar of the community who took a personal interest in the well-being of his men, faced by far the fewest desertions of the four companies. Clearly with regard to desertions, the Native Cavalry is an example of the proverbial fish that rots from the head.

APPENDIX E

Lieutenant de la Guerra Pursues Deserters, December 1864

This document is an example of something that is unfortunately rare regarding the Native Cavalry, namely a written report. As has been mentioned, the neglect of documentation and correspondence by the battalion's officers was noted by contemporaries on more than one occasion.

This report details an effort to apprehend deserters in the rugged country south and east of Los Angeles, an area including the hinterlands of San Diego County and what later became Orange County. At the time the region was, while not wilderness, largely undeveloped and sparsely populated.

In early December 1864 Colonel Curtis ordered Lieutenant Santiago de la Guerra, a corporal, and two lancers to ride south toward San Diego in pursuit of deserters.[1] It is unclear what specifically prompted this mission, as desertions in the Native Cavalry had been a continuous problem for the unit's entire service at Drum Barracks, and the deserters named here had absconded months earlier. De la Guerra may have been ordered south to assist Lieutenant George Haycock of the 4th California Infantry, who was already in the field with a detachment pursuing deserters from both his own post of San Diego and Drum Barracks. Haycock received reports that the errant soldiers were in Baja California, perhaps as far south as Cabo San Lucas, so he crossed the border in an effort to arrest them and to recover horses they had stolen. While south of the line, Haycock reported some frustration with the reluctance of Mexican officials to hand over Spanish-speaking deserters from the Native Cavalry, regarded as fellow countrymen despite their U.S. uniforms, though they were eager to assist in the case of Anglo-American absconders.[2] This situation was echoed in some ways at Magdalena several months later.

The Californio lieutenant and his soldiers were in the field for a month, which seems to have been longer than some expected. In their absence a rumor started that they had been waylaid in the mountains and killed in a confrontation with secessionists. By the time this tale saw print in the press, however, the detachment had already returned to Drum Barracks.[3]

The following document is interesting for a few reasons. First, it tends to put the lie to Senator Hill's earlier criticism of Lieutenant de la Guerra as an illiterate who spoke little or no English. Both the physical report and the interactions with other officers described therein imply otherwise. Beyond this, the report provides insight into what was involved in this sort of rather routine and mundane mission.

> Persuant [*sic*] to Special Order No. 218, dated Head Quarters Drum Barracks Cal. Dec. 3rd 1864, left Drum Barracks at 3 o'clock A.M. of Dec. 4th in persuit [*sic*] of deserters and proceeded direct to San Juan [Capistrano] a distance of (57) fifty-seven miles, at which place we arrived between the hours of seven and eight P.M. After making enquiries I ascertained that the parties of which we were in persuit had pass[ed] through there five days previous en rout for San Diego.
>
> Left San Juan at 6 o'clock A.M. of December 5th and proceeded directly to the Rancho de las Flores, where I arrived at 12 o'clock A.M. having travelled a distance of (24) twenty four miles, at this place made further enquiries and learned that the parties of which we were in persuit were six days in advance, having fed and rested our horses, started at 3 o'clock P.M. for the mission of San Luis Rey, at which place we arrived between the hours of seven and eight P.M. having travelled a distance of (15) fifteen miles. Being informed at that place that a man living at the Rancho de San Pascual had passed through there with two men answering to the description of those of which we were in persuit left San Luis Rey at five o'clock A.M. of Dec. 5th "en route" for San Pascual, arrived at the Rancho Escondido between the hours of 6 and 7 P.M. having travelled a distance of (24) twenty four miles over a mountainous district and learning that forage for our horses could not be obtained until we should arrive at the Rancho de Santa Ysabel, remained there that night. Leaving the Rancho Escondido at six o'clock A.M. of December 7th proceeded direct to San Pascual at which place we arrived at nine o'clock A.M. having

San Diego, California.
From Bartlett, *Personal Narrative,* vol. 2.

travelled a distance of (8) eight miles, upon making enquiries at that place, I learned that a man by the name of Antonio Alvarado had purchased a saddle and bridal from one of the men of which we were in persuit [*sic*]. I immediately ordered his arrest, and questioned him as to where he had seen or heard of the parties from whom he had obtained said property.

He replied that if I would furnish him with a horse that he would conduct me to their place of concealment, I immediately ordered search to be made for horses, but there were none to be obtained at that Rancho.

The prisoner then informed me that he had a horse that would last as far as the Rancho de Santa Ysabel, where others might be procured.

I started immediately for that place "with the prisoner in charge" where I arrived about (8) o'clock P.M. having travelled a distance of twenty-four miles.

Upon my arrival I was informed that there were three deserters at that place. I succeeded in arresting one by the name of Teodocio Vuelna [*sic*],[4] who was recognized as belonging to Company "D" 1st Battalion Nat. Cav. But after diligent search I could not find no trace of the other two, they probably upon

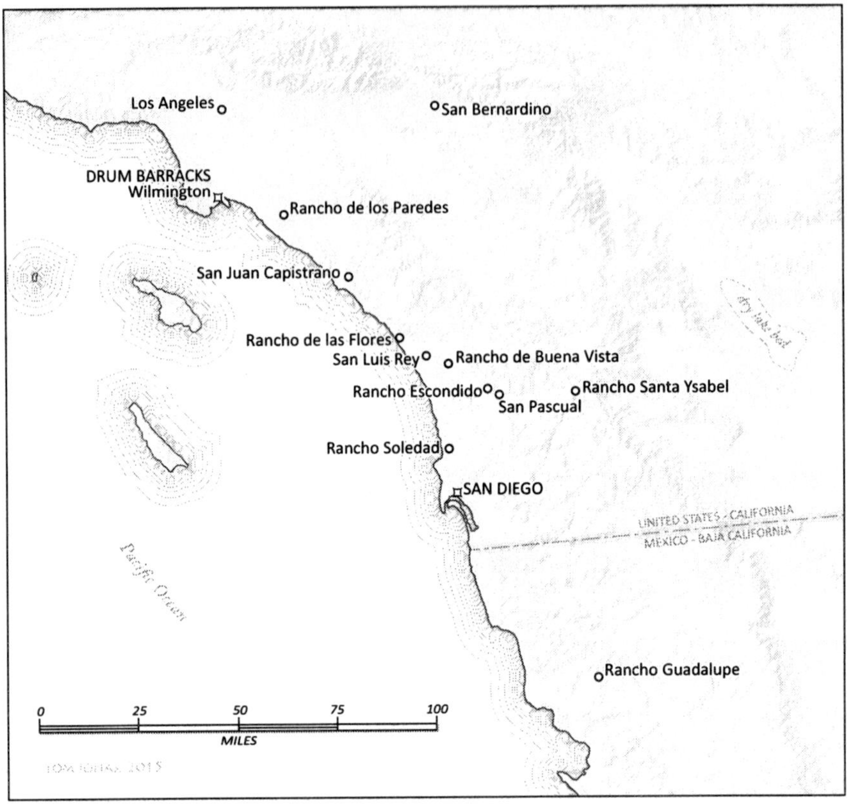

Lieutenant de la Guerra's mission in the
San Diego backcountry, December 1864–January 1865.
Map by Tom Jonas. Copyright © 2015 by the University of Oklahoma Press.

hearing of our arrival had concealed themselves somewhere in the neighborhood mountains.

Upon the following morning (Dec. 8th) I was informed that one of the men of which I was in persuit had been seen upon the road to Buena Vista,[5] for which place I immediately started when I arrived at (5) o'clock P.M. having travelled a distance of (15) fifteen miles, but could not learn nothing of the man of which I was in persuit.

While at this Rancho there arrived a Government Train under command of Captain Sherman[6] with whom I made arrangements to forward the man Vuelna to Drum Barracks.

I immediately returned to Santa Ysabel and upon the following morning (Dec. 9th) forwarded the prisoner to Buena Vista.

I concluded to remain at Santa Ysabel for the space of four or five days, in order to refresh the horses, which were completely done up.

Upon the 12th it commenced raining in which state the weather continued for two days, when it changed to snow, making it impossible for us to leave untill the (18th), upon which day we started for Rancho Escondido "en route for San Diego" when we arrived between the hours of six and seven P.M. having travelled a distance of (30) thirty miles.

Upon the following morning, Dec. 19th, left Rancho Escondido at (5) five O'clock A.M. and arrived at the camp of Capt. Grant [commander, San Diego][7] at (5) five o'clock P.M. having travelled a distance of thirty-six miles.

December 20th dispatched Private Ysidro Alta Mirano [*sic*], Co. "D" 1st Batt. N.C.C.V.[8] to the Rancho de Guadalupe[9] at which place Lieut. Haycock was encamped, to identify some deserters detained by that officer, he recognized two, one by the name of Andres Verdugo, Company "D" Nat Cav.[10] and one by the name of Ernest Bossart, Company ([?]) 4th Infty, C.V.[11] December 28th Lieut. Haycock arrived with the prisoners in charge.

Left camp Dec. 29th at (12) 12 o'clock A.M. prisoners en route for Drum Barracks, arrived at Rancho de Soledad at 5 o'clock P.M. having travelled a distance if sixteen miles.

Left Soledad at 7 o'clock A.M. of Dec. 30th and arrived at the Mission of San Luis Rey at 7 O'clock P.M. having travelled a distance of (36) thirty six miles. Left the Mission of San Luis Rey at (6) six o'clock A.M. of Dec. 31st and arrived at San Juan [Capistrano] at (6) six o'clock P.M. having travelled a distance of (36) thirty six miles.

January 1st 1865, remained in San Juan to refresh the horses, they being unable to proceed farther.

Left San Juan at (7) seven o'clock A.M. of January 2nd and arrived at the Rancho de los Paredes, having travelled a distance of (30) thirty-six miles.

Left Rancho de los Paredes at (7) seven o'clock A.M. of January 3rd and arrived at Drum Barracks at 12 o'clock A.M. having travelled a distance of (27) twenty seven miles.

I have the honor to be, sir, very respectfully,
your obedient servant,
Santiago de la Guerra
1st Lieut., Co. "D," 1st Batt,
Nat. Cav.

Notes

Abbreviations

AGC Adjutant General's Corrspondence, Military and National Guard Collection, California State Archives

CSR Compiled Service Records, Record Group 94, National Archives, Washington, D.C.

CWVR Civil War Volunteers Records, Military and National Guard Collection, California State Archives

NA National Archives, Washington, D.C.

OR U.S. War Department. *The War of Rebellion: A Compilation of the Official Records of the Union and Confederate Armies.* Ser. 1, vol. 50 (in 2 parts), *Operations on the Pacific Coast.* 1897.

RG Record Group

Introduction

1. Orton, *Records of California Men,* 304.
2. Pitt, *Decline of the Californios.*

Chapter 1

Epigraph. *Alta California,* June 10, 1863.

1. Pitt, *Decline of the Californios,* 52–53. Californios were entirely outnumbered after the arrival of over 100,000 migrants in 1849 alone. Pitt estimates that they were outnumbered by immigrants from other parts of Mexico by 1850.
2. Dana, *Two Years before the Mast,* 92.
3. Ibid., 92–93.
4. William Henry Brewer and Francis P. Farquhar, eds., *Up and Down California in 1860–1864: The Journal of William H. Brewer, Professor of Agriculture in the Sheffield Scientific School from 1864–1903* (New Haven, Conn.: Yale University

Press, 1930), 27, 157. Brewer served as the expedition's botanist and second in command. He does not seem to have minded Guirado's departure from the party as he was considered "by far the least valuable member of our crew." Ibid., 19.

5. Orton, *Records of California Men,* 98. Lieutenant Guirado commanded the detachment that first entered Tucson in June 1862. After three years of active service with the California Column in Arizona and New Mexico, he served on the staff of Brig. Gen. Joseph R. West in Arkansas as a lieutenant in the 11th Missouri Cavalry.
6. Pitt, *Decline of the Californios,* 229–30, 233–40.
7. For a good summary of the events of the French Intervention, particularly in relation to American foreign policy, see Miller, *Arms across the Border,* 5–8.
8. Hayes-Bautista and Chamberlin, "Cinco de Mayo's First Seventy-Five Years," 23–64.
9. Ibid.; *Alta California,* June 10, 1863.
10. Pacheco later served California as governor and represented the state in Congress. A complete account of his remarkable life and career can be found in Genini, *Romualdo Pacheco.*
11. *Sacramento Union,* Jan. 28, 1863.
12. Orton, *Records of California Men,* 304.
13. One of the few comprehensive studies of warfare in this era is Phelps, "On Comic Opera Revolutions," 44–63.
14. Thiele, "Some Notes on the Lance and Lancers," 31–37.
15. A Benicia Arsenal lance in the Arizona Historical Society collection in Tucson differs from the McClellan pattern described by Thomas Thiele in that the metalwork is entirely steel rather than a mix of brass and steel parts. See "Some Notes on the Lance and Lancers."
16. The Battle of San Pasqual occurred in California on December 6, 1846, in the hills thirty miles inland from San Diego. It is regarded as the only clear defeat the United States suffered at the hands of Mexican forces during the Mexican-American War (1846–48). For a detailed and colorful account, see Woodward, *Lances at San Pasqual.*
17. Phillips, *Chiefs and Challengers,* 113; Pitt, *Decline of the Californios,* 158–59, 169–70.
18. Orton, *Records of California Men,* 304.
19. Maj. William P. "Bill" Reynolds was purportedly the son of a Massachusetts merchant seaman and a Malaysian woman. He was born in the Philippines and educated in the United States. He arrived in California some years before the Mexican War when the Hawaiian merchant ship he was on shipwrecked near Redondo. In addition to his service in the state militia, he worked as a surveyor and was known as an authority regarding Spanish and Mexican land grants. He was described as having a "tremendous intellect" and a "trenchant

sense of humor." His interest in the Native Cavalry might be explained by his personal relationship with some of its officers, sympathies stemming from his own mixed-race heritage, or a desire for a commission in the new organization. See Bell, *On the Old West Coast,* 209–11.

20. McKittrick, "Salvador Vallejo," 309–31.
21. Salvador Vallejo, "Notas Historicas," 154. Despite the Spanish title, this memoir is largely written in awkward and flowery English. The work was dictated to an assistant of Hubert Howe Bancroft who may have translated it as well.
22. Rosenus, *General Vallejo,* 227.
23. Vallejo, "Notas Historicas," 155.

Chapter 2

Epigraph. Pico to Stanford, San Jose, Jan. 30, 1863, Box 6, AGC.

1. Though he was baptized José María de la Natividad y Reymundo Pico y Bernal, contemporary accounts and official records call him "José Ramón." He seems to have referred to himself this way as well, so this name is used here. J. R. Pico's grandfather and Andrés Pico's father were brothers born in Sonora who came to California as children with the Anza expedition in 1775. Modern English-language kinship conventions would call José Ramón the first cousin, once removed of Andrés. Contemporary accounts call Andrés the younger Pico's uncle, which was consistent with how Spanish-speaking people of the time would have referred to the relationship.
2. Alice B. Maloney, "Ranchero Cavalry," *Western Horseman* 8, no. 3 (May–June 1943): 18, 39–43.
3. *Alta California,* Oct. 7, Nov. 2, 1860; *Sacramento Union,* Oct. 22, 1860.
4. *Sacramento Union,* June 4, 1855, Jan. 14, 1859.
5. Pico to Stanford, San Jose, Jan. 2, 1863, Box 6, AGC.
6. Ibid.
7. *El Voz de Méjico,* Mar. 3, 1863. There were similar advertisements in English-language newspapers as well. See, for example, *Alta California,* Mar. 3, 1863. These were still appearing regularly as late as May.
8. *Alta California,* Mar. 11, 1863. The newspaper account reports that this speech was made in Spanish.
9. Ibid.
10. Pico to Stanford, May 12, 1863, San Jose; and Pico to Weeks, May 23, 1863, Box 6, AGC. An active and well-connected Republican, Pico lobbied Gov. Leland Stanford in person for additional funds.
11. A survey of the Civil War–era expansion of the Presidio can be found in Thompson and Woodbridge, *Special History Study: Presidio of San Francisco,* 21–28.
12. Various officers to Stanford, Oct. 10, 1863, Presidio of San Francisco, Box 6, AGC.

13. "Proceedings of a Court of Inquiry which Convened at Benicia Barracks, Calif.," Apr. 22, 1865, in CSR, Capt. José Ramón Pico (hereinafter referred to as "Court of Inquiry").
14. Pico to Drum, Feb. 29, 1864, Fort Gaston, in CSR, Capt. José Ramón Pico.
15. *Alta California*, July 6, 1863.
16. The gifts seem to have been counted against Ibarra's twenty-five-dollar enlistment bounty.
17. Initial Muster Roll, Co. A, 1st Battalion of Native Cavalry, CWVR.
18. Pico to Drum, Dec. 29, 1863, San Francisco, in CSR, 1st Lt. Crisanto Soto.
19. *San Francisco Bulletin*, July 8, 1865.
20. Pico to Stanford, May 12, 1863, San Jose, Box 6, AGC.
21. Various officers, Presidio of San Francisco, to Governor Stanford, Oct. 10, 1863, ibid.
22. "Court of Inquiry."
23. Ibid.
24. Ibid.
25. Ibid.
26. Marchande to Purdy, Dec. 2, 1863, San Francisco, in CSR, Capt. José Ramón Pico.
27. Ibid.; Pico to Drum, Dec. 8, 1863, Presidio of San Francisco, ibid.
28. Marchande to Drum, Dec. 9, 1863, San Francisco, ibid. "Jeremy Diddler" was the name of a character in *Raising the Wind*, an 1803 farce by James Kenny. The name had become a popular slang term to refer to a swindler or con man and remained so throughout the nineteenth century.
29. Steel to Purdy, Dec. 12, 1863, San Francisco, ibid.
30. Orton, *Records of California Men*, 307–10.

Chapter 3

Epigraph. "Proceedings of a Court of Inquiry which Convened at Benicia Barracks, Calif.," Apr. 22, 1865 in CSR, Capt. José Ramón Pico (hereinafter referred to as "Court of Inquiry").

1. Special Orders 286, Headquarters, Department of the Pacific, Dec. 26, 1863, *OR*, 50(2):709. A good summary of this conflict is in Nelson, *Our Home Forever*, 78–91.
2. Brinckerhoff, "Last of the Lancers."
3. *Alta California*, Jan. 3, 1864.
4. *Humboldt Times*, Jan. 9, 23, 1864. The 1st Battalion of Mountaineers was composed of six companies raised between May 1863 and February 1864 in the northern counties as a part of California's authorized Federal quota. Because so many local settlers were at best ambivalent toward the Union cause, they were recruited with the understanding that they were not to serve outside of

the state and would be mustered out at the end of hostilities in the region. They were armed, equipped, and uniformed as other California Volunteer infantry. Orton, *Records of California Men,* 826–31.

5. Lippitt to Drum, Apr. 21, 1864, Fort Humboldt, Calif., OR, 50(1):1026–28.
6. *Humboldt Times,* Feb. 6, 13, 1864; Whipple to Drum, Jan. 29, 1864, Fort Gaston, OR, 50(1):243. Alternate spellings of Tseweñaldiñ include "Ceonaltin" and "Seranaltin."
7. *San Jose Patriot,* Oct. 26, 1864.
8. The detachment may have been posted to Redwood Ranch near Camp Anderson, a site on Redwood Creek recently ordered to be reoccupied by a detachment of the mountaineers from Fort Gaston. Bledsoe, *Indian Wars of the North-West,* 434–35.
9. Eglize, Le Blond, and Querloy to McDowell, Dec. 1, 1864, Fort Alcatraz, RG 94, NA. Pvts. Michael Eglize, Henry Le Blond, and Pierre Querloy deserted from Fort Gaston in February 1864, making off with a horse and robbing a civilian home in the process. They were quickly recaptured and eventually allowed to rejoin the company, though Eglize and Le Blond later deserted again. *Sacramento Union,* Feb. 26, 1864; "Court of Inquiry"; Orton, *Records of California Men,* 307–309.
10. Whipple to Ulio, Feb. 20, 1864, Fort Gaston, OR, 50(2):762–63. Whipple was elected to represent Humboldt County in the California State House and was granted leave to attend the legislative session at Sacramento.
11. Special Order 13, Mar. 6, 1864, Fort Gaston, ibid., 781.
12. Nelson, *Our Home Forever,* 86–88.
13. "Court of Inquiry."
14. Ibid.
15. *Humboldt Times,* Oct. 15, 1864.
16. *San Jose Patriot,* Oct. 26, 1864.
17. Douglas to Drum, Aug. 18, 1864, Fort Wright, OR, 50(2):950–51.
18. Tassin, "Chronicles of Camp Wright," 24–32.
19. *San Jose Patriot,* Oct. 26, 1864.
20. "Court of Inquiry."
21. Pico to Whipple, Dec. 10, 1864, Cahto, Calif., in CSR, Capt. José Ramón Pico.
22. "Court of Inquiry."
23. Ibid.
24. Ibid.
25. Ibid. The Native Cavalry's Sharps carbines used a .52-caliber cartridge, while the Springfield rifles issued to the infantry fired a .58-caliber ball, thus ammunition could not be shared between the companies at Camp Wright.
26. Ibid.
27. Pico to Drum, Feb. 15, 1865, Fort Wright; Pico to Drum, Mar. 24, 1865; and Pico to McDowell, Mar. 28, 1865, in CSR, Capt. José Ramón Pico.

28. *Sacramento Union,* Feb. 27, 1865.
29. Ibid., Apr. 10, 1865.
30. Ibid., Apr. 18, 1865.
31. Ibid., Apr. 25, 27, 1865.
32. Ibid. *Alta California,* Apr. 25, 1865; The prisoners were later transferred to Alcatraz Island, where they awaited trial for treason, which carried a maximum penalty of death. Under the terms of an order from General McDowell, they were pardoned in exchange for agreeing to take an oath of loyalty to the United States. The bad blood in Green Valley continued, however, and as late as September there was a "shooting affray" arising from apparent retaliation against a resident who had reported the activities of local secessionists to officers at Benicia. *Sacramento Union,* June 19, Sept. 7, 1865.
33. Orton, *Records of California Men,* 305.
34. "Court of Inquiry."
35. Ibid.; *Sacramento Union,* May 1, 1865.
36. "Court of Inquiry."

Chapter 4

Epigraph. *Pajaro Times* (Watsonville, Calif.), Apr. 1, 1865.

1. Orton, *Records of California Men,* 310–14.
2. *San Jose Patriot,* Jan. 18, 1865.
3. Pico to Stanford, Sept. 9, 1863, Box 6, AGC.
4. Statement of George H. Ringgold, Feb. 1, 1864, in CSR, Capt. Ernest H. Legross.
5. Vallejo to Mason, Jan. 18, 1864, ibid. Fitch was a nephew of Major Vallejo's wife. He does not seem to have been related to Capt. Joseph Ives Fitch, an officer in the 4th California Infantry.
6. *San Jose Patriot,* Jan. 18, 1865. The Chasseurs d'Afrique were a French corps of light cavalry composed of native African soldiers commanded by European officers. Several of these units served with the French expeditionary forces supporting Maximilian, and there is evidence to suggest that some of the "veterans" who enlisted in the Native Cavalry and other California units had deserted from the "Mexican adventure."
7. Unger had served with Company D, 2nd California Cavalry at Camp Babbitt at Visalia, California. He was dismissed from the service by court-martial on January 21, 1864, after being implicated in a fraud scheme that also resulted in the removal of all three of the company's commissioned officers. *Sacramento Daily Union,* Feb. 9, 1864.
8. "Proceedings of a general court-martial held at Camp Low, San Juan, Cal. Pursuant to Brigade S.O. No. 19 dated Brigade Hd. Qrs. Dist of Cal. Sacramento, Feby 7th, 1865," in CSR, Capt. Ernest Hypolite Legross (hereinafter cited as Legross court-martial).

9. *San Jose Patriot,* Jan. 18, 1865.
10. Thompson and Woodbridge, *Special History Study: Presidio of San Francisco,* 21–23.
11. Ibid.
12. Muster rolls, June 30–Aug. 31, 1864, Co. B, 1st Battalion of Native Cavalry, CWVR.
13. Soennichsen, *Miwoks to Missiles,* 39–51. Established in September 1863, Camp Reynolds was named for Maj. Gen. John Reynolds, who was killed by a Rebel sharpshooter during the Battle of Gettysburg two months earlier.
14. Muster rolls, Co. B, CWVR. A newspaper report about a deserter gives some insight into how the soldiers might have absconded from Angel Island. "John Jackson, the soldier of the Third Artillery who has been in the habit of swimming from Angel Island across Raccoon Straits and back, nightly, for his whiskey, was picked up by a sloop this morning, chilled through, and died a few minutes after." *Sacramento Union,* Feb. 22, 1865.
15. Legross to Mason, Feb. 15, 1864, San Francisco, Box 7, AGC.
16. *Alta California,* July 13, 1864.
17. CSR, Zebina N. Streeter.
18. Muster rolls, Co. B, CWVR; *Los Angeles Times,* May 22, 1904.
19. *San Jose Patriot,* Jan. 18, 1865.
20. Ibid.
21. Legross court-martial.
22. Special Order 246, Department of the Pacific, Nov. 12, 1864, *OR,* 50(2):1155–56.
23. *San Jose Patriot,* Jan. 18, 1865.
24. Wright to Low, Dec. 14, 1864, Sacramento, Box 8, AGC.
25. Secrest, *Lawmen and Desperadoes,* 173–76, 215–18.
26. Wright to Low, Dec. 14, 1864, Sacramento, Box 8, AGC; *Monterey Gazette,* Jan. 20, 1865.
27. O'Brien to Low, Feb. 1, 1865, Box 8, AGC.
28. *Pajaro Times* (Watsonville, Calif.), Jan. 14, 1865.
29. Ibid., Jan. 14, Apr. 1, 1865; Mylar, *Early Days at the Mission San Juan Bautista,* 118–19.
30. *Pajaro Times* (Watsonville, Calif.), Feb. 25, Oct. 28, 1865; General Order 21, Department of California, Oct. 19, 1865, Bound Records, 1st Battalion of Native Cavalry, CWVR. The company was in Arizona, with Perras in confinement there, while he was tried in absentia at Camp Low. He apparently escaped confinement shortly after learning that he was sentenced to death, the records listing him as having "deserted" in December 1865.
31. Mylar, *Early Days at the Mission San Juan Bautista,* 119.
32. *Alta California,* Jan. 24, 1865.
33. O'Brien to Low, Feb. 1, 1865, Box 8, AGC.
34. CSR, Capt. Ernest H. Legross.
35. *Alta California,* Jan. 24, 1865; muster rolls, Co. B, CWVR. The Presidio of

Monterey was established during Spanish rule in 1770 and remained an active military post for Mexico and then the United States until it was abandoned in 1856. After reoccupation during the Civil War, it was again abandoned in 1866 but remained a military reservation until the post was reestablished in 1902.

36. *Sacramento Union,* Mar. 18, 1865.
37. Angustias and her brothers feuded bitterly over her inheritance after the death of their father, Don José Antonio Julián de la Guerra y Noriega, in 1858. It is not clear if this affected Porfirio's relationship with his uncle Antonio during their service together in the Native Cavalry. Pubols, *Father of All,* 292–93.
38. Ibid.; Bancroft, *Works,* 692. Dr. Ord was the brother of Edward O. C. Ord, an army officer who had also served in California and would rise to the rank of major general during the Civil War.
39. Bancroft, *Works,* 692; Sherman to de la Guerra, Dec. 15, 1856, De la Guerra Archives, Mission Santa Barbara, Calif. Sherman and both Ord brothers had been boarders and close acquaintances of Angustias during their service in California. Pubols, *Father of All,* 262. Sherman's subsequent military career is sufficiently well known that it does not need to be recounted here. His involvement with the younger Jimeno's education happened largely during his civilian career as a bank manager in San Francisco (1853–58).
40. Altschuler, *Cavalry Yellow and Infantry Blue,* 178–79.
41. Jimeno to de la Guerra, Oct. 18, 1864, Jimeno File, De la Guerra Archives, Mission Santa Barbara, Calif. (translated from Spanish).
42. *Alta California,* Apr. 12, 13, 1865.
43. Ibid., May 16, 1865; Secrest, *Lawmen and Desperadoes,* 176, 217. Mason and Henry separated because of an argument over a woman sometime around August 1865. Henry was killed in a shootout with a sheriff's posse of civilians and soldiers near San Bernardino the following month. Mason was killed by a potential recruit at Tejon Canyon as he tried to organize a new gang in April 1866.
44. Thrapp, *Encyclopedia of Frontier Biography,* 342–43. Karl Friedrich Hieronymus, Freiherr von Munchhausen, was an eighteenth-century German nobleman and cavalry officer known for his tall tales and exaggerated accounts of his exploits. *The Surprising Adventures of Baron Munchausen,* a satirical and embellished account by Rudolf Erich Raspe, a contemporary of the baron, was still in print and remained popular through Cremony's time. In fairness Cremony's exaggerations pale before those attributed to Munchausen, though his first-person accounts are often regarded with some skepticism by historians.
45. *Pajaro Times* (Watsonville, Calif.), Apr. 29, 1865.
46. *Alta California,* May 14, 1865; *Monterey (Calif.) Gazette,* June 9, 1865; Mylar, *Early Days at the Mission San Juan Bautista,* 119. The *Sacramento Union* reported on April 27, 1865, that thirty persons were being held by the provost marshal in San Francisco "for using expressions of joy at the assassination of President Lincoln."

Chapter 5

Epigraph. *Los Angeles Times,* Dec. 20, 1940.

1. Wright to Stanford, Mar. 2, 1863, Box 6, AGC; Pitt, *Decline of the Californios,* 244–47.
2. Streeter, "Recollections," 157–59. Born in Spain in 1779, the elder de la Guerra arrived in California in 1793, when he was posted to the Presidio of San Diego as a cadet. He was assigned to the Presidio of Santa Barbara in 1815 and served there through Mexican independence, becoming commander in 1827. By the time he retired to civilian life in 1842, he was the leading citizen of the community, having served a term in the Mexican Congress and commanding a ranching empire of more than half a million acres.
3. *Los Angeles Times,* June 23, 1913.
4. Muster and descriptive roll, Co. C, 1st Battalion of Native Cavalry, Box 6, AGC; Vallejo to Low, Nov. 2, 1864, Box 8, AGC.
5. Pablo de la Guerra to Low, May 26, 1864; and Still to Low, May 27, 1864, Box 7, AGC. As late as November 1864, Captain de la Guerra was still trying to get reimbursed for the expenses he incurred maintaining the recruits. See Vallejo to Low, Oct. 29, Nov. 2, 1864, Box 8, AGC. Giussepe "José" Lobero was an Italian immigrant who opened his saloon early in 1864. Eventually, his enterprise moved and expanded to become the Lobero Theater.
6. Hill to Kibbe, May 16, 1864, Box 7, AGC.
7. Pablo de la Guerra to Low, May 26, 1864, ibid.
8. Streeter, "Recollections," 169.
9. Hill to Low, Apr. 24, 1864, Box 7, AGC. Hill and Jimeno had a longstanding association, having attended school together while on the East Coast.
10. Frost, Huse, and Sturgeon to McDowell, Nov. 17, 1865, Santa Barbara, De la Guerra Archives, Mission Santa Barbara, Calif.
11. Muster and descriptive roll, Co. C, Box 6, AGC.
12. *Alta California,* Sept. 11, 1864.
13. Hill and Parks, *Santa Barbara Tierra Adorada,* 66.
14. Ibid.
15. *Alta California,* Sept. 11, 1864.

Chapter 6

Epigraph. Curtis, endorsement on Vallejo to Drum, Apr. 1, 1864, Box 7, AGC.

1. For more background, see Robinson, *Los Angeles in Civil War Days.*
2. Ibid., 55, 127.
3. Scammell, "Military Units in Southern California," 229–49.
4. Ibid.
5. Sanchez to Mason, Sept. 9, 1864, Box 7, AGC.
6. Still to Low, May 27, 1864, ibid.
7. Sanchez to Mason, Sept. 9, 1864, ibid.

8. Muster rolls, Co. D, 1st Battalion of Native Cavalry, CWVR. Still et al. to Curtis, Mar. 1, 1864, Box 7, AGC.
9. Muster rolls, Co. D, CWVR.
10. Jimeno to de la Guerra, Oct. 9, 1864; and Jimeno to de la Guerra, Oct. 27, 1864, Jimeno File, De la Guerra Archives, Mission Santa Barbara, Calif. (translated from Spanish).
11. Reynolds to Low, Mar. 28, 1864, Box 7, AGC; Robinson, *Los Angeles in Civil War Days,* 156.
12. Hunt, *Army of the Pacific,* 44; Reynolds to Low, Mar. 28, 1864, Box 7, AGC.
13. Vallejo to Drum, Jan. 16, 1865, in CSR, Maj. Salvador Vallejo.
14. Curtis to Drum, Jan. 17, 1865, Drum Barracks, in ibid.
15. Reynolds to Low, June 9, 1864, Box 7, AGC; Sanchez to McDowell, Jan. 12, 1865, in CSR, Maj. Salvador Vallejo.
16. Curtis to Low, July 2, 1864, Box 7, AGC.
17. Because of the similarity of their names, some sources confuse Francisco with his brother, José Juan Francisco de Jesús Guirado, who was a lieutenant in the 1st California Cavalry. At the time Company D was posted at Drum Barracks, José Guirado was serving on the staff of Brig. Gen. Joseph R. West in Arkansas as a lieutenant in the 11th Missouri Cavalry.

Chapter 7

Epigraph 1. *Alta California,* Nov. 28, 1864. This may refer to Pvt. Feliciano Verdugo of Company D, a nineteen-year-old Californio vaquero who is shown on official rolls as having been "shot by accident in the town of Wilmington 19 Nov 1864."

Epigraph 2. Lee to de la Guerra, May 21, 1865, in CSR, Antonio Maria de la Guerra.

1. Curtis to Drum, Nov. 13, 1864, Box 7, AGC.
2. Drum to Curtis, Dec. 18, 1864, ibid.
3. *Alta California,* Aug. 23, 1864.
4. Drum to Low, Sept. 7, 1864, Box 7, AGC.
5. Curtis to Drum, Aug. 4, 1864, Drum Barracks, *OR,* 50(2):927. See also Robinson, *Los Angeles in Civil War Days,* 153.
6. Curtis to Drum, Aug. 4, 1864, Drum Barracks, *OR,* 50(2):927.
7. Special Order 65, District of Southern California, Oct. 30, 1864, ibid., 1035–36.
8. Special Order 67, District of Southern California, Nov. 5, 1864, ibid., 1047.
9. Drum to Low, June 9, Sept. 8, 1864, Box 7, AGC.
10. *Sacramento Union,* Dec. 22, 1864.
11. Rouse, "Civil War Volunteers," 58.
12. *Los Angeles News,* Feb. 25, 1865; Jimeno to de la Guerra, Feb. 23, 1865, De la Guerra Collection, Santa Barbara Mission Archives.
13. Casebier, *Mojave Road,* 131–40.

14. Drum to Curtis, Apr. 21, 1864, *OR*, 50(2):823.
15. Jimeno to de la Guerra, Oct. 27, 1864, Jimeno File, De la Guerra Archives, Mission Santa Barbara, Calif.
16. Monthly returns, Feb. 1865, in CSR, Santiago de la Guerra; Curtis to Drum, Mar. 2, 1865, Drum Barracks, *OR*, 50(2):1150–51.
17. Coues, *On the Trail of a Spanish Pioneer,* 242n16. Bale's company was housed in seven Sibley tents per Special Order 17, District of Southern California.
18. Lee to Bale, Mar. 3, 1865, Drum Barracks, *OR*, 50(2):1153.
19. The local newspaper reported the death of a soldier of the 4th California Infantry, who had been ill for two months due to heat stroke suffered while serving at Camp Cady. *Wilmington (Calif.) Journal,* Mar. 25, 1865. While there is no evidence that any soldier of the Native Cavalry was similarly struck, this speaks to the sort of conditions the men had to face on the Mojave River.
20. Order 5, Camp Cady, Bound Records, 1st Battalion of Native Cavalry, CWVR. Bitter Springs was a campsite located approximately eighteen miles north of Camp Cady along the route to Salt Lake City, which joined the Mojave Road at a place known as Road Forks nine and a half miles west of the post.
21. Though Carmen Duarte, wife of Cpl. José Victor Corona, later reported that her husband, who she accompanied to Camp Cady, participated in a "battle" against "California Indians," there are no official records of such a skirmish during Company D's service there. Pension File, Joseph V. Corona, RG 94, NA.
22. *U.S. v. Rodney Stetson, Co. H, 4th Inf.,* Civil War General Court-Martial Case File MM2342, RG 153, Records of the Office of Judge Advocate General (Army), NA.
23. Bugler Soto, a native of Santa Barbara, enlisted in July 1864 as a twenty-three-year-old ranchero.
24. Despite his last name, Private Robinson was a Californio and a member of the de la Guerra family. At enlistment he identified himself as a thirty-six-year-old farrier from Santa Barbara. Private Bermudez (also spelled "Vermudez") was a twenty-seven-year-old native of Santa Barbara who listed his occupation as ranchero.
25. *U.S. v. Rodney Stetson;* Pension File, Pvt. Ysmael Soto, RG 94, NA.
26. General Orders 24, Department of California, Nov. 22, 1865, in *U.S. v. Rodney Stetson.* Stetson was apparently an ongoing discipline problem. On this occasion he had absconded from the post to avoid fatigue duty and stabbed a fellow soldier in the process. The sentence specified the size of the ball each was to wear, with Stetson's weighing twelve pounds and Shearer's weighing twenty-four.
27. *Los Angeles Times,* Dec. 20, 1940.
28. Robinson, *Los Angeles in Civil War Days,* 159.
29. *Los Angeles Times,* Dec. 20, 1940.
30. *Wilmington (Calif.) Journal,* Apr. 15, 1865.

31. Curtis to Drum, Apr. 16, 1865, Drum Barracks, *OR*, 50(2):1197. On April 24, 1865, the *Sacramento Union* reported rumors of "trouble in San Bernardino," including a skirmish between "guerillas and a small detachments of troops." This is not corroborated by other sources.
32. *Wilmington (Calif.) Journal*, Apr. 15, 2011; Robinson, *Los Angeles in Civil War Days*, 161.

Chapter 8

Epigraph. Cremony, "Santa Cruz," 337.

1. *Sacramento Union*, Apr. 21, 1865.
2. *Alta California*, Apr. 12, 1865. These men disembarked at Drum Barracks and remained behind, having been replaced by a detachment from the 1st California Cavalry, as General Mason continued on to Arizona. They rejoined Company B when the latter arrived at Drum Barracks.
3. Mason to Drum, Feb. 24, 1865, San Francisco, *OR*, 50(2):1142–43.
4. *Sacramento Union*, Mar. 18, 1865.
5. Curtis to Drum, Jan. 17, 1865, Drum Barracks, in CSR, Maj. Salvador Vallejo.
6. Lee to Vallejo, Feb. 1, 1865, Drum Barracks; Vallejo to Curtis, Feb. 2, 1865, Drum Barracks; and de la Guerra to Lee, Feb. 3, 1865, Drum Barracks, ibid.
7. Vallejo, "Notas Historicas," 155.
8. Orton, *Records of California Men*, 307.
9. Ibid. As a battalion rather than a full regiment, the Native Cavalry's "field and staff" consisted of only two officers: the major commanding and an assistant surgeon. The assistant surgeon was equivalent to a first lieutenant but could be promoted to captain, whereas a surgeon was equivalent to a major. Two other positions, adjutant (first lieutenant) and quartermaster (first lieutenant), were never filled, though Lieutenants Codington and Lafferty, respectively, would act in these battalion-level capacities later.
10. Gelcich to Drum, Apr. 28, 1865, Drum Barracks, in CSR, Vincent Gelcich. Gelcich married María Petra Celestina Pico y Bernal, Captain Pico's sister, at Santa Clara on December 19, 1863.
11. *Wilmington (Calif.) Journal*, May 27, 1865.
12. Bale to Curtis, Apr. 30, 1865, Drum Barracks, in CSR, Capt. Edward Bale.
13. *San Jose Patriot*, May 31, 1865. This park later became the site of San Jose State University.
14. Soto to Drum, May 29, 1865, San Jose, in CSR, 1st Lt. Crisanto Soto.
15. *Wilmington (Calif.) Journal*, June 10, 1865.
16. *Monterey (Calif.) Gazette*, June 9, 1865; Mylar, *Early Days at the Mission San Juan Bautista*, 119.
17. *Monterey (Calif.) Gazette*, June 16, 1865; *San Francisco Bulletin*, July 8, 1865.
18. *Alta California*, Apr. 24, 1865.

19. *Wilmington (Calif.) Journal,* July 1, 1865.
20. Ibid., July 8, 1865.
21. *San Francisco Bulletin,* July 8, 11, 1865. The town of San Buenaventura is now commonly called Ventura.
22. *Alta California,* July 15, 1865; *Wilmington (Calif.) Journal,* July 15, 1865.

Chapter 9

Epigraph. Jimeno to de la Guerra, Aug. 3, 1865, Fort Yuma, Calif., De la Guerra Collection, Santa Barbara Mission Archives. The Spanish portion of this quote translates, "We have had a lovely trip from Drum Barracks to this place." The remainder of the quote was written in English as shown.

1. *Los Angeles Tri-Weekly News,* Oct. 24, 1865.
2. Ibid.
3. Muster rolls, Co. D, 1st Battalion of Native Cavalry, CWVR. Robarts seems to have been what historian Leonard Pitt refers to as a "Mexicanized Gringo." See Pitt, *Decline of the Californios,* 19.
4. *Los Angeles Tri-Weekly News,* Oct. 24, 1865.
5. *San Francisco Bulletin,* July 8, 1865.
6. *Wilmington (Calif.) Journal,* July 29, 1865.
7. *Los Angeles Tri-Weekly News,* Oct. 24, 1865; *Wilmington (Calif.) Journal,* Aug. 5, 1865. The teamster was identified as "Mr. Hollister, who was formerly engaged as a baker in Wilmington." The Overland Trail crossed the international border at present-day Calexico, reentering the United States near the modern community of Vicente Guerrero (Algonones). Two campsites along the route, Alamo Mocho and Cooke's Wells, were in Baja California and had been well-known landmarks since the Mexican-American War. See Tom Jonas, "Wells in the Desert: Retracing the Mexican War Trails of Kearny and Cooke through Baja California," *Journal of Arizona History* 50, no. 3 (Autumn 2009): 269–96.
8. Jimeno to de la Guerra, Aug. 3, 1865, Fort Yuma, Calif., De la Guerra Collection, Santa Barbara Mission Archives. This particular letter was written largely in English. The last line translates, "It is impossible to give a description of this place." Established at the edge of the Colorado Desert, Carrizo Creek Station was the last reliable water source until Cooke's Wells. Marcy, *Prairie Traveler,* 292.
9. *Wilmington (Calif.) Journal,* Aug. 5, 1865.
10. *Los Angeles Tri-Weekly News,* Oct. 24, 1865.
11. Ibid.
12. Ibid.
13. Ibid.
14. Ibid.

15. Ibid., Sept. 30, 1865. The awkward Spanish translates into equally awkward English: "Notice—The Cavalry Company of Native Californians of Los Angeles Arrived at this place on 4 September, 1865, and leaves tomorrow, the 5th for Calabazas on the border. The men of the company Send blessings to their family and friends in Los Angeles. All goes well."
16. Ibid., Oct. 24, 1865.

Chapter 10

Epigraph. Jimeno to de la Guerra, Oct. 30, 1865, Fort Mason, Ariz., De la Guerra Collection, Santa Barbara Mission Archives. The quote translates into English as, "This is a sad country, ugly and almost without civilized people."

1. Fontana, *Calabazas of the Rio Rico.*
2. Reid, *Reid's Tramp,* 187–88.
3. Ibid.; Mason to Drum, June 18, 1865, Tubac, *OR,* 50(2):1261–63.
4. Hunt, *Army of the Pacific,* 142–44. The 7th California Infantry was organized in early 1865, and recruits were largely miners from the Sierra Nevadas. The regimental flag, which had been carried to California around Cape Horn by the 7th New York Volunteers during the Mexican-American War, flew over the post's parade ground.
5. Underhill, "History of the First Arizona Volunteer Infantry," 20–25.
6. *Sacramento Union,* Oct. 19, 1865; muster rolls, Co. D, CWVR.
7. Thomas Edwin Farish, *History of Arizona,* 8 vols. (Filmer Brothers: San Francisco, 1916), 4:99–110.
8. Jimeno to de la Guerra, Fort Mason, Oct. 30, 1865, De la Guerra Collection, Santa Barbara Mission Archives. Here, Jimeno's Spanish translates awkwardly into English. The last sentence reads "Deberas hasta rabia da," a Spanish colloquialism that literally translates as "Truly, it gives one rabies."
9. *Sacramento Union,* Oct. 19, 1865; *San Francisco Bulletin,* Oct. 23, 1865.
10. *Sacramento Union,* Oct. 19, 1865.
11. Ibid.; *San Francisco Bulletin,* Oct. 23, 1865. José Moreno Bustamante was prefect of the Department of "Arizona," which included much of northern Sonora, under the imperial government. In 1857 he held a similar post at Caborca, where he commanded the forces that defeated and executed a band of American filibusters commanded by former California state senator Henry Crabb. Having fought in several battles, he fled across the northern border after Maximilian was defeated. Bustamante was killed in a skirmish in 1867 after he returned to Sonora with a band of partisans to fight the new order. Almada, *Diccionario de Historia,* 489–90.
12. *San Francisco Bulletin*, Oct. 13, 1865.
13. Ibid.
14. Ibid.

15. Ibid.; *Los Angeles Tri-Weekly News,* Oct. 24, 1865.
16. *Sacramento Union,* Oct. 19, 1865. Contemporary writers often referred to all imperialist forces as "French" even in Sonora, where the bulk of the men fighting for the empire were Mexican. French regulars apparently never ventured north of Ures.
17. Ibid.
18. Post returns, Fort Mason, Records from U.S. Military Posts, 1800–1916, RG 94, M617, Roll 1524, NA; Pension File, Capt. José Ramón Pico, RG 94, NA (hereafter cited as Post returns, Fort Mason).
19. *Los Angeles Tri-Weekly News,* Oct. 24, 1865; Ronstadt, *Borderman,* 4–5. Later the patriarch of a prominent family in Tucson, Arizona, Frederick Augustus Ronstadt was a German engineer born in Hanover in 1816. He immigrated to North America to flee a new regime in his homeland, arriving in Sonora by the early 1850s. He became an officer in the state's national guard in 1858. After the overthrow of Maximilian, Ronstadt continued to serve Sonora in various military and civil capacities until 1874, when he went into the mining business there and in Baja California. In 1886 he joined his family in Tucson, where he died in 1889.
20. *Los Angeles Tri-Weekly News,* Oct. 24, 1865; Ronstadt, *Borderman,* 4–5. Many sources place Pesquiera's party at Tubac, but it is clear from contemporary accounts that he remained at Calabazas during his exile. A native of Sonora, Pesquiera used his popularity as a military hero to become governor in 1856, being in and out of that office until 1875. Characterized as moody, he was criticized for a dictatorial approach to governing that tended to run counter to his reform-minded liberal sentiments. See Acuña, *Sonoran Strongman.*
21. *San Francisco Bulletin,* Oct. 23, 1865; *Sacramento Union,* Oct. 19, 1865.
22. *Los Angeles Tri-Weekly News,* Oct. 24, 1865; Special Orders 17, 18, Southern Sub-District of Arizona, Sept. 17, 1865, Fort Mason, RG 94, NA.
23. Post returns, Fort Mason; Jimeno to de la Guerra, Oct. 30, 1865, Fort Mason, De la Guerra Collection, Santa Barbara Mission Archives. This is not the modern town of Patagonia but a mining camp in the adjacent mountains. Its Mexican owners sold the site to a former army officer named Sylvester Mowry in 1860. He made improvements and worked the mine successfully until it was seized by Union forces in 1862 due to suspicions of secessionist sympathies. The place appears on modern maps as "Mowry." At the time of the Native Cavalry's occupation, it was only being worked sporadically due to Apache attacks, though more extensive operations would resume later.
24. Post returns, Fort Mason; Acuña, *Sonoran Strongman,* 87. Colonel Ronstadt was the only member of Pesquiera's party who did not fall ill, and he cared for the others. Ronstadt, *Borderman,* 4.
25. José María García to Señora Doña Joaquina Uribes de García, Nov. 11, 1865, Fort Calabazas, in Pension File, Pvt. José María García, RG 94, NA.

26. Muster roll, field and staff, Aug. 31–Oct. 31, 1865, 1st Battalion of Native Cavalry, CWVR.
27. Special Order 21, Nov. 4, 1865, Bound Records, 1st Battalion of Native Cavalry, CWVR.
28. *Wilmington (Calif.) Journal,* Dec. 30, 1865; Cremony, "Santa Cruz," 336–40. The Ópata were a Uto-Aztecan speaking people of northeastern Sonora. They sided with the imperialists due to grievances against the republic, Governor Pesquiera in particular, and a notion that Maximilian's government would better serve tribal interests. Some sources identify Tanori as a general, but this promotion seems to have occurred later. He is generally regarded by historians as the last great leader of the Ópata as a discreet tribe, for they had largely assimilated by the twentieth century. See Yetman, *Ópatas,* 242–45. The pickets may well have been the same ones posted to the Santa Cruz road in September.
29. *Wilmington (Calif.) Journal,* Dec. 30, 1865. A native of Sonora with a long military career, Gen. and Acting Gov. Jesús García Morales was left in charge of what remained of republican forces in the state, an estimated two hundred poorly armed men, after Pesquiera fled. He coordinated what amounted to a guerilla campaign from northern Sonora with little success until help arrived from neighboring states. He later served in the Mexican Senate and is honored with a statue on the Paseo de Reforma in Mexico City. Almada, *Diccionario de Historia,* 300–303.
30. Lieutenant Codington later described the village of San Rafael as "a very feeble attempt at a small town situated about one and one half miles from the boundary line and about nine miles North from Santa Cruz." Codington to Lewis, Feb. 11, 1866, Fort Mason, in Book of Scouts, Dist. of Arizona, E29, RG 393, NA; See also Cremony, *Life among the Apaches,* 56–58.
31. Acuña, *Sonoran Strongman,* 87–92. During the exile, Colonel Ronstadt secured $24,000 from prominent Tucsonans to raise and equip a new republican force. Ronstadt, *Borderman,* 5. The French completely withdrew from Sonora by August 1866, and Tanori attempted to escape across the Gulf of California with a band of partisans. He was captured and executed in September. Almada, *Diccionario de Historia,* 679–80.

Chapter 11

Epigraph. Jimeno to de la Guerra, Oct. 30, 1865, Fort Mason, Ariz., De la Guerra Collection, Santa Barbara Mission Archives. This passage roughly translates into English as "All that is spoken of is Apaches, Apaches."
1. Cremony to Mason, Jan. 1, 1866, Fort Mason Letterbook, RG 393, NA.
2. Sweeney, *Cochise,* 233.
3. Jimeno to de la Guerra, Oct. 30, 1865, Fort Mason, in Pension File, Pvt. Feliciano de la Osa, RG 94, NA.

4. José María García to Señora Doña Joaquina Uribes de García, Nov. 11, 1865, Fort Calabazas, in Pension File, Pvt. José María García, RG 94, NA.
5. General Order 11, District of Arizona, Oct. 31, 1865, RG 393, NA.
6. Ibid.
7. *Alta California,* Dec. 31, 1865.
8. Cremony to Mason, Jan. 1, 1866.
9. Jimeno to Lewis, Jan. 23, 1866, Fort Mason; and Codington to Lewis, Feb. 11, 1866, Fort Mason, in Book of Scouts, Dist. of Arizona, E29, RG 393, NA (hereinafter cited as Scout Reports).
10. Cremony to Mason, Jan. 1, 1866.
11. Scout Reports. Babocómari was a ranch that dated back to the 1820s. The site was vulnerable to Apache raids and was abandoned by the time of the Mexican-American War. The fortified headquarters buildings were largely in ruins by the 1850s, but the place remained important as a campsite. Barnes, *Arizona Place Names,* 34; Officer, *Hispanic Arizona,* 109–10.
12. Scout Reports. Given the era, it is likely that Jimeno had no map. In his report he misidentifies the valley between the Santa Rita and Whetstone Mountains as the San Rafael Valley.
13. Ibid. Jimeno's campsite was at or near the place marked on contemporary maps as San Pedro Crossing, which is near the modern town of Benson.
14. Ibid. The Spanish army post known as the Presidio of Santa Cruz de Terrenate was originally established at the headwaters of the San Pedro River in 1741. The garrison was moved multiple times during its history but always retained the name regardless of location, which leads to occasional confusion. The presidio moved to this site in 1775, then relocated farther south in 1780. In 1787 it was moved to the upper Santa Cruz River at the site of what became the town of Santa Cruz. Jimeno correctly identifies the campsite, but some contemporary maps erroneously call it the Presidio of San Pedro.
15. Ibid.
16. Ibid. Edwin Sweeney identifies the West Stronghold as the location of this rancheria. See *Cochise,* 239.
17. Scout Reports; Meketa and Meketa, *One Blanket and Ten Days Rations,* 20. Norton's scout was part of the campaign ordered by Mason. The party left Fort Bowie on December 9 and returned on December 23, covering a loop of about 210 miles.
18. Scout Reports. A native of Chihuahua and a staunch unionist who was a partner in a successful freighting operation, Estevan Ochoa was one of the most prominent business and political leaders in Tucson. He is generally credited with creating Arizona's public school system. Sheridan, *Los Tucsonenses,* 42–48. On the way to Bowie, Ochoa's wagons were accompanied by an escort that included a corporal and eight Native Cavalry troopers of Company A. Special Order 127, Fort Mason, Dec. 22, 1865, Bound Records, 1st Battalion of Native Cavalry, CWVR.

19. Scout Reports. The 1st New Mexico Infantry was one of the units formed when the volunteer forces in that territory were reorganized after the collapse of the Confederate invasion of 1862. Company A was recruited in and around Santa Fe by Capt. Nicolas Quintana in the fall of 1863 and had been posted at Fort Bowie since June 1864. Bowie was established by soldiers of the 5th California Infantry in 1862 and retained its primitive character until 1868, when it was relocated to adjacent higher ground. For more on the New Mexico Volunteers at Fort Bowie, see Meketa and Meketa, *One Blanket and Ten Days Rations,* 3–25.
20. Scout Reports. Merejildo Grijalva was an Ópata from Sonora who was captured by Chiricahua Apaches at the age of ten. He escaped captivity in 1859 and soon became a well-regarded scout and interpreter, remaining active with the army in one capacity or another for the duration of the Apache Wars in Arizona. See Sweeney, *Merejildo Grijalva.*
21. Scout Reports. Edwin Sweeney identifies this as Rucker Canyon. See *Cochise,* 239.
22. Scout Reports; Velasco, *Sonora,* 72–73. Fronteras was established as a presidio by the Spanish in 1692 and remained the site of a garrison under Mexican rule through the end of the Apache Wars. Almada, *Diccionario de Historia,* 163–64, 281–82.
23. Scout Reports.

Chapter 12

Epigraph. Huse, Sturgeon, and Frost to McDowell, Nov. 17, 1865, Santa Barbara, De la Guerra collection.

1. *Los Angeles Tri-Weekly News,* Nov. 4, 1865; *Los Angeles Semi-Weekly News,* Dec. 15, 1865.
2. Post returns, Fort Mason, Records from U.S. Military Posts, 1800–1916, U.S. Adjutant General's Office, M617, Roll 1524, NA; Pension File, Capt. José Ramón Pico, RG 94.
3. *Wilmington (Calif.) Journal,* Feb. 17, 1866; *San Francisco Bulletin,* Mar. 30, 1866.
4. Charles A. Wyckoff, "Journal of Company C, Seventh Infantry, California Volunteers, May 20, 1865 to March 26, 1866," n.d., Sharlot Hall Museum, Prescott, Ariz., typescript by Aurora Hunt of original at Sutter's Fort Museum, Sacramento, Calif. Port Isabel, a landing on a muddy flat on the Sonoran coast two and a half miles south of the mouth of the Colorado River, was built in 1864 for the transfer of goods and passengers between riverboats and seagoing vessels. The journey described here was typical of commerce between California and the Colorado River during the era before railroads.
5. Ibid. A crewman went overboard in rough seas a day out of Cabo San Lucas.
6. *Sacramento Union,* Mar. 27, 1866. These were both officers of Company B, 1st Arizona Infantry Battalion. This was the same company being raised at

Maricopa Wells when the Native Cavalry passed through there on the way to Fort Mason the previous August. Underhill, "History of the First Arizona Volunteer Infantry," 25–27.

7. *Alta California,* Mar. 26, 27, Apr. 4, 1866.
8. Hill and Parks, *Santa Barbara Tierra Adorada,* 66.
9. Vallejo, "Notas Historicas," 155–57.
10. Cleland and Hardy, *March of Industry,* 174–75.
11. *Los Angeles Daily Times,* June 6, 1885.
12. Pico to Low, Aug. 20, 1866, Box 9, AGC.
13. *Sacramento Union,* Apr. 17, 1873.
14. *San Francisco Call,* Oct. 21, 1902.
15. *Pacific Rural Press,* Dec. 8, 1877.
16. *San Francisco Call,* June 29, 1896, Jan. 4, 1902.
17. Ibid., Feb. 2, 1905.
18. "Major J. R. Pico," 618–19. Captain Pico was not, in fact, the last to have the family name. A cousin named Pío Pico was living in Tanque Verde, Arizona, and passed away in the 1920s.
19. Thrapp, *Encyclopedia of Frontier Biography,* 1378–79. For a complete account of Streeter's exploits, see Bailey, *White Apache.*
20. Jimeno to de la Guerra, Apr. 6, 1867, Mazatlan, Mex., De la Guerra Archives, Mission Santa Barbara, Calif. Jimeno switches between English and Spanish in this letter. The Spanish portions quoted translate as follows: "Tell my grandmother (poor little thing) that . . . '*in the mode of the country.*' The population is entirely Mexican, the appearance and everything is truly Mexican, the temperature is good but in the middle of the day it is much hotter, finally they say that from eleven until three none are on the streets but. . . ." A *chacual* (plural, *chacuales*) is a type of either a gourd cup or a hide basket used in playing traditional indigenous Mexican ball games. In this context the first meaning seems more likely.
21. Ibid.
22. Altschuler, *Cavalry Yellow and Infantry Blue,* 178; death announcement, n.d., De la Guerra Archives.
23. Dibblee Poett, *Rancho San Julian,* 42.
24. *Los Angeles Times,* Dec. 20, 1940.
25. *Los Angeles Herald,* July 31, 1890, Aug. 23, 1891; *Los Angeles Times,* July 27, 1910.
26. *Sacramento Union,* Apr. 16, 1866.
27. The veterans home at Yountville opened in 1884. It was established after a fundraising campaign by the Lincoln Post (San Francisco) of the GAR and built on land that had once belonged to Salvador Vallejo. The home was taken over by the State of California in 1896 and still operates today.
28. Pension Files, Bernard Means and Timothy Means, RG 94, NA. The Pension Bureau considered their discharge date to be September 27, 1865, the day that

they deserted from Fort Mason. No explanation exists for this retroactive change.

29. John Boessenenecker, *Bandido: The Life and Times of Tiburcio Vasquez* (Norman: University of Oklahoma Press, 2010), 400–401.
30. *Santa Barbara Daily News,* Oct. 6, 1897.
31. Pension File, Pvt. Ysmael Soto, RG 94, NA.
32. *Santa Barbara Morning Press,* Aug. 6, 1899.
33. Ibid., Nov. 15, 1916.
34. *Los Angeles Times,* July 18, 1894.
35. Pension File, Pvt. Joseph V. Corona, RG 94, NA.
36. Pitt, *Decline of the Californios,* 249–50.

Appendix A

1. It is assumed that his death must have occurred before April 1864 since his name does not appear on muster rolls after that date.
2. Does not appear on any company muster rolls.
3. Disappears from the muster rolls after June 1865.
4. Private Luis was arrested by civilian authorities for a near-fatal stabbing of a Chinese woman with “unadulterated cussedness” during a “drunken frolic” in San Francisco’s China Alley during the last week of March 1865. For some reason, he does not seem to have been discharged on December 5, 1865, with the other troopers who remained in California.
5. Dismissed from the service by a general court-martial on January 21, 1864, and enlisted as a private in Company B two weeks later.
6. Father of Pvt. Juan Carrillo.
7. Son of Sgt. José Carillo.
8. Private Moreau was a Mexican of French descent.
9. According to an obituary in the *Santa Barbara Morning Press,* Aug. 6, 1899, Private Ponce de León “was a descendant of the famed explorer” Juan Ponce de León.
10. Duarte was found with a gunshot wound at Fort Mason on October 22 and died the next day. A coroner’s jury of officers at the post was empaneled, but nothing came of the matter. He was a brother-in-law to Cpl. José Victor Corona and Pvt. José María Corona.

Appendix B

1. Elizabeth Salas, *Soldaderas in the Mexican Military: Myth and History* (Austin: University of Texas Press, 1990), 33–34.

Appendix D

1. Lonn, *Desertion during the Civil War,* 234–35; Orton, *Records of California Men,* 307–13.
2. Scammell, "Military Units in Southern California," 236.

Appendix E

1. Post Order 218, Drum Barracks, Dec. 3, 1864, in CSR, Lt. Santiago de la Guerra. Company muster rolls do not mention a corporal on detached service during this time, so it seems that Lieutenant de la Guerra was accompanied only by two privates, forty-four-year-old Clemente Espinoza and thirty-seven-year-old Francisco Lugo. Both men were rancheros and natives of Santa Barbara.
2. *Alta California,* Dec. 29, 1864. The post at San Diego was variously called New San Diego, New San Diego Barracks, San Diego Barracks, and just San Diego. Ruhlen, "San Diego Barracks," 15–23.
3. *Sacramento Union,* Jan. 4, 1865.
4. Private Teodocio Buelna was mustered in to Company D in April 1864. He deserted on July 17. After his arrest and return to Drum Barracks, he escaped on December 30. Orton, *Records of California Men,* 318.
5. Rancho de Buena Vista is now the city of Vista, California.
6. Captain Matthew Sherman of Company F, 4th California Infantry. Orton, *Records of California Men,* 637.
7. Captain Alfred S. Grant of Company G, 4th California Infantry commanded the military post at San Diego. Ruhlen, "San Diego Barracks."
8. Private Isidro Altamirano was a twenty-three-year-old Californio who worked as a vaquero prior to his enlistment in Company D in February 1864. He later deserted again at Fort Yuma en route to Arizona Territory. Orton, *Records of California Men,* 318.
9. Rancho Guadalupe was about forty miles south of the border in Baja California. It was once owned by San Diego pioneer Juan Bandini and held a special place in the histories of both Californias, having been a refuge for Gov. Pío Pico during the American conquest and serving as a base for the resistance against the Walker filibuster of 1854. Long, "Annals of the Rancho Ex-Misión de Guadalupe," 129–33.
10. Private Andres Verdugo, a nineteen-year-old laborer and native of California, was one of the original volunteers recruited into Company D by Captain Sanchez early in 1864. He deserted from Drum Barracks on July 9. Any record of what happened to him after his arrest is lost, but it is clear that he did not return to the service.
11. This may refer to Pvt. Henry E. Bosser of Company E, 4th California Infantry. He was later dishonorably discharged. Orton, *Records of California Men,* 631.

Bibliography

Archive Collections

Military & National Guard Collection, California State Archives, Sacramento.
- Adjutant General's Correspondence, Boxes 6–8
- Civil War Volunteers Records, 1st Battalion, Native Cavalry

De la Guerra Archives, Mission Santa Barbara, California.
- Porfirio Jimeno File

National Archives, Washington, D.C.
- Post Returns, Microfilm Publication M617
  - Drum Barracks, California
  - Fort Mason, Arizona
- Record Group 94, Records of the Adjutant General's Office, 1780–1917
  - Battalion Returns, 1st Battalion, Native Cavalry
  - Company Returns, 1st Battalion, Native Cavalry
  - Compiled Service Records
    - Edward Bale
    - J. C. Cox
    - Vincent Geleich
    - A. M. de la Guerra
    - Santiago de la Guerra
    - Porfirio Jimeno
    - John Lafferty
    - Ernest H. LeGross
    - J. R. Pico
    - J. A. Sanchez
    - Crisanto Soto
    - Zebina N. Streeter
    - Salvador Vallejo

Pension Files

Santos Avila

Hermingildo Balderamos

Nicolas Cordova

José María García

John Lafferty

Ernest H. LeGross

Feliciano de la Osa

José Picasso

José Ramón Pico

Pedro Romero

Ysmael Soto

Record Group 393, Records of U.S. Army Continental Commands, 1821–1920

Book of Scouts, District of Arizona

Articles

Browne, John Ross. "A Dangerous Journey." Pts. 1 and 2. *Harper's Magazine,* May 1862, 741–58; June 1862, 6–19.

———. "A Tour through Arizona." Pts. 1–5. *Harper's Magazine,* October 1864, 553–74; November 1864, 689–711; December 1864, 22–33; January 1865, 137–49; February 1865, 283–93.

Cremony, John C. "How and Why We Took Santa Cruz." *Overland Monthly,* April 1871, 336–40.

Hayes-Bautista, David E., and Cynthia L. Chamberlin. "Cinco de Mayo's First Seventy-Five Years in Alta California: From Spontaneous Behavior to Shared Memory, 1862–1937." *Southern California Quarterly* 89, no. 1 (Spring 2007): 23–64.

Long, Robert W. "Annals of the Rancho Ex-Misión de Guadalupe." In *Brand Book Number Four,* edited by Abraham S. Nasatir, 129–33. San Diego: San Diego Corral of the Westerners, 1976.

"Major J. R. Pico." *Sunset* 14, no. 6 (April 1905): 618–19.

McKittrick, Myrtle M. "Salvador Vallejo." *California Historical Society Quarterly* 29, no. 40 (December 1950): 309–31.

Phelps, Robert. "On Comic Opera Revolutions: Maneuver Theory and the Art of War in Mexican California, 1821–45." *California History* 84, no. 1 (Fall 2006): 44–63.

Rouse, Stella Haverland. "Civil War Volunteers." *Noticias* (Santa Barbara Historical Society) 27, no. 3 (Fall 1981): 58.

Ruhlen, George. "San Diego Barracks." *San Diego Historical Society Quarterly* 1, no. 2 (April 1955): 15–23.

Scammell, J. M. "Military Units in Southern California, 1853–1862." *California Historical Society Quarterly* 29, no. 3 (1950): 229–49.

Streeter, William A. "Recollections of Historical Events in California, 1843–1878 (Continued)." Edited by William Henry Ellison. *California Historical Society Quarterly* 18, no. 2 (June 1939): 157–59.

Tassin, A. G. "Chronicles of Camp Wright, Part I." *Overland Monthly and Out West* 10, no. 55 (August 1887): 24–32.

Thiele, Thomas F. "Some Notes on the Lance and Lancers in the United States Cavalry." *Military Collector and Historian* (Summer 1955): 31–37.

Books and Manuscripts

Acuña, Rodolfo. *Sonoran Strongman: Ignacio Pesquiera and His Times.* Tucson: University of Arizona Press, 1974.

Almada, Francisco R. *Diccionario de Historia, Geografía y Biografía Sonorenses.* Chihuahua, Mex.: N.p., 1952.

Altshuler, Constance Wynn. *Cavalry Yellow and Infantry Blue: Army Officers in Arizona between 1851 and 1886.* Tucson: Arizona Historical Society, 1991.

Bailey, Lynn R. *White Apache: The Life and Times of Zebina Nathaniel Streeter.* Tucson, Ariz.: Westernlore, 2010.

Bancroft, Hubert Howe. *The Works of Hubert Howe Bancroft.* Vol. 21, *History of California: Pt. IV, 1840–1845.* 1890. Reprint, New York: Arno, [1967].

Barnes, Will C. *Arizona Place Names.* Tucson: University of Arizona Press, 1988.

Bartlett, John Russell. *Personal Narrative of Explorations and Incidents in Texas, New Mexico, California, Sonora, and Chihuahua: Connected with the United States and Mexican Boundary Commission, during the Years 1850, '51, '52, and '53.* 2 vols. New York: D. Appleton, 1854.

Bell, Horace. *On The Old West Coast: Being Further Reminiscences of a Ranger.* New York: W. Morrow, 1930.

Bledsoe, Anthony Jennings. *Indian Wars of the North-West: A California Sketch.* San Francisco: Bacon, 1885.

Brinckerhoff, Sidney B. "Last of the Lancers." Unpublished manuscript at Arizona Historical Society, Tucson.

Brown, Rodney Hilton. *American Pole Arms, 1526–1865: The Lance, Spontoon, Pike, and Navy Boarding Weapons.* N.p.: N. Flayderman, 1967.

Casebier, Dennis G. *The Mojave Road.* Norco, Calif.: Tales of the Mojave Road, 1975.

Cleland, Robert Glass, and Osgood Hardy. *March of Industry: California.* Los Angeles: Powell, 1929.

Coues, Elliot, ed. *On the Trail of a Spanish Pioneer: The Diary and Itinerary of Francisco Garcés in His Travels through Sonora, Arizona, and California, 1775–1776, Translated from an Official Contemporaneous Copy of the Original Manuscript, and Edited with Copious Critical Notes.* Vol. 1. New York: Francis P. Harper, 1900.

Cremony, John C. *Life among the Apaches.* New York: A. Roman, 1868.

Dana, Richard Henry, Jr. *Two Years before the Mast: A Personal Narrative.* Boston: Fields, Osgood, 1869.

Dibblee Poett, A. *Rancho San Julian: The Story of a California Ranch and Its People.* Santa Barbara, Calif.: Fithian, 1990.

Fontana, Bernard L. *Calabazas of the Rio Rico.* Smoke Signal 24. Tucson, Ariz.: Tucson Corral of Westerners, 1971.

Genini, Ronald. *Romualdo Pacheco: A Californio in Two Eras.* San Francisco: Book Club of California, 1985.

Gray, Andrew B. *Survey of a Route for the Southern Pacific R.R., on the 32nd Parallel, by A. B. Gray, for the Texas Western R.R. Company.* Cincinnati: Wrightson, 1856.

Hill, Laurence Landreth, and Marion Parks. *Santa Barbara Tierra Adorada: A Community History.* Los Angeles: Security-First National Bank of Los Angeles, 1930.

Hunt, Aurora. *The Army of the Pacific: Its Operations in California, Texas, Arizona, New Mexico, Utah, Nevada, Oregon, Washington, Plains Region, Mexico, etc. 1860–1866.* Glendale, Calif.: Arthur H. Clark, 1951.

Lonn, Ella. *Desertion during the Civil War.* Lincoln: University of Nebraska Press, 1998.

Marcy, Randolph B. *The Prairie Traveler: A Hand-Book for Overland Expeditions with Maps, Illustrations, and Itineraries of the Principal Routes between the Mississippi and the Pacific.* New York: Harper & Brothers, 1859.

Meketa, Charles, and Jacqueline Meketa. *One Blanket and Ten Days Rations: 1st Infantry New Mexico Volunteers in Arizona.* Globe, Ariz.: Southwest Parks and Monuments Association, 1980.

Miller, Robert Ryal. *Arms across the Border: United States Aid to Juarez during the French Intervention in Mexico.* Transactions of the American Philosophical Society, vol. 63, pt. 6. Philadelphia: American Philosophical Society, 1973.

Mylar, Isaac L. *Early Days at the Mission San Juan Bautista.* San Juan Bautista, Calif.: San Juan Bautista Historical Society, 1994.

Nelson, Byron, Jr. *Our Home Forever: The Hupa Indians of Northern California.* Salt Lake City: Howe Brothers, 1988.

Officer, James E. *Hispanic Arizona, 1536–1856.* Tucson: University of Arizona Press, 1987.

Orton, Richard H., comp. *Records of California Men in the War of the Rebellion, 1861 to 1867.* Sacramento: Office of the Adjutant General, 1890.

Phillips, George H. *Chiefs and Challengers: Indian Resistance and Cooperation in Southern California.* Berkeley: University of California Press, 1975.

Pitt, Leonard. *The Decline of the Californios: A Social History of the Spanish-Speaking Californians, 1846–1890.* Berkeley: University of California Press, 1966.

Pubols, Louise. *The Father of All: The de la Guerra Family, Power and Patriarchy in Mexican California.* Berkeley: University of California Press, 2009.

Reid, John Coleman. *Reid's Tramp; or, A Journal of the Incidents of Ten Months Travel through Texas, New Mexico, Arizona, Sonora, and California, including Topography,*

Climate, Soil, Minerals, Metals, and Inhabitants, with a Notice of the Great Inter-Oceanic Rail Road. Selma, Ala.: John Hardy, 1858.

Robinson, John W. *Los Angeles in Civil War Days, 1860–1865.* Los Angeles: Dawson's Book Shop, 1977.

Ronstadt, Edward, ed. *Borderman: The Memoirs of Federico José María Ronstadt.* Albuquerque: University of New Mexico Press, 1993.

Rosenus, Alan. *General Vallejo and the Advent of the Americans.* Albuquerque: University of New Mexico Press, 1995.

Secrest, William B. *Lawmen and Desperadoes: A Compendium of Noted Early California Peace Officers, Badmen, and Outlaws, 1850–1900.* Spokane, Wash.: Arthur H. Clark, 1994.

Sheridan, Thomas E. *Los Tucsonenses: The Mexican Community in Tucson, 1854–1944.* Tucson: University of Arizona Press, 1986.

Soennichsen, John. *Miwoks to Missiles: A History of Angel Island.* Tiburon, Calif.: Angel Island History Association, 2001.

Sweeney, Edwin R. *Cochise: Chiricahua Apache Chief.* Norman: University of Oklahoma Press, 1991.

———. *Merejildo Grijalva: Apache Captive, Army Scout.* El Paso: Texas Western Press, 1992.

Thompson, Erwin M., and Sally B. Woodbridge. *Special History Study: Presidio of San Francisco: An Outline of Its Evolution as a U.S. Army Post, 1847–1990.* Denver: National Park Service, 1992.

Thrapp, Daniel. *Encyclopedia of Frontier Biography.* Glendale, Calif.: Arthur H. Clark, 1988.

Underhill, Lonnie E. "A History of the First Arizona Volunteer Infantry, 1865–1866." Master's thesis, University of Arizona, 1979.

U.S. War Department. *The War of Rebellion: A Compilation of the Official Records of the Union and Confederate Armies.* Ser. 1, vol. 50 (in 2 parts), *Operations on the Pacific Coast.* 1897. Reprint, Harrisburg, Penn.: National Historical Society, 1971.

Vallejo, Salvador. "Notas Historicas Sobre California por El Mayor Salvador Vallejo." Sonoma, Calif., 1874. Unpublished handwritten manuscript, H. H. Bancroft Collection, Bancroft Library, University of California, Berkeley.

Velasco, José Francisco. *Sonora: Its Extent, Population, Natural Productions, Indian Tribes, Mines, Mineral Lands, Etc., Etc. Translated from the Spanish of Francisco Velasco by William F. Nye.* San Francisco: H. H. Bancroft, 1861.

Woodward, Arthur. *Lances at San Pasqual.* San Francisco: California Historical Society, 1948.

Yetman, David A. *The Ópatas: In Search of a Sonoran People.* Tucson: University of Arizona Press, 2010.

Newspapers

Alta California (San Francisco)
Humboldt Times
La Voz de Mejico
Los Angeles Herald
Los Angeles Times
Los Angeles Semi-Weekly News
Los Angeles Tri-Weekly News
Monterey (Calif.) Gazette
Pacific Rural Press (San Francisco)
Pajaro Times (Watsonville, Calif.)
Sacramento Union
Santa Barbara Daily News
Santa Barbara Morning Press
San Francisco Bulletin
San Francisco Call
San Jose Patriot
Wilmington (Calif.) Journal

Index

Page numbers for illustrations and maps are in italicized type.